Economic Dualism in Zimbabwe

This book identifies the root causes of income inequality in underdeveloped economies and proposes new solutions for structural reform in economies that have long neglected and exploited working people. It focuses on the case of Zimbabwe, a classic example of an African post-colonial state continuing with dualistic economic structures while simultaneously laying the blame for the initiation of this form of underdevelopment with colonialism. The book explores the colonial roots of economic dualism, in which traditional sectors run alongside newer forms of wage employment, and suggests ways for Zimbabwe to move beyond the ingrained inequalities and asymmetries in production and organisation that it generates.

Using a combination of theoretical and empirical approaches, *Economic Dualism in Zimbabwe* demonstrates how economic dualism can be eliminated through structural transformation of the traditional agricultural sector and reallocation of labour across sectors. The author comprehensively discusses the origins of dualism in Zimbabwe, how it developed in land, labour, credit and financial markets, who stands to gain and lose from it, and ultimately what reforms are needed to eliminate dualism from the economic system. The book aims to complement efforts made by both North and South to transform this structurally embedded cause of underdevelopment and seeks to motivate change in the collective development agenda mindset.

This book will be of interest to graduate-level students, scholars, researchers and policy practitioners in the fields of Development Studies, Economics, Agricultural Policy, Labour Policy, Economic Planning and African Studies.

Daniel B. Ndlela is a Lead Researcher and Team Leader with Zimconsult, Zimbabwe, formerly taught economics at the University of Zimbabwe, and was Senior Regional Adviser on economic co-operation and integration for the United Nations Economic Commission for Africa (UNECA).

Routledge Studies in African Development

Political Transition and Inclusive Development in Malawi
The Democratic Dividend
Edited by Dan Banik and Blessings Chinsinga

National Liberation Movements as Government in Africa
Edited by Redie Bereketeab

Hunger and Poverty in South Africa
The Hidden Faces of Food Insecurity
Jacqueline Hanoman

Extractive Industries and Changing State Dynamics in Africa
Beyond the Resource Curse
Edited by Jon Schubert, Ulf Engel and Elísio Macamo

Peacebuilding in Contemporary Africa
In Search of Alternative Strategies
Edited by Kenneth Omeje

The Challenge of Governance in South Sudan
Corruption, Peacebuilding, and Foreign Intervention
Edited by Steven C. Roach and Derrick K. Hudson

African Peacekeeping Training Centres
Socialisation as a Tool for Peace?
Anne Flaspöler

Corporate Governance in Tanzania
Ethics and Accountability at the Crossroads
Peter C. Mhando and Andulile J. Mwakalyelye

Economic Dualism in Zimbabwe
From Colonial Rhodesia to Post-Independence
Daniel B. Ndlela

Economic Dualism in Zimbabwe

From Colonial Rhodesia to Post-Independence

Daniel B. Ndlela

Routledge
Taylor & Francis Group
LONDON AND NEW YORK

First published 2019
by Routledge
2 Park Square, Milton Park, Abingdon, Oxon OX14 4RN

and by Routledge
52 Vanderbilt Avenue, New York, NY 10017

Routledge is an imprint of the Taylor & Francis Group, an informa business

British Library Cataloguing-in-Publication Data
A catalogue record for this book is available from the British Library

Library of Congress Cataloging-in-Publication Data
Names: Ndlela, Daniel Boda, editor.
Title: Economic dualism in Zimbabwe : from colonial Rhodesia to post-independence / edited by Daniel B. Ndlela.
Description: Abingdon, Oxon ; New York, NY : Routledge, 2019. | Series: Routledge studies in African development | Includes bibliographical references and index.
Identifiers: LCCN 2019005035 (print) | LCCN 2019007405 (ebook) | ISBN 9780429054921 (eBook) | ISBN 9780367150860 (hardback)
Subjects: LCSH: Economic development–Zimbabwe–History. | Zimbabwe–Economic conditions. | Zimbabwe–Economic policy.
Classification: LCC HC910 (ebook) | LCC HC910 .E26 2019 (print) | DDC 330.9681–dc23
LC record available at https://lccn.loc.gov/2019005035

ISBN: 978-0-367-15086-0 (hbk)
ISBN: 978-0-429-05492-1 (ebk)

Typeset in Goudy
by Wearset Ltd, Boldon, Tyne and Wear

For my wife, Thando, and my sons, Kwazakele, Mongezi and Mlandeli.

Contents

Figures

Tables

1 Introduction

Background

In setting the foundations of the present book, the introduction chapter locates economic dualism from colonial Rhodesia in both its historic and geographical location terms at the end of the nineteenth century, as having formed the foundation and cradle of its distorted economic structure and underdevelopment, which has continued to be so well into the twenty-first century. The chapter also spells out the origin and central task of the study of dualistic development in the Zimbabwean economy.

With a land area of approximately 390,000 square kilometres,[1] Zimbabwe is bordered by Mozambique to the east, South Africa to the south, Botswana and Namibia (the Caprivi Strip) to the west and Zambia to the north and north-west. Zimbabwe's distinctive physical characteristic is the high plateau, the 'high-veld' that runs from the south-west to the north-east through the centre of the country; it is about 650 kilometres long and 80 kilometres wide and lies mostly on an altitude of between 1,200 and 1,500 metres above sea level. Areas on both sides of the plateau lying at an altitude between 600 and 1,200 metres are called the, 'middle–veld', and the lowest part at an altitude below 600 metres, the 'low-veld', which consists of the Zambezi Valley, the Limpopo Valley and the Sabi Basin.

The climate corresponds to the altitude pattern with temperate climate in the high plateau and middle-veld and more extreme temperature variations in the low-veld. The country's natural regions strongly influence the pattern of agricultural cropping. As will be seen, land distribution under the colonial rule also followed the landscape and the climatic variations as well as the natural resource endowment patterns. Thus, the majority of the African settlements were moved from the high- and middle-veld areas to the generally arid low-veld, where both agricultural cropping and livestock farming are hazardous for lack of rainfall and vegetation. On the other hand, the plateau became the centre of European settlement because of its good climate, rainfall, vegetation and proximity to most of the commercial mineral deposits.

While the white settler politically induced land distribution remained a sore point to the indigenous people whose only hope was the expected independence which ushered majority rule. The country's climatic condition and attractiveness has remained a permanent feature. According to an International Quality of Life Index, published in January 2011 ranking 192 countries, Zimbabwe ties with the Mediterranean island of Malta for having the best climate on Earth.[2] Zimbabwe scored 100 per cent on climate, 75 per cent on leisure and culture and 67 per cent on cost of living.[3] The crime rate in Zimbabwe was ranked as very low. The country, however, did not do as well on the economy, politics and infrastructure.

Summary

While uneven distribution of wealth has been characteristic of most post-colonial economies, the situation in Southern Africa with particular focus on Zimbabwe, South Africa and Namibia took its own special dimension and characteristics. This book constitutes a continuation and update of my earlier book *Dualism in the Rhodesian Colonial Economy* (1981). The motivation behind the book is to address the structural problem of the distribution of income of the masses in the rural segment of underdeveloped economies, especially as a result of land alienation in the Southern African economies, with special focus on the Zimbabwean settler colonial economy, then known as Rhodesia. The central task of the book is to demonstrate from both theory and empirical evidence that the dualistic economic development was the result of consistent efforts of the colonial governments' economic policies and monopoly power possessed by large-scale operators and employers of labour in the modern sector. The racially determined ownership of land was entrenched in the early twentieth century by legislation which included the Land Native Act of 1913 in South Africa, the Land Settlement Proclamation of 1920 in Namibia, the Land Apportionment Act of 1930 and the Land Tenure Act of 1969 in Zimbabwe. As will be shown in detail in the case of Zimbabwe, the aim was to hold back any prospects of development in the indigenous African economy in order to extract cheap labour from these communities.

As the capitalist mode of production to dominate the economy, positive steps were taken to both reduce the competitiveness of African agriculture and to establish a permanent labour supply from the impoverished indigenous population. A similar and even more robust economic dualism divide took place in the South African case. Thabo Mbeki contends that, on one hand, there was the first economy, the modern economy, producing the bulk of the country's wealth and this first economy was integrated within the global economy. On the other hand, the second economy (also known as the marginalised economy) characterised by under-development, contributed little to the Gross Domestic Product (GDP). The latter economy, contained a big percentage of our population, incorporating the poorest of the country's rural and urban population, structurally disconnected from both the first and global economy, and was incapable of self-generated growth and development.[4]

The current book while re-stating the key positions taken in my earlier publication,[5] discusses and adds new trends that have taken place since the publication of the earlier volume. The views being developed in this volume will continue to directly affect the politics and development genre of many countries in the African region, at least until the key issues raised in the book have been addressed. The focus is built on the theoretical and empirical foundations of economic dualism in the literature. This is in order to find solutions towards structural transformation, an inclusive social order and sustainable development.

It will be argued in the rest of the book that, the Zimbabwean experience of continuation with the colonial economic dualism is a typical and even 'classic' example of the African post-colonial state's 'normalising the abnormal'. In the Zimbabwean case, the post-independent state has continued with dualistic structures of the economy as a new normal, while loudly blaming colonialism and imperialism for having planted and perpetrated this form of underdevelopment. This social formation, typically of Zimbabwe and South Africa has historically been characterised by an articulation of modes of production – the pre-capitalist and capitalist modes of production. But it is widely agreed that this situation, has to change, however formidable the historical and continued structural disconnection between the modes of production, which best analyses the processes of economic development in these economies.

What this book hopes to do differently, is to show how economic dualism can be eradicated through structural transformation of the colonial entrenched pre-capitalist 'traditional' agricultural sector and creation of conditions for the reallocation of labour across sectors. The book also addresses the wide spread of economic dualism that has in the post-independence period penetrated the economy through the growth of the informal sector.

The key motivation of the book is to change the mind-set of society's tolerance of underdevelopment, and urge the present generation of political leadership, academia and other societal actors to unleash and unshackle the existing economy by liberal economic reforms. Accompanied by structural transformation of the economy, this is expected to lower existing trade barriers and tax rates, and break the post-independent established and enhanced state monopolies. In this way, these economies can be structurally transformed towards industrialisation, competitiveness, and hence open them to regional economic integration and fair trade with the rest of the world.

The foundations of the present study

Economic dualism manifests itself in many ways and is an inherent part of the subject matter of underdevelopment. Economic dualism is still with us and has continued to be so until well into the twenty-first century. The subject of economic dualism has been dealt with at length and in various forms in the literature of development economics. It is essential to note that revisiting the subject is not only justifiable but it is essential for our understanding of the binding relations behind the phenomenon of underdevelopment. The term underdevelopment in the relevant literature refers to the generally less favourable indices that characterise the lower level of productive forces of the countries of the Third World – the present day underdeveloped countries. By today's designations some of the countries are in the category of Least Developed Countries (LDCs). The latter term is connected with the theory according to which these countries have fallen behind in the process of their historical development or 'have lost time and tempo, and consequently are now at an earlier, lower stage of general process of growth'.[6]

According to the United Nations the world's most impoverished and vulnerable countries, the LDCs group of countries have been classified as 'least developed' in terms of their low gross national income (GNI), their weak human assets and their high degree of economic vulnerability.

My original and central task of the study was to demonstrate that the dualistic economic development in Zimbabwe was the result of consistent efforts of the colonial government's economic policies and monopoly power possessed by large-scale operators and employers of labour in the modern sector. These forces tended to hold back any prospects of development in the traditional agrarian economy. Policies of land alienation, discrimination and low wage levels in the wage employment sector, unequal provision of capital inputs between the African peasant farmers and the large-scale white farmers as well as discriminatory marketing arrangements in the produce market formed a system of causation that constitutes the interrelationships of dualism. The essential feature of economic dualism in the Zimbabwe is that causation runs from imperfections in the land market to the other factor markets. This results in a downward causation of interlocking components starting from population pressure on the designated African farming lands, land degradation and soil erosion, low productivity, and ending in low and falling incomes per capita both in the rural African areas and in the modern sector. Riddell also emphasised that

> the effect of measures taken to restrict the competitiveness of African agriculture together with an increasing population farming a fixed area of land had been that the majority cannot provide enough for the needs of their families and so they are forced to work outside the Reserves.[7]

Teboho P. Bojabotseha recently highlighted that the idea that South African society is characterised by dual socio-economic structures is once more gaining ascendancy.[8] Its key advocates include the former President of the Republic of South Africa – Thabo Mbeki – and the majority of members of the ANC-dominated judiciary, legislative and executive assemblies.[9] Like in the case of Zimbabwe, the dualist interpretation in the context of development is presented as a 'correct' way of understanding reality in South Africa and problems that beset it. In these circumstances, in general there is an irresistible temptation to adopt dualist propositions as they appear to be self-evidently true.

Recent advances in empirical knowledge of underdeveloped economies show convincing evidence that the distribution of income of the rural masses in such economies as well as their absolute standard of living are highly dependent on the degree of concentration of landed wealth. There is also evidence that rapid growth in such enclave economies does not guarantee that those in the bottom deciles of socio-economic strata can improve their relative, or even their absolute position. This is because the economic policies employed have pronounced class bias which tends to disfavour the poor and those who own little property. In the specific conditions of Zimbabwe, this concentration of land-ownership was fostered by land alienation policies of successive colonial governments as well as by racial discrimination by law. The existing stock of assets, especially land resources, was acquired by whites through alienation of the African lands and property, especially African livestock.[10] From the stand point of origin, Zimbabwe's economic dualism has its roots in the land alienation by white settlers. This was buttressed by the subsequent colonial legal system. In general terms, dualism on the social and economic level became entrenched as the enclave economy, i.e. the mining and plantation sector became superimposed on the African pre-capitalistic economy.

As soon as the British Colonial Office realised and had misgivings about the BSA Company's conduct, it set out the 1898 Southern Rhodesia Order-in-Council which required the Company to ensure that sufficient land was set aside as reserves for the Africans' traditional agricultural requirements 'within which the life of the natives might be continued under protection and control'.[11] It was under this provision that the first native reserves were demarcated. As will be shown in Chapters 2 and 3, thereafter, a succession of land commissions progressively entrenched the division of land between Europeans and Africans. This created staggering differences between black subsistence smallholders and white commercial farmers. This development conclusively eliminates the sometimes widely held myth in Rhodesia and elsewhere that the African agriculture practised in the post-colonial Reserves from the end of the 1890s to early 1900s, and later to be called Tribal Trust Lands (TTLs) up to the country's independence in 1980 was the 'traditional and continuous farming methods' used before the arrival of the white farmers.

Once inaugurated, the policies of government frequently reinforce particular social structures. This, of course, comes as no surprise 'since governments are part of the society and respond to pressures exerted by those who possess political and economic power'.[12] One major consequence of these pressures manifests itself in the so called 'anti-rural bias'. However, many such policies have a greater stance on a class rather than a locational or sector bias.[13] In the modern era, the class bias of these policies is often seen in the channelling of scarce foreign exchange resources towards well established economic units of the modern sector to the disadvantage of small producers and potential competitors. Similarly, the low real interest rates on loans from the banking system and associated lack of credit rationing policies encourage the adoption of capital-intensive methods of production both in industry and in agriculture. Because of the structure of factor endowments (the amounts of factors of production that the country possesses) in an underdeveloped country and the inferior capacity of the small economic units, notably small farmers, policies tend to be inefficient in terms of allocation of the resources and have a negative impact on equity.[14]

This chapter sets out the background of the low and extremely unequal growth of the economy from the colonial to post white settler economies. This has continued to be a subject of interest and focus for scholarly research. In the chapters below we attempt to develop and elaborate the argumentation of how the persistence of dualism was created, and sustained throughout the colonial period to post independent Zimbabwe.

Notes

1 For a Standard book on the Zimbabwean geography, see Kay, 1970.
2 *International Living Magazine*, 2011.
3 Ibid.
4 Mbeki, 2004:29.
5 Ndlela, 1981.
6 Szentes, 1976:131; see also Thomas, 1974:25.
7 Ibid.
8 Bojabotseha, 2011:1.
9 Ibid.
10 A figure of 30,000 cattle was entered into the books of the Native Commissioner as representing cattle taken for 'for the use of settlers' before the final distribution in December 1895 in which the British South Africa Company (BSAC) helped itself to an additional 35,000 head. Stigger, 1977:20.
11 Palmer, 1977:58.
12 Griffin, 1976:5.
13 Ibid.
14 Lipton, 1977:75.

References

Bojabotseha, T.P. 2011. 'Dualism and the Social Formation of South Africa', *African Journal of Hospitality, Tourism and Leisure*, Vol. 1, No. 3:2.

Griffin, Keith. 1976. *Land Concentration and Rural Poverty*. London: Macmillan.

International Living Magazine. 2011. *Quality of Life Index*, January publication.

Kay, George. 1970. *Rhodesia: A Human Geography*. London: University of London Press.

Lipton, Michael. 1977. *Why Poor People Stay Poor: Urban Bias in World Development*. London: Temple Smith.

Mbeki, T. 2004. 'Meeting the Challenge for the Second Economy', *New Agenda: South African Journal of Social and Economic Policy*, Issue 14, Second Quarter:29.

Ndlela, Daniel Boda. 1981. 'Dualism in the Rhodesian Colonial Economy', *Lund Economic Studies*, 22, Lund, Sweden: Department of Economics, University of Lund.

Palmer. 1977. *Land and Racial Domination in Rhodesia*. London: Heinemann.

Stigger, P. 1977. 'Volunteers and the Profit Motive in the Anglo-Ndebele War, 1893', *Rhodesian History*, Vol. 2:20.

Szentes, Tamas. 1976. *The Political Economy of Underdevelopment*. Third, Revised and Enlarged Edition, Budapest: Akademia Kiado.

Thomas, Clive Y. 1974. *Dependence and Transformation: The Economics of the Transition to Socialism*. New York and London: Amazon.

2 The origins of dualism in Zimbabwe

The roots of dualism during Zimbabwe's colonial period

The chapter sets out the roots of dualism on the Zimbabwean colonial economy starting with the country's invasion and disruption of the traditional pre-colonial economy. The chapter provides the background to the main features of the pre-colonial economy – the Gold trade and the agricultural and grazing activities – leading to the origins of the colonial laws that set out land alienations. It also sets the background to the enactment of the Land Apportionment Act of 1930, which became the legal and institutional basis of the dualistic structure of the economy.

Without the understanding and appreciation of Zimbabwe's pre-colonial and colonial economy, many aspects of the present economy will be lost. Most of the characteristics of the contemporary social and economic life in Zimbabwe cannot be adequately appreciated without some knowledge of the society that existed before the advent of the Rhodesian colonialism. It is therefore a good idea to review briefly the development of the 'original' traditional economy before the colonisation of the country.

A great deal of research, particularly during the colonial period, enables us to reconstruct the main features of the social and economic life in pre-colonial Zimbabwe.[1] In this chapter, we will concentrate on how the socio-economic system worked. Within its geographical boundaries, pre-colonial Zimbabwe was a comparatively closed system with its own internal dynamics. The bulk of the people were engaged in the production for subsistence (in agricultural and pastoral activities based on communal ownership of land), and production for exchange. Some long-distance trade, via the East African coast, to destinations as far apart as China, India and Portugal existed.[2] In this sense, pre-colonial Zimbabwe was already connected with the world economy through the exchange of goods.

Gold trade

The most important traded product entering the international trade produced in Zimbabwe was gold. Gold reef mining that had started by the twelfth century, continued and developed steadily up to the nineteenth century.[3] During a large part of this period, gold constituted the most important export product though it was gradually overtaken by ivory. There were some other export products as well, such as copper.[4] Though gold mining was restricted to those areas where the ore existed, and though it was limited by the state of technical progress, the Zimbabweans had made remarkable achievements in the field of mining before colonisation during the end of the nineteenth century. This is confirmed by David Beach:

> All work was carried out by the Shona village communities, which mined, washed and milled gold and reduced it to a condition suitable for export; thus by the 1840s in the south-west and at least the 1890's elsewhere, they had worked out very nearly all payable reef gold, though it was possible to wash for gold in certain areas after this.[5]

The single most important determining factor in Zimbabwe's colonial invasion and subsequently conquest was in search of the territory's overestimated gold deposits. Though the much expected gold deposits eluded the expectations of the colonialists, a rich and diversified mineral sector came to characterise Zimbabwe to date. Over 40 minerals are mined, with the number of operating mines reaching between 800 and 900. This situation contrasts sharply with the situation in most African countries. Most mining countries in Africa depend on one single or possibly two or three minerals, dominated by a few large-scale mines, and only a handful transnational companies dominating the industry or there is a large state ownership.

It is therefore not an accident that the political boundaries of Zimbabwe had to coincide almost completely with the geological boundaries of the Zimbabwean Craton and are intersected by the Great Dyke. Both are geological phenomena with large reserves of several economic interesting minerals.

More recent studies have proven that the structural geology of Zimbabwe is dominated by the Zimbabwean craton, cut by the Great Dyke and surrounded by rift valleys in the north and north-west (Zambezi Rift) and mobile belts in the north (Zambezi Belt) and south (Limpopo Belt). The craton is overlain in the north, north-west and east by Proterozoic sedimentary basis.[6] In geological terms, the craton was formed during the early Archaean (3.6 to 2.5 billion years ago) and consists of granites and gneisses that contain few economic minerals except for vein (pegmatite) deposits near contacts, but the craton also contains economically important schist belts also known as greenstone or gold belts which comprise volcano-sedimentary sequence containing most of the mineral deposits currently exploited. These include the vast majority of gold deposits, the nickel-copper-cobalt deposits, the podium chromite deposits, the iron-ore deposits, numerous limestone deposits, asbestos, etc.[7]

Agricultural and grazing activities

Agriculture and grazing activities were much more important than international trade in minerals and ivory. Though Zimbabweans also relied on hunting and gathering activities the latter were secondary to the reliance upon agriculture and herding which were the primary sources of food.[8] The method of cultivation consisted of a shifting system of cultivation or a land rotation system. (This was probably the result of accumulated knowledge about the conditions of soil fertility and nutriments so that the 'traditional' cultivators had learned the methods of restoring soil fertility though reverting land to fallow.) Indeed the techniques of deep ploughing and the shift from a 'land rotation system' to a continuous system of cultivation emphasising crop rotation rather than fallow, had disastrous effects on soils lacking chemical properties to sustain continuous cultivation. The new techniques produced inferior yields to those of the African peasants who still had access to shifting cultivation until well after the Second World War 'when the agricultural revolution of manufactured fertilisers, herbicides and pesticides, of efficient motorised machinery and crop strains, finally gave a decisive advantage to large-scale capital intensive production'.[9]

Zimbabwe's modern economy was built upon the land alienation policies that followed the country's colonisation by white settlers organised by the British South Africa (BSA) Company in 1890. Though the primary motive of the colonisation by the BSA Company was the pursuit of rich gold deposits, failure to realise this original dream turned the Company towards the exploitation of land and related agricultural resources. Already by the early twentieth century, African peasant agriculture was being vigorously organised to provide food for commercial settlements, namely mines and urban centres. By the beginning of 1900, three types of land categories were in existence in Rhodesia, reserves set aside for the exclusive use by Africans; land alienated to mines and farms, sometimes occupied, sometimes in the hands of absentee landowners or companies; and un-alienated land that the BSA Company (the settler colonial administration) regarded as its own until the Privy Council decision of 1918 conferred it to the Crown.

Though the division of the land into European areas and African reserves had demarcated following the decision of the 1890 Southern Rhodesia Order in Council, in the early years of the twentieth century, there was no clear policy on the agricultural sector of the Rhodesian colony. But from 1908–1914 a so-called 'white agricultural policy' further launched an attack on the African reserves with the intention of recovering the best land and making it available for European settlement.[10] The hallmark of the BSA Company rule was the enactment of racial discriminatory laws, which set aside the reserves for the exclusive use and habitation by Africans, even though this was against the law that had stated that the rest of the land areas in the colony were open for purchase by members of all races. For instance, the BSA Company refused to sell land to leading Ndebele households who needed it. The Company also refused to sell land to the Fingo Community (migrants from South Africa who had been invited by Rhodes to settle in Rhodesia).[11]

As already hinted in Chapter 1, it is not correct that Zimbabwe's problem of dualism emanated from its cultural constraints that prevented land occupied under traditional farming from getting onto the market. The pre-colonial 'traditional' farming system 'consisted of a shifting system of cultivation' described above, not the colonial farming system as prescribed by the African reserves. The primary motive of creating and setting aside reserves was the most important means of acquiring labour from the impoverished African farmers. What followed this pattern was the increasing population farming a fixed area of land that forced Africans to look for work outside the reserves. This became a continuous process as reported by the Chief Native Commissioner by 1923 that movements to the reserves consisted of a continuous stream.[12] At the end of the 1920s, the first reports of the reserves being full were being received.[13] This was by any other means 'overpopulation' of African people within their allocated territories within the reserves.

In these circumstances, there was no resistance by African chiefs to fight for traditional 'cultural' authority in the Tribal Trust Lands in Rhodesia so that they could allocate lands. As Giovanni Arrighi noted

> Native Commissioners or Inspectors of Police called on the various chiefs and headmen, informing the villagers that a certain per centage must work for the white man in return for a minimum wage of 10s. per month as well as board and lodging; these orders were enforced by African policemen who often exceeded their authority.[14]

In 1908, the Department of Agriculture was reorganised to give technical support to white farmers. A Land Bank was set up in 1912 with a share capital of £250,000 to make credit facilities available to white farmers only.[15] Bank loans up to £2,000 for the purchase of farms, livestock, and other agricultural equipment were made available to white farmers, and no loans were made available to black farmers until 1945 when the Land Bank initiated a scheme of advancing loans to farmers in the African Purchase Areas (APAs). The APAs was a very small proportion of farm land in the country, occupying only 8 per cent of the total land area in 1961.[16] Because of the alleged lack of collateral security among African peasant farmers, the African reserve farmers were not considered for the Land Bank loans.

The Southern Rhodesia Order in Council of 1898, Article 83, had stated that 'a Native may acquire, hold, encumber and dispose of land on the same conditions as a person who is not a Native ...'.[17] This condition was, however, removed at the recommendation of the 1925 Land Commission, which prepared the stage for the Land Apportionment Act of 1930, and consequently also laid the foundations for a permanent division of the country into African and European areas. In the period up to 1930 the laws had set aside reserves for the exclusive use and habitation by African local population. The rest of the land areas were open for purchase by members of all races, although in practice this was not always the case.[18]

These developments laid the foundations for the permanent division of the country into African and European areas. The Land Apportionment Act was the first legal sanction by Parliament to confirm the BSA Company practice and provide for the areas reserved for whites and blacks. The Land Apportionment Act not only legally sanctioned land alienation policies and the creation of African reserves. It was also used to prevent the African peasant farmer from becoming a competitor to the white settler farmers or plantation owners. In many ways it was also used to impoverish the African peasantry to such an extent that the majority of the adults would be compelled to work for white farmers in mines or farms.[19]

African peasant agricultural production thus was severely curtailed. During the 1920s a given African labour effort in the produce market gave a lower return than 20 years earlier. Whereas at the beginning of the twentieth century African produce sales accounted for 70 per cent of their total cash earnings, by 1932 the figure had fallen to 20 per cent.[20] A stagnant peasant agriculture within the framework of dualism in the economy had emerged as a result of the black peasant farmers being increasingly evicted from the more-fertile lands and from the areas within easy reach of markets. The discriminatory and dualistic political and economic framework developed during the previous periods, especially with regards to land policy, was further entrenched under the Native Land Husbandry Act of 1951. When the Land Apportionment Act of 1930 was superseded by the Land Tenure Act of 1969, all the main provisions of the former were confirmed.

The development of a specific policy on agricultural prices was triggered by a deep slump in Rhodesian cattle and maize prices that occurred in 1921–1923. This slump had far more devastating effects than previous economic depressions. In 1920, the African grain sales to 'white' traders was estimated at 19,800 tonnes[21] at 10s per bag. By 1921 the average price had fallen to approximately 5s per bag, at which prices sales of grain became uneconomic in many districts. As a result, and notwithstanding the bumper harvest that year, only 43,000 bags (4,300 tonnes) were purchased from African peasant farmers, a drop of 78 per cent in sales.

A similar reduction was reported in sales of African cattle. From an estimate of at least 20,000 head of cattle sold in 1919 at prices in the order of £7 to £8, by 1921 the demand for African cattle had declined and practically ceased to exist. The trend of decline over time was spectacular. At the beginning of the century, 70 per cent of Africans' total earnings came from produce sales, but by 1932 it had fallen to 20 per cent. This change was not just a cyclical phenomenon but rather a 'deep-seated' structural change based on the development of policy and institutional changes that had taken place in the country. The African peasant farmers had moved en masse to the more remote reserves, cut off from the rail line, other transport systems and credit facilities. Thus, as peasant production for marketed surplus was further curtailed, the forced evictions of Africans into the reserves were aggravated by falling prices in the produce market.[22]

As is evident from the situation just described in respect of maize, agricultural pricing policies came to be closely tied to the institutions set up to regulate agricultural activity. In the 1920s the white farmers called for the establishment of statutory marketing agencies in order to stabilise and guarantee agricultural producer prices and help find domestic and foreign markets for their produce. The slump in the prices in the wake of the great depression of the early 1930s made the case for statutory marketing institutions even more necessary. Thus, the sudden decline in the price of maize at the beginning of 1931 became the main reason for the setting up of the Maize Marketing Board, established by the Maize Control Act of 1931. It became compulsory for all maize marketed in the urban areas (except for sales between Africans in the same administrative area) to be sold to the Board.

With the enactment of the Maize Control Amendment Act of 1940, a new price system was instituted whereby the government guaranteed a fixed price to the producers based on the estimated costs of production plus some profit.[23] In 1943, the government guaranteed a price of 13 shillings and six pence and a bonus of two shillings for all maize delivered to the government maize marketing agency. The Maize Control Board, provided that maize was grown under certain conditions of sound farming practices. These conditions were that the area under maize cultivation should be protected from soil erosion, and that in the first season, one-third of the area (and one-half of the following season) under cultivation should be planted with green manure crop. These conditions obviously discriminated against the African farmers, since the digging of contour ridges for the protection of soil erosion only started in earnest after 1951, under the Native Land Husbandry Act.

Maize marketing had thus become a controlled product and the government had established a monopoly over the marketing of maize into the urban areas. The Maize Marketing Board functioned until 1950 when it was replaced by the Grain Marketing Board (GMB), created under the Grain Marketing Act (No. 31). Since its formation, the GMB has controlled the purchase and sale of various products including sorghum (from 1950), groundnuts (from 1951), soybeans (from 1969), wheat (from 1970) and coffee (from 1971).[24] Following the opening-up of the economy in the 1990s most of the controls were scrapped – but then they were re-introduced from the year 2001.

Entrenchment of economic dualism through distortions in agricultural markets

As shown above, economic dualism in the Zimbabwean economy was manifested first and foremost in the land market. This was as a result of successive policy interventions of the colonial state, starting from the beginning of settler colonial rule by the BSA Company in the late 1890s. Thereafter, dualism was entrenched through successive land commissions and actions in other factor markets (labour and capital) and in product markets. Dualism was also achieved mainly via discrimination in the marketing arrangements of agricultural produce. These relationships interacted to create economic impoverishment of the African agricultural producers and the African labour force. The following interlocking forces contributed to that outcome: land alienation policies and discrimination in the provision of infrastructure and services; population pressure in the African rural areas and land-degradation in the African reserves; low productivity; and migrant labour discrimination as well as low African wages.[25]

Zimbabwe's land tenure was split into various distinct farming systems, operated under different land tenure rules, each having its own characteristic farming system. From the colonial period, legislation restricted produce transactions within each category as well as labour and product movements between categories.

Economic dualism also emerged from the biases in factor and product markets, and through the institutional and political mechanisms created by the colonial state. These actions undermined the participation of the African peasant farmers in marketing agricultural produce. The conduct of the marketing institutions that emerged after the depression of the early 1930s was important in this regard, as was the dualistic structure of the transport services in relation to the marketing of agricultural produce. Only 30 per cent of the land assigned to Africans, as against 75 per cent of that alienated to Europeans, was within 25 miles of the railway line and therefore within reach of markets for agricultural goods in the towns and mines.

From the early years of colonial administration, the policy was to locate the European farms within a radius of 25 miles of the railway line so that white farmers had easy access to the country's transport system. Peasant farmers, by contrast, were cut off from the markets. When railway costs were added, grain crops could not bear the costs of more than 15 miles of ox-wagon transport.[26] Thus the general movement of Africans into the more-remote reserves not only reduced the inland resources both in terms of size and quality, but also progressively reduced their ability to compete in grain markets. In order to access export markets from a land-locked situation, Zimbabwe's railways and roads were created with the aim of assisting transit routes to the sea-ports. Virtually all the exports of bulk products (mainly minerals and agricultural products) generally went through the Mozambican ports of Beira and Maputo or the South African port of Durban.[27]

In the wake of the drastic fall of export prices of maize in 1931, the government introduced a dual price system, one for the local market (or local pool) and the other for the export pool. Through this quota system, the amount of output allocated to the local pool was that deemed sufficient to meet local demand. The price paid for the local pool was 30 to 50 per cent above world prices with the local pool thereby constituting a support price scheme for producers. The remaining surplus was sold to the export pool at whatever prices could be realised in the world market. That is, the quota system served to reduce the marketing of produce of the African majority farmers, a tendency that was further reinforced under the marketing levies applied to African products during the 1950s.

There was also discrimination in prices between different price categories of farmers, namely small-scale white farmers, the large-scale white farmers and the African peasant farmers. The small-scale white farmers were allocated 80 per cent of all their deliveries to the high-priced local market, compared with just 20 per cent for both the large-scale white farmers and the African peasant producers. Both communal and African Purchase Area (APA) farmers (small-scale black commercial farmers) were lumped together for their deliveries to the high-priced internal market. In other words, though the African peasant farmers were invariably small-scale producers, they were largely excluded from the price incentives enjoyed by the small-scale white farmers. If there had not been a discriminatory price policy, the African peasant farmers would have received higher prices for 80 per cent of their deliveries to the higher-priced internal market.

The implications of the maize quota system on farm productivity are obvious, as this was the most important crop produced by both black and white farmers up to the 1950s (after which tobacco became the country's leading crop). In addition, with the clear separation of land settlement between African farmers and farmers of European origin, it was possible to direct capital expenditure in roads, dams, communication systems, and other infrastructure to widen the differential in overall productivity between the two racial groups.

Thus, Zimbabwe's modern economy was built on the land alienation policies that followed the colonisation in 1890. As shown above, once the colonialists were disappointed by the failure to reap the much expected gold deposits in the new colony, the company turned towards exploitation of the land and agricultural resources. White farmers were given exclusive rights to the best farmland, together with various forms of support and assistance, while the majority African producers were confined to areas much less suitable for agriculture and were subject to discriminatory policy measures designed to subordinate African agriculture. The areas in which Africans were required to remain were initially known as Native Reserves, but were subsequently referred to as Tribal Trust Lands (during the 1960s and 1970s) and communal lands after independence in 1980.

The demand for land distribution that fed the desire for the liberation war culminated in a negotiated settlement for independence in 1980 with land reform as a key issue in the country's resolution for peace and reconstruction. At independence in 1980, the new government recognised the need to redistribute lands owned by the white to the landless blacks and peasant farmers who had been pushed to arid land areas. The Lancaster House negotiated settlement stipulated that for the first ten years land could only be acquired from the commercial farmers by the state on a "willing buyer-willing seller" basis. Hence, the planned Phase One Land Resettlement Programme (1980–1999) managed to acquire and redistribute some 3.6 million hectares to 76,000 families, who included beneficiaries that had been displaced by the war, former occupants of overcrowded communal lands and other landless persons.

By the time of its independence in 1980, Zimbabwe had inherited a dual agrarian structure that had seen white commercial farmers prosper in good farming areas while hundreds of thousands of poor black families continued to struggle to subsist on smallholdings in the communal areas, much of it in semi-arid areas with poor soils. It was estimated that there were nearly three times more people living in the communal areas than the land could sustain. Initially, the Zimbabwe Government prioritised the communal areas for development by intensifying agriculture and initiating a programme of resettlement and migration to decongest them.

The above measures led to the smallholder sector making significant gains, surpassing the commercial sector in maize and cotton production in the mid-1980s. This followed ambitious plans by government to intensify production by land-use reorganisation and establishing consolidated villages in which to concentrate physical and social infrastructure. The resettlement programme aimed to resettle 162,000 families, while over 300,000 families were expected to migrate to towns and cities. But these hopes had faded by the end of the 1980s. Output declined, village planning stalled, the rate of resettlement slowed to a trickle, and the expected migration of households to urban centres failed to materialise.

The continued economic dualism in Zimbabwe's post-independence period will be discussed in Chapters below.

Notes

1 Blake, 1977; Gann, 1969; Beach, 1976:6, 1977, 1980; Moyana, 1975; Palmer and Parsons, 1977; Phimister, 1974; Bhebhe, 1974; Bhila, 1972.
2 'In 1600 Portugal traded with the central African kingdom of Monomotapa as well as with Japan', Wallerstein, 1974:301.
3 For details see Makoni, 1980, and Ndlela, 1980.
4 Phimister, 1974:447.
5 Beach, 1980:26.
6 Jourdan *et al.*, 2012.
7 For details, see Paul Jourdan. Ibid.
8 Beach, 1977:40.

9 Palmer, 1977:15.
10 Palmer, ibid.:89.
11 Loney, 1975:54.
12 Palmer, 1977:80.
13 Palmer, 1968:39.
14 Arrighi, 1970:208.
15 Palmer, ibid.:89.
16 Ibid.
17 Southern Rhodesia, 1926:3.
18 Loney, 1975.
19 Ndlela, 1981:72.
20 Arrighi, 1970:216.
21 This is equivalent to 198,000 bags and each bag weighed 200 lb.
22 Arrighi, 1970:216.
23 Yudelman, 1964:273.
24 Some other products were initially controlled and later removed from the controls list: beans in 1959, bulrush millet in 1962 and finger millet (rapoko) in 1965.
25 Ndlela, 1981:58–59.
26 Ibid.
27 Beef, however, is exported through Cape Town.

References

Arrighi, Giovanni. 1970. 'Labour Supplies in Historical Perspective: A Study of the Prelotarianization of the African Peasantry in Rhodesia', *The Journal of Development Studies*, Vol. 6, No. 3:6.

Beach, D.N. 1976. 'Second Thoughts on the Shona Economy: Suggestions for Further Research', *Rhodesian History*, Vol. 7:6.

Beach, D.N. 1977. 'The Shona Economy: Branches of Production', in Robin Palmer and Neil Parsons (eds), *The Roots of Rural Poverty in Central and Southern Africa*. London: Heinemann.

Beach, D.N. 1980. *The Shona and Zimbabwe 900–1850*. Gwelo: Mambo Press.

Bhebhe, Ngwabi M.B. 1974. 'Ndebele Trade in the Nineteenth Century', *Journal of African Studies*, Vol. 1, No. 1:87–100.

Blake, Robert A. 1977. *A History of Rhodesia*. London: Eyre Methuen.

Bhila, H.H.K. 1972. 'Trade and the Survival of an African Polity: The External Relations of Manyika from the Sixteenth to the Early Nineteenth Century', *Rhodesian History*, Vol. 3:17.

Gann, L.H. 1969. *A Study of Southern Rhodesia: Early Days to 1934*. New York: Penguin Books.

Jourdan, Paul, Chigumira, Gibson, Kwesu, Isaac and Chipumho, Erinah. 2012. *Mining Sector Policy Study*. Harare, Zimbabwe: Zimbabwe Economic Policy Analysis Unit (ZEPARU).

Loney, M. 1975. *Rhodesia: White Racism and Imperial Response*. Harmondsworth: Penguin Books Ltd.

Makoni, T. 1980. *The Rhodesian Economy in a Historical Perspective' Part II. UN – United Nations. Zimbabwe, Towards a New Order: An Economic and Social Survey* Working Papers, Vol. 2, United Nations.

Moyana, H.V. 1975. *Land Apportionment in Rhodesia*. Unpublished PhD Thesis Colombia, New York.

Ndlela, D.B. 1980. *The Rhodesian Economy in a Historical Perspective, Part I. UN – United Nations. Zimbabwe, Towards a New Order: An Economic and Social Survey.* Working Papers, Vol. 2, United Nations.

Ndlela, D.B. 1981. 'Dualism in the Rhodesian Colonial Economy', *Lund Economic Studies*, 22, Department of Economics, University of Lund, Sweden, Lund.

Palmer, R.H. 1968. *Aspects of the Rhodesian Land Policy, 1890–1936.* The Central African Historical Association, Local Series No. 22. Salisbury.

Palmer, R.H. 1977. *Land and Racial Discrimination in Rhodesia*. London: Heinemann.

Palmer, Robin and Parsons, Neil. 1977. (eds). *The Roots of Rural Poverty in Central and Southern Africa*, London: Heinemann.

Phimister, I.R. 1974. 'Alluvial Gold Mining and Trade in Nineteenth Century South Central Africa', *Journal of African History*, Vol. 15, No. 3:450.

Southern Rhodesia. 1926. *Report of the Land Commission, 1925: Presented to the Legislative Assembly*. Salisbury.

Wallerstein, Immanuel. 1974. *The Modern World-System: Capitalist Agriculture and the Origins of the European World – Economy in the Sixteenth Century*. New York and London: Kindle Edition.

Yudelman, M. 1964. *Africans on the Land: Economic Problems of African Agricultural Development in Southern Central and East Africa, with Special Reference to Southern Rhodesia*. Cambridge, MA: Harvard University Press.

3 Land tenure and economic dualism

Introduction

The first foundation of this chapter is to give an account of the origin of and the initial conditions for the creation of economic dualism through land alienation policies. The policies gave rise to land concentration among white farmers side by side with acute shortages of land in the country's African segregated land areas. It is also demonstrated that it was the colonial legal sanction that set aside the African reserves for the exclusive use and habitation by the indigenous population. Further, that it was this continued feature of economic dualism that spread from the land market to all other factor markets, thus constituting the basic problem for transformation of these economies.

The chapter goes beyond the discussion of dualism during the colonial period. It traces dualism in the form of continued structural disarticulation of the main economic sectors in the post-colonial economy. The most distinct feature of the Zimbabwean economy and that of most post-colonial African economies is the lop-sided nature of their pattern and size of production, consumption and trade. This continued feature of 'modern dualism' constitutes the basic problem for transformation of these economies.

By giving dualism its historicity and theoretical underpinnings, it is argued that it cannot be eradicated without purposive Government actions and interventions. As will be shown in Chapter 9, structural transformation of economic dualism has to go beyond the land to other factor markets, into the whole structure of economic dualism pitting the modern formal sector against the backward non-formal sector of the economic divide.

Generous land grants – based on alienation of the high-quality African lands on Zimbabwe's high-veld, coupled with financial protection for the white farmers were given the sanction of law. With the enactment of the Land Apportionment Act of 1930 and the Land Tenure Act of 1969, the practice of land alienation and the division of the country into European and African areas were sanctioned by law. The per capita land area occupied by the Africans was a tiny fraction of the European land area. With an increasing population, this led to a rising man–land ratio in the designated African areas.

As will be seen, the initial conditions for the creation and maintenance of the post-colonial dualism were already present in the foundations of colonial economy. Under the specific conditions of the entry of foreign capital or colonisation in Zimbabwe, most of the lands hitherto possessed and occupied by the indigenous African population were alienated into the white or the so called European areas. This policy of land alienation in combination with low-wage policies of the mines and plantations were eventually to form the basis for the creation of a distinct 'modern' sector that came to co-exist and thrive by the maintenance of the low productivity and relatively stagnant African 'traditional' sector. Thus, the existing distribution of assets, especially the land concentration in the hands of the whites and the scarcity of agricultural land in the African areas, initially called native reserves, as a result of the alienation of African traditional property rights, virtually became a permanent feature of the Zimbabwean economic landscape.

Dualism was also exacerbated by the allocation of high- and low-quality land areas so that the relatively poor African farmers were forcibly evicted into poor arid areas with less rainfall. Thus, from an historical perspective, dualism in the Rhodesian economy had its basis on dualism in the land market. Thus in the early 1960s Floyd observed that 'although modifications have certainly been made over the intervening years, the basic pattern of land allocation has persisted without radical change from the turn of the century down to the present time'.[1]

By the time of Zimbabwe's independence in 1980, the situation had remained the same. About 5,600 white commercial farmers had access to 15.5 million hectares of the more productive farmland held under freehold tenure, while over 760,000 African smallholder farmers had to earn livelihoods from 16.4 million hectares of communal land held under customary tenure, much of it in the arid areas with poor soils. It was this dual economy – an impoverished traditional sector, the other a thriving modern sector – was the single most enduring feature of Zimbabwe's agrarian structure.

The origins of dualism in the land market

The development of dualism in Zimbabwe's land market cannot be fully appreciated without some knowledge of the nature, motivation and methods used in the scramble for land by the advancing European settler community who spearheaded colonisation in the country. In this section we show how the colonial system was consolidated and describe the methods used in shaping the emerging land settlement pattern.

The scramble for land following the colonisation of Zimbabwe inherited the Cape Dutch system of land tenure under which Europeans were given free hand to peg out their own farms, and also the South African system of 'war and tenure'.[2] As the Europeans spread inwards into the African hinterland, a tradition was quickly established whereby after a defeat of the Africans in warfare, Europeans parcelled out the surrounding land tracts for themselves. The Rhodesian land scramble, however, differs from the South African pattern in its initial aims and context. In South Africa, the settlers needed land for stock-raising and farming. The Rhodesian land annexations were meant to attract settlers whose initial mission was a gold hunting expedition. The prime motivation for the occupation was the hope of significant gold discoveries and an increase in the European settler population.

The land rights were, therefore, initially held as a speculative asset rather than as a production factor. The members of the Pioneer Column – the paramilitary force that was organised by Cecil John Rhodes' British South Africa Company (the BSA Company) – who had been recruited from all over South Africa were each promised 3,000 acres of land and the right to 15 gold claims at the end of the trek.[3]

Second, the BSA Company expedition was perpetrated in a commercial and speculative context. To the Company directors and most of the pioneers, gold claims were more highly prized than land and cattle claims, and indeed most pioneers sold off their land rights to speculators while still on the march to Rhodesia. Immediately after their arrival at Fort Salisbury (Harare) in 1890, the Pioneer Column disbanded and the search for gold and new farms began. By February 1891 (only four months after their arrival), some 7,000 gold claims had been marked off.[4] But within a short time this turned out to be a fiasco for there was no second Rand in Mashonaland (the eastern part of Zimbabwe, which had been occupied by the BSA Company). The settler land rights, on the other hand, had depreciated in value from £100 at the time of occupation to the point whereby April 1893 they were changing hands at only £55 to £60 each.[5]

Because of the relative neglect of agriculture, the settler agricultural economy was characterised by low land values, limited occupations and stagnation, to the point where it was held that there were no more than six active white farmers in the whole territory at the end of the 1892–1893 season.[6] This situation turned the Company interest to the conquest of Matebeleland in the hope that perhaps mineral resources there would be greater. Its fertile lands and well-stocked high-veld also provided an added inducement.[7]

The BSA Company doubled its inducement fund in order to attract volunteers. Everyone taking up arms was promised a free farm of 3,000 morgen[8] anywhere in Matebeleland[9] and the right to 15 reef and five alluvial gold claims. In addition, the cattle loot from the Matebele was to be shared equally, with one half going to the Company and the other half to be shared among officers and men.[10] But as soon as the settlers had obtained their land rights, they began pressing for the right not to occupy them, since their interest lay elsewhere – in the gold claims – and a nominal annual quit-rent of £1 per 1,500 morgen farm fostered the country's long tradition of absentee landlordism.[11] Thus a land glut had been conferred to people whose immediate interest was not occupying the land. This led to intensified speculation in the land rights. Within the first month of the defeat of the Matebele, in 1893, land rights changed hands at £75 and even lower, compared with official price of £450 set by the Company.[12]

The degree of speculation in land rights can be seen from the fact that out of 948 land rights established after the 1893 Anglo-Ndebele war, only 275 such located farms and 33 unlocated rights remained individually owned by 1899. The balance of 640 located farms and further unlocated rights were held in blocks by individuals or under the control of companies.[13] Former volunteers of all ranks disposed of their rights to speculators with eagerness. Those who gained most by speculation in land rights were quasi-aristocrats, speculative companies, fortune hunters, military men and missionaries. For example, among the military men, Major Sir John Willoughby who was seconded from the Royal Horse Guards to act as chief of staff in the Pioneer Column accumulated 7.3 million acres for his own Willoughby Consolidated Company. He was also allotted 8,850 head of the Ndebele cattle by the Loot Committee.[14]

Of the fortune hunters, Dunbar Moodie virtually became a feudal lord of the Melsetter District where he curved a huge estate of over 60,000 acres together with a large head of cattle.[15] By the turn of the century, Christian missionaries had also carved for themselves around a quarter of a million acres, with Catholics taking nearly half of this amount. Naturally, the missionaries had to insulate themselves morally while grabbing land. 'Knight Bruce, the Anglican Bishop of Mashonaland argued that the mission lands were intended as native reserves in case Africans were squeezed off their lands.'[16]

The impact of land encroachment on the property rights of indigenous Africans was disastrous. Within a few months of the arrival of the white settlers, all the African lands, including the whole of the their most valued region – the high-veld – ceased to be their patrimony and passed into private estates of white individuals or became property of commercial companies. It then became necessary to demarcate certain areas of the country for the protection of African peoples.

Thus, the African reserves were created with the objective of protecting Africans from further European encroachment on their lands. By the Matebeleland Order in Council of July, 1894, the Colonial Office gave authority to a Land Commission that established the first reserves in Matebeleland. In 1898, the Southern Rhodesia Order in Council extended native reserves to the whole country 'within which life of the native might be continued under protection and control'. The reserves were subsequently entrenched in the 1923 Southern Rhodesia constitution, which gave self-rule to the settlers.[17] The areas in which Africans were required to remain were initially called Native reserves and were subsequently referred to as Tribal Trust Lands (during the 1960s and 1970s) and as communal lands (after independence in

1980). Like in the original BSA Company colonial model, in these areas traditional communal land tenure prevails. From the beginning of colonial administration, native reserves (now communal lands) were set aside for exclusive use by Africans. These reserves (now called communal lands) have continued to be administered directly by central government, albeit remaining 'traditional' in that traditional leaders retain the rights to allocate arable plots among local households, while grazing land is open to those households. Methods of cultivation have remained the same to those used before colonialism, but now with much higher population densities and therefore with lower levels of production.[18] In this sense, the concept of reserves is closely associated with settler colonialism as it was its creation. The reserves, therefore, deliberately created the dualistic economic structure with a socio-legal segregation based on reserved land categories.

The native reserves concept reached its extreme case in the South African apartheid and Rhodesian racialist systems. A similar view of dual economy is also to be found in some form (based on class rather than race) in many other underdeveloped countries. But in the latter, there were no 'lands' set out as reserves.

In South Africa, the reserves were originally to protect the Khoikhoi ('Hottentots') whose lands had been transferred into white hands, leaving them with the unpalatable choice of taking up low paid jobs in the white service, going into the reserves (the first of which were created in 1801), or moving into the territory of other Africans.[19] The reserves were later on extended to other African areas in Natal and Transkei. The Rhodesian reserves like those of South Africa and, to a lesser extent, those of Kenya and Northern Rhodesia (Zambia), were also indicative of the degree of land alienation in these territories. Where massive land alienation did not take place, like in Tanganyika (mainland Tanzania) and Nyasaland (Malawi), there arose no need to create reserves. In these territories the African majority occupied a greater proportion of the country, their land areas being referred to as public land and native trust land respectively.

Going back to the Rhodesian experience, we find that the basis for a dual economy along the racial division of land was laid in the first ten years of the settler colonial occupation. Already by the turn of the nineteenth century, three types of land categories were in existence, namely: (a) reserves – land set aside for the exclusive use by Africans; (b) land alienated to mines and farms, sometimes occupied, sometimes in the hands of absentee land owners or companies; (c) un-alienated land that the BSA Company regarded as its own until the Privy Council decision of 1918 conferred it to the Crown.

In the Zimbabwean case, the tenure regime instituted in the colonial era has continued to the country's independence in 1980 and beyond. While white commercial agricultural farming areas used the "freehold" system to use, mortgage, raise capital from banking institutions, dispose and acquire as well as bequeath as inheritance there were differences in the other tenure regimes. In the large-scale commercial farming (LSCF) areas there was a vibrant land market, which was predicated on the 'freehold' rights pertaining to that tenure regime. Individuals and corporates were able to buy and dispose of their 'commercial' properties, with legal basis ensuring that these transfers were recorded with the Registrar of Deeds under the Ministry of Justice and Parliamentary Affairs.

The legal basis of dualism in the Rhodesian experience

In this section we show how the contemporary dualistic land market was actually created historically by the land legislation of the colonial governments. As we have seen, the apportioning of land by race began as soon as the BSA Company hoisted the British flag in Zimbabwe. But it was only in 1930 when the Land Apportionment Act became the first legal sanction by Parliament to provide reserved areas for whites and blacks throughout the country.

The land distribution under the Land Apportionment Act (1930) broadly followed the division of land that had been made in the 1890s, i.e. during the first decade of colonisation. The European land area rose from 20 per cent of total in 1911, to 32.6 per cent in 1925, and to 50.8 per cent in 1931. The Land Apportionment Act had, thus, allocated over 50 per cent of the total land area to the whites (3 per cent of the population) and only 30 per cent to the blacks (97 per cent). Thus, the seeds for future confrontation leading to the protracted war of liberation and the land battles that have continued long after Zimbabwe's independence were laid.

The Land Apportionment Act was in force for 39 years, when it was finally superseded by the Land Tenure Act of 1969. All the main provisions of the former Act were confirmed. These two Acts form the pivotal legislations on which the whole of the Rhodesian land policies rest.

All the known mineral resources and major transport networks, including all the railways and paved roads, were carefully confined to the European Areas, as was a large part of fertile land with good rainfall.[20] All urban areas also lay within the European Area. The undetermined area, which also lay under European ownership, consisted of 0.1 per cent of total land area, which, if the owners so desired, could be transferred to Africans and become incorporated into the Native Purchase Area.[21] The Forest Area consisted of land set aside for the development as Forest reserves, more or less as a national asset. The unassigned land was generally poor and inhospitable land left under the government jurisdiction to be distributed later among any of the categories.[22]

Under the colonial legislation, no African was allowed to purchase or occupy land in the European Area. The Land Apportionment Act of 1930 provided that:

a No African shall acquire, lease or occupy land in the European Area.
b No owner or occupier of land in the European Area, or his agent shall:
  i dispose or attempt to dispose of any such land to an African;
  ii lease any such land to an African; and
  iii permit, suffer or allow any African to occupy such land.[23]

These provisions of the Land Apportionment Act were retained in the Land Tenure Act of 1969. Under the revised Act, an equal amount of land, approximately 46 per cent of the total land area in each case, was allocated to Africans and Europeans. However, since the Africans were 96 per cent of the population, whereas the Europeans were only 4 per cent, this works out in theory at around three hectares for each black person, compared with 60 hectares for a white. 'In practice, most of the European land was concentrated in a few hands, with huge farms being owned by a comparatively small number of the wealthiest white farmers and businessmen'.[24] This will be discussed in detail in the subsection below of the farm-size distribution. Also under the Land Tenure Act, an additional 7 per cent of the total land area was designated as National Land, consisting of national parks and game reserves.

On the other hand, the land area occupied by Africans had been severely limited by the same laws. Under the Land Apportionment Act of 1930 the African Land Area was divided into Native Reserves and Native Purchase Areas (later called African Purchase Areas (APAs) and subsequently renamed Small-Scale Commercial Farms (SSCF) in the post-independence era).

However, under the colonial land laws, administratively the land was no longer vested in the Chief as it was in the traditional system, since the traditional powers of the Chief had been subordinated to those of the European Native Commissioners. Under both the Land Apportionment Act of 1930 and the Land Tenure Act of 1969, powers that gave consent to the occupation and use of land by Africans in the Reserves (now called the Tribal Trust Lands) were vested in the colonial government authorities.[25]

The APAs were reserved for acquisition as farms by individual Africans, and regarded as compensation for the loss of the right to purchase farmland anywhere in the country. Africans were only allowed to buy and own land individually in the APAs, the purpose of which was to encourage the development of a limited number of cash crop farmers. Thus, only 10 per cent of the total land area allotted to the black majority under the Land Tenure Act of 1969 was made up of the APAs, while around 90 per cent consisted of the Tribal Trust Lands.[26]

With the enactment of the Maize Control Amendment Act of 1940, a new price system was instituted whereby the government guaranteed a fixed price to the producers based on the estimated costs of production plus some profit.[27] In 1943, the government guaranteed a price of 13 shillings six pence and a bonus of two shillings for all maize delivered to the government maize marketing agency, the Maize Control Board, provided that maize was grown under certain conditions of sound farming practices. These conditions were that the area under maize cultivation should be protected from soil erosion, and that in the first season, one-third of the area (and one-half of the following season) under cultivation should be planted with green manure crop. These conditions obviously discriminated against the African farmers, since the digging of contour ridges for the protection of soil erosion only started in earnest after 1951, under the Native Land Husbandry Act.

As is evident from the situation just described in respect of maize, agricultural pricing policies came to be closely tied to the institutions set up to regulate agricultural activity. In the 1920s the white farmers called for the establishment of statutory marketing agencies in order to stabilise and guarantee agricultural producer prices and help find domestic and foreign markets for their produce. The slump in the prices in the wake of the great depression of the early 1930s made the case for statutory marketing institutions even more necessary. Thus, the sudden decline in the price of maize at the beginning of 1931 became the main reason for the setting up of the Maize Marketing Board, established by the Maize Control Act of 1931. It became compulsory for all maize marketed in the urban areas (except for sales between Africans in the same administrative area) to be sold to the Board.

Maize marketing had thus become a controlled product and the government had established a monopoly over the marketing of maize into the urban areas. The Maize Marketing Board functioned until 1950 when it was replaced by the Grain Marketing Board (GMB), created under the Grain Marketing Act (No. 31). Since its formation, the GMB has controlled the purchase and sale of various products including sorghum (from 1950), groundnuts (from 1951), soybeans (from 1969), wheat (from 1970) and coffee (from 1971).[28] Following the opening up of the economy in the 1990s, most of the controls were scrapped, – but then they were re-introduced from the year 2001.

From the early years of colonial administration, the policy was to locate the European farms within a radius of 25 miles of the railway line so that white farmers had easy access to the country's transport system. Peasant farmers, by contrast, were cut off from markets. When railway costs were added, grain crops could not bear the costs of more than 15 miles of ox-wagon transport.[29] Thus, the general movement of Africans into the more-remote reserves not only reduced the inland resources both in terms of size and quality, but also progressively reduced their ability to compete in grain markets. In order to access export markets from a land-locked situation, Zimbabwe's railways and roads were created with the aim of assisting transit routes to the sea-ports. Virtually all the exports of bulk products (mainly minerals and agricultural products) either go through the Mozambique ports of Beira and Maputo or the South African port of Durban.

From the discriminatory pricing system and provision of infrastructure shown above, there was a continuation and deepening of dualism in the

Zimbabwean economy, which started first and foremost in the land market and was entrenched through other factor markets (labour and capital) and in product markets, mainly via discrimination in the marketing arrangements of agricultural produce. These relationships interacted to create economic impoverishment of the African agricultural producers and the African labour force. The following interlocking forces contributed to the following outcome: land alienation policies and discrimination in the provision of infrastructure and services; population pressure in the African rural areas and soil erosion; low productivity; and migrant labour discrimination and low wages.[30]

Dualism also emerged from the biases in factor and product markets, and through the institutional and political mechanisms created by the colonial governments to undermine the participation of the African peasant farmers in marketing agricultural production. The conduct of the marketing institutions that emerged after the depression of the early 1930s was important in this regard, as was the dualistic structure of the transport services in relation to the marketing of agricultural produce.

By the time of Zimbabwe's independence in 1980, some 6,600 white farmers occupied 15.5 million hectares of prime land, while some seven million African people were crowded in the marginal and drier parts of the country. As will be seen in the following chapters, it is this dualism in the land market that forms the basis of the current and continuing dualism in the Zimbabwean economy.

Land distribution by natural regions and farm-size

Zimbabwe's agricultural land distribution closely follows that of the country's three major landscapes: the high-veld, the middle-veld and the high-veld.[31] Rainfall, but not necessarily land quality, also closely follows the country's landscape with the highest rainfall found in the high-veld and lowest precipitation in the low lying areas of the country.

The country's farming systems was carefully designed to according to its five agro-ecological regions, namely:

Region I, lies on the eastern border, predominantly in the Melsetter and Chipinge areas (eastern highlands), and has the highest effective rainfall. The eastern border area is mostly mountainous and cool with a high summer rainfall which spreads for longer duration around the year so that dry months may range zero to three months. This region is the most suitable for specialised – intensive and diversified farming – beef and dairy farming and plantation crops.

Region II, largely, on the high-veld, is the main area suitable for intensive cropping in Zimbabwe. It has good summer rainfall but winters are dry. There are some dry spells during the rainy season. Large-scale maize cropping and tobacco farming as well as mixed farming are found in this region. Intensive forms of agriculture have developed within easy reach of the towns to satisfy the specialised needs of the urban markets.[32]

Region III, situated in the middle-veld, has a drier and warmer climate than Natural Region II. There is greater risk of drought as the rainy season is relatively short so that more reliance must be placed on drought resistant crops and cattle as the main production. Region III is most suitable for semi-intensive crop production as well as mixed farming.

Region IV, in the middle-veld and high-veld, is only recommended for semi-intensive farming. Rainfall is considerably low and there are frequent dry spells during the rainy season. The risk of drought is considerable for crop production, which cannot be recommended without supplementary irrigation, though there is still production of drought resistant staples and cash crops on some suitable sites. Cattle production dominates the agricultural industry.

Region V, predominantly in the high-veld, is only suitable for extensive farming. The incidence of drought is very high and the ecologically dry season is the longest. Cattle ranching and other livestock, especially goats, have remained the dominant form of agriculture. Region IV, also in the high-veld, has most of the characteristics of Region V, but is unsuitable for crop production, except under irrigation. The fact that this classification is based on effective rainfall makes the feasibility of irrigation and cattle feeding important factors in transforming land from one region to another.[33]

According to the extent of land distribution per each natural region, 38 per cent of the total land area is suitable for crop production (Natural Regions I–III) and approximately 60 per cent is suitable for livestock production (Natural Regions IV–V).[34] The unequal distribution of land most suitable for agriculture was very clear. In total, 71 per cent of Natural Region I, 69 per cent of Region II, and 45 per cent of Region III was allocated to the European Area during the colonial period.

Four defining features of Zimbabwe's communal sector can be listed as follows.[35]

a Its relatively poor agricultural potential, which is in contrast to the most productive land in Natural Regions I and II held by large scale commercial farmers, while most of the communal farming areas, c.60 per cent fell into Natural Regions IV and V, with very limited agricultural potential.[36]

b Its burgeoning population operating within a traditional system of agriculture dominated by land tenure arrangements whereby local leaders allocate arable land to households and their families on a usufruct basis. Effectively, this means that land cannot be officially rented, bought and sold. Another drawback is the continual subdivision of land into smaller and less viable holdings as the population grows. This is due to the absence of a land market, which allows a mechanism to consolidate small plots into more viable farm sizes. As the population builds up households must access land in more marginal farming areas unsuitable for cultivation, setting in motion a debilitating process of extensive and shifting cultivation.[37]

c Households' entitlement to common property resources, such as water for household use and irrigation, woodlands for firewood and building, and pastures for grazing cattle and other livestock. Herein lies the problem of communities trying to devise rules – that involve high transaction costs and which are continually buffeted by powerful but perverse economic incentives for individuals to benefit by their unsustainable use of natural resources.[38]

d Finally, the main defining feature of Zimbabwe's communal areas is their stunted urban growth coupled with very poor infrastructure and services. Typically, the communal settlement pattern consists of tiny scattered farms, punctuated every few kilometres with the so called 'growth points', usually small run-down rural centres that serve the immediately surrounding communities.

Given the above described situation, the inequitable land distribution by race was exacerbated if we take into account that the land most suitable for intensive agriculture was allocated to the European farmers, a group with most of the capital resources, while the land suitable for semi-intensive and semi-extensive livestock production went to the African Area.

The discriminatory and dualistic political and economic framework developed during the previous periods, especially with regards to land policy, was further entrenched under the subsequent land laws, e.g. the Native Land Husbandry Act of 1951. This ensured that the pattern of land distribution in Zimbabwe remained the same throughout the colonial period. This uneven distribution of the land was the driving force of the war of liberation that engulfed the country from the 1960s to 1980, culminating with negotiations for independence from the colonial master, at Lancaster House, London, England in 1979. By 1997, nearly two decades after Zimbabwe's independence in 1980, the historical fact of extreme concentration of land ownership had remained intact. Although the number of white commercial farmers had decreased to about 4,500, they still held over 30 per cent of the country's most productive land under freehold.[39]

The main conclusion from this section is that the existing structure of the distribution of landed wealth in Zimbabwe owes its origin to the historical process of colonial land policies. The chief characteristic of economic dualism in Zimbabwe's agricultural economy was manifested in the concentration of land among the country's whites and the depressed tiny holdings of peasant agriculture in the 'native reserves'. As shown above, African peasants had been forcibly evicted from their good quality lands and resettled into the designated African reserves (later called Tribal Trust Lands).

What made this dualistic structure of land distribution become unacceptable was the fact that, while the majority of the Africans were facing growing overpopulation, landlessness and land degradation and increasing poverty in these overcrowded and overgrazed African areas, much of the land held by whites remained unutilised.

Notes

1 Floyd, 1962:231.
2 Lundahl and Ndlela, 1980:110.
3 Ibid.:130.
4 Palmer, 1977:25.
5 Stigger, 1971:12.
6 Ibid.
7 Palmer, 1977:28.
8 A land measure formerly used in the Netherlands and still used in South Africa, equal to about 2 acres Palmer, 1977:82.
9 One morgen = 2.1 acres = 0.85 hectares.
10 A figure of 30,000 cattle was entered in the books of the Native Commissioner as a figure representing cattle taken 'for the use of settlers' (sic) before the final distribution in December 1895 in which the Company helped itself to an additional 35,000 head. Stigger, 1971:20.
11 Palmer, 1977:35.
12 Stigger, 1971:14.
13 Ibid.
14 Palmer, 1997:36.
15 Ibid.
16 Ibid.
17 Rifkind, 1972:55.
18 Riddell, 1978:6–11.
19 Davenport, 1969:293.
20 International Commission of Jurists Report, 1976:12.
21 Kay, 1970:51.
22 Ibid.
23 Southern Rhodesia, *The Land Apportionment Act* (1930), section 42(1) (a).
24 IDAF, 1977:9.
25 Ushewokunze, 1980:181.
26 IDAF, 1977:9–10.
27 Yudelman, 1964:273.
28 Some other products were initially controlled and later removed from the controls list: beans in 1959, bulrush millet in 1962 and finger millet (rapoko) in 1965.
29 Arrighi, 1970:217.
30 Ndlela, 1981:58–59.
31 The 'high-veld' consists of a high plateau that stretches from south-west to south-east through the centre of the country. The 'high-veld' lies in an altitude of between 1,200 and 1,500 metres above sea level. Next to the 'high-veld' is the 'middle-veld' which has an altitude of between 900 and 1,200 metres above sea level. Land below 900 metres above sea level forms the 'low-veld' and consists of the Zambezi Valley, the Limpopo Valley and the Sabi Basin.
32 Metcalfe, 1971:86.
33 The Sabi–Limpopo scheme and the Tuli scheme among others have shown that land classification as dry land could turned into massive agricultural production when the appropriate irrigation infrastructure is made available, thus, the Sabi Basin at Chiredzi normally in Natural Region V was made suitable for growing citrus fruit, sugar cane, wheat and cotton.
34 Riddell, 1978:1, Table 1.

35 Dore, 2009:1–2.
36 Vincent and Thomas, 1961.
37 Lele and Stone, 1989, quoted in Dore, ibid.
38 Dore aptly observes that 'despite four decades of critiques of Hardin's Tragedy of the Commons (1968), the basic tenets of his argument still hold true today. Deforestation, overgrazing, and the silting of dams in the communal areas bear witness to the externalisation of environmental costs as individuals benefit from using a public resource but bear few of the costs.' Ibid.
39 Kanyenze *et al.*, 2011:77.

References

Arrighi, Giovanni 1970. 'Labour Supplies in Historical Perspective: A Study of the Prelotarianization of the African Peasantry in Rhodesia', *The Journal of Development Studies*, Vol. 6, No. 3:217.

Dore, Dale. 2009. *The Recovery and Transformation of Zimbabwe's Communal Areas*. Comprehensive Economic Recovery in Zimbabwe, Working Paper Series. Working Paper 4. United National Development Programme, UNDP. Zimbabwe.

Davenport, T.R.H. 1969. 'The Consolidation of a New Society: The Cape Colony', in M. Wilson and L. Thompson (eds), *Oxford History of South Africa, Vol. 1, South Africa to 1970*. Oxford: Clarendon Press.

Floyd, B. 1962. *Land Apportionment in Southern Rhodesia*, in R. Prothero (ed.), *People and Land in Africa*. London: Oxford University Press.

IDAF. 1977. *International Defence and Aid Fund. Zimbabwe: The Facts about Rhodesia* London: IDAF.

International Commission of Jurists Report. 1976. *Racial Discrimination and Regression in Southern Rhodesia*. Geneva: United Nations.

Kanyenze, G., Kondo, T., Chitambara, P. and Martens, J. (eds). 2011. *Beyond The Enclave: Towards a Pro-poor and Inclusive Development Strategy for Zimbabwe*. Harare: Weaver Press.

Kay, George. 1970. *Rhodesia: A Human Geography*. London: University of London Press.

Lele, U. and Stone, S. 1989. *Population Pressure, the Environment and Agricultural Intensification*. MADIA Discussion Paper 4. World Bank, Washington, DC.

Lundahl, Mats and Ndlela, Daniel B. 1980. 'Land Alienation. Dualism, and Economic Discrimination: South Africa and Rhodesia', *Economy and History*, University of Lund, Vol. 23, No. 2. London, Pretoria: The Human Sciences Research Council (HSRC) Press,

Metcalfe, C.B. 1971. *A Guide to Farming in Rhodesia*. Salisbury: Rhodesian Farming.

Ndlela, Daniel Boda. 1981. 'Dualism in the Rhodesian Colonial Economy', *Lund Economic Studies*, Department of Economics, University of Lund, Sweden, Lund.

Palmer, Robin. 1977. *Land and Racial Discrimination in Rhodesia*. London: Heinemann.

Riddell, Roger C. 1978. *The Land Problem in Rhodesia. Alternatives for the Future*. Mambo Occasional Papers, Socio-Economic Series No. 11, Gwelo.

Rifkind, M.L. 1972. 'Land Apportionment in Rhodesia', *Rhodesian History*, Vol. 3:55.

Southern Rhodesia. 1930. *The Land Apportionment Act*. Salisbury: Government Printers.

Stigger, P. 1977. 'Volunteers and the Profit Motive in the Anglo-Ndebele War, 1893', *Rhodesian History*, Vol. 2:11–23.

Ushewokunze, C. 1980. 'A Survey of Legal Aspects of Land Tenure, Mineral Production and Manufacturing Industries, Including Aspects of Economic Sanctions', in UN – United Nations. *Zimbabwe, Towards a New Order: Economic and Social Survey*. Working Papers, Vol. 1, United Nations.

Vincent, V. and Thomas, R.G. 196. *Agricultural Survey of Southern Rhodesia*. Harare: Government Printer.

Yudelman, Montague. 1974. *Africans on the Land: Economic Problems of African Agricultural Development in Southern, Central and East Africa, with Special Reference to Southern Rhodesia*. Cambridge, MA: Harvard University Press.

4 Dualism in agricultural credit and produce markets

Background

The chapter sets out to show that the volume of credit funds was much higher in the white farming sector than in the African sectors, and explores the reasons for the low level of credit in African peasant sector. It also shows that while the European agricultural sector received ample amounts of credit from both the private banks and the public financial sources, there was virtual scarcity of credit to the African farmers.

In the produce market, the chapter shows that at the beginning of colonial rule, African peasant farmers were able to produce for surplus and trade a variety of produce (grain, sweet potatoes, pumpkins and groundnuts) to the incoming white settlers. But this was soon nipped in the bud as their land areas were alienated to the white settler farmers. Further discriminatory practices were reinforced by the government's establishment of statutory marketing agencies, which were meant to stabilise prices for the white farmers, especially during the world depression of the early 1930s.

In Part I of the chapter, the Rhodesian agricultural credit market will be explained with reference to the development of the institutional sources of credit. The section ends with an analysis of interest rates, which indicates that lending rates were determined by government policy and were unimportant in the allocation of credit.

In Part II on dualism in the Agricultural Produce Markets, we discuss the development of the agricultural produce market, paying particular attention to the institutions and price policies that affected the marketing of the produce of European farmers and African peasants. This section focuses on the decline in participation of the African peasantry in the produce market. As will be seen, developments in the produce market strongly reinforced dualism in the land market, and contributed to unlimited supplies of labour to the modern economy. We provide an account of the marketing institutions in the Rhodesian economy as they emerged after the great depression of the early 1930s, and the discriminatory price policies that were administered under these marketing institutions. Further, these price policies had the effect of limiting the marketing opportunities for African produce.

Finally, we analyse the dualistic structure of the transport services in relation to the marketing of agricultural produce.

Part I: agricultural credit

The demand for credit

The demand for credit in the agricultural sector of underdeveloped countries is frequently connected with consumption needs between the planting and harvesting periods, and, in addition, with both long-term 'fixed capital' needs and short-term requirements, like variable capital inputs (fertilisers, seeds and fuel). While the demand for credit for consumption purposes was almost exclusively concentrated in the African peasant sector, this experience has affected both the white commercial farming sector and the emerging African peasantry. In this sub-section, our purpose is to determine the extent of the demand for credit in the European and African farming sectors.

It is well known that the whites in Rhodesia were generally better off with regard to savings than Africans. This was because the white farmers had higher per capita incomes than Africans, since increases in per capita incomes are an important source of savings. It can, therefore, be concluded that the former had better possibilities for saving and accumulating capital formation than the latter. This, however, did not prevent the white farmers from demanding credit. In fact, despite their better position for accumulating savings, the white farmers needed credit facilities for their farming operations. The demand for credit by the white farmers to purchase farms, livestock and agricultural equipment and improvements such as fencing and irrigation works led to the establishment of a Land Bank in 1912.[1] (The success of this scheme in Rhodesia led white settlers elsewhere – notably Kenya where one similar bank was established in 1930 – to demand similar facilities for white farmers.[2])

In combination with the demand for pure credit facilitates, the white farmers in Rhodesia also pressed for more government subsidies and extension services.[3] The combination of these factors created an unfair competition between the 'heavily subsidised European farmers' and the African peasant farmers who were, in addition, being pushed away from the lands with easy access to the markets.[4] The demand for credit facilities by the whites in the agricultural sector led the government to establish the Land and Agricultural Bank in 1924, which replaced the previously established Land Bank, to provide medium- and long-term credit for European agriculture and short-term loans for agricultural production.

Another reason for the establishment of the Land and Agricultural Bank was the recognition by the government that private commercial banks could not be relied upon to provide long-term and intermediate credit to the agricultural sector. This institution served the demand for white farmers during the whole period from 1924 to 1971 when it was replaced by the Agricultural

Finance Corporation (AFC) of Rhodesia. Available estimates indicate that 80 per cent of all European farmers had actually demanded loans at one time or another by 1954.[5] Table 4.1 shows loans granted for a wide variety of purposes for the white farmers in 1969. The loans ranged from the purchase of land, erection of buildings, irrigation works and equipment to cropping activities. The Land and Agricultural Bank's loans fell into the three categories of long-term, short-term and drought relief loans.

The demand for credits by the white farming sector also led to the private banking system to grant credits, especially short-term loans to white farmers. The operations of the private banks will be discussed when we come to the supply of credit.

Turning our attention to the demand for credit in the African sector, we can also postulate that the African peasants needed credit for a variety of purposes including buying land as well as for short-term requirements. The colonial government put great obstacles in the way of those Africans who had resources to buy land.[6] This was due to the fear of white settlers of African competition in the land and produce markets, and any demand for credit by the African farmers was frustrated. But this by itself could not stop the Africans from demanding more credit.

In his book *Development in Rhodesian Tribal Areas*, a Rhodesian economist, A.J.B. Hughes, denied the need for credit by the African farmers.

Table 4.1 Purposes for which credit was granted to white farmers

	1969 ($)	*15 Months ended 31-3-71 ($)*
Purchase of land	1,411,324	2,439,354
Erection of buildings	112,234	170,059
Erection of fencing	164,620	130,818
Construction of dip-tanks/spray races	9,620	9,710
Construction of water and soil conservation	13,630	39,166
Sinking of wells and boreholes	15,382	24,332
Irrigation works and equipment	125,000	197,125
Repayment of bonds:	269,302	203,247
Land bank	176,830	184,517
Others	54,566	38,254
Payment of sundry liabilities	1,307,530	1,470,893
Purchase of livestock	640,634	625,222
Purchase of implements	11,262,116	11,649,906
Crop production expenses	**$15,562,788**	**$17,182,603**
Three categories of loans	$	$
Long-term loans	3,840,766	5,185,549
Short-term loans	9,329,680	8,407,895
Drought relief loans	2,392,342	3,589,159
	$15,562,788	**$17,182,603**

Source: Rhodesia – Report of the Operation of the Land and Agricultural Bank, 1971:2.

on rather subjective grounds.[7] He states that there was growing realisation in many quarters that the assumption of credit by individual tribal farmers was a non-essential prerequisite for agricultural advancement.[8] Hughes emphasises that the Tribal Trust Land (TTL) farmers must take positive steps to save up money in advance to pay for the agricultural inputs required for more sophisticated agricultural practises.[9]

This dismissive and patronising view is an incorrect view. The neglect of the need for credit by African farmers has been shown to have adverse effects on development. Under the so-called community development scheme of the colonial government, the TTLs were required to raise revenue by local taxation and fees for certain services.[10] However, due to the impoverishment of these areas, this policy resulted in community services, e.g. schools, being closed down for lack of funds.

Mats Lundahl[11] points out that in a rural economy where incomes are close to subsistence level, credit demand arises for a wide variety of purpose. Lundahl distinguishes two kinds of loans; those taken to protect the borrower against unforeseen contingencies, precautionary loans in the Keynesian terminology, and those taken to cover expenses actually incurred or to be incurred during the loan period. The small farmer is thus more or less constantly faced with the problem of cash flow and risk management without large flows of cash.

There is no quantification of the relative extent of 'precautionary' loans and 'actual expense' loans in the Zimbabwean peasant agricultural sector. Although it is not possible to know the relative importance of the demand for credit for unpredictable events and loans to meet the operating expenses of the households, some popular assets such as livestock (which is relatively liquid) are kept as a reserve to fall back upon in times of need. In practice, it may be cheaper to go into debt once an unforeseen event has happened. But, it is probable that the demand for precautionary loans was less significant when compared to the demand for loans to meet current expenditure.[12]

One of the most important categories of loans demanded by the Zimbabwean African farmers arose out of the need to purchase capital inputs. The demand for the latter may well have been intensified among Africans during the 1930s since the Land Apportionment Act of 1930 put a definite limit on the land available for settlement by the Africans, thus creating the necessary conditions for a transformation from the 'traditional' system of cultivation to permanent or continuous cultivation. Given the techniques employed by the African farmers and the types of soils allocated to them, the transformation towards a continuous system of cultivation produced soil erosion and declining land productivity. In these circumstances, in order to raise their output per capita, African farmers needed to intensify production. Although cattle dung and compost manure had begun to be applied to cultivated land during the early 1940s, other means of intensification – fertilisers, improved seed, insecticides, and farm equipment – had to be purchased. As we have seen in the above section, household savings in the

African sector presumably were invariably low. In an analysis of the Rhodesian situation, Montague Yudelman observed that 'All available evidence indicates that net returns after cash outlays for supplies' (especially fertiliser) were higher than when producers did not use these supplies.[13] According to an estimate of the Native Land Husbandry Act of 1951, a farm holding of eight cultivated acres with six head of cattle and 60 acres of grazing land was expected to yield a profit of £98 if the producer uses £22 worth of fertiliser. But, in 1960, less than 3 per cent of the producers in the African areas used fertilisers.[14]

Thus, we may safely conclude that the demand for credit for agricultural production purposes among the Africans (both APAs and TTLs) is quite high judging by the needs of the African farmers to borrow in order to purchase capital inputs. Of, course, this postulated high demand by African farmers for productive credit may, in practice, be lessened somewhat if one takes into account the general lack of knowledge about investment opportunities and managerial skills, which make the peasants fail to take advantage of the agricultural incentives, which were generally available to the white farmers and also to the few progressive APA farmers. In addition, the peasant is not likely to be a dynamic risk taker because any unsuccessful innovation in his sphere of production is likely to lead to starvation among his family given the subsistence nature of his farming enterprise

The supply of credit

In general there are two types of credit markets in underdeveloped countries: the informal credit market and the formal credit markets. The former are usually operated by moneylenders (generally under unwritten contracts), but their presence is quite widespread in many poor peasant societies. In the Zimbabwean colonial experience these sources of loans were noticeably lacking so that the African peasant farmers had no choice but to seek credit in the formal credit markets. Though there are no studies exploring the reasons why the informal credit markets did not mushroom under the Rhodesian colonial era as they had done elsewhere, it is generally known that the creation of the African reserves under the strict surveillance of the colonial administration prevented the emergence of the informal money markets. First, from the early years of colonial rule, a practice quickly grew up whereby an inadequate level of cash income from the sale of surplus produce could be supplemented by income from wage labour Second, the relative lack of storekeepers (who could afford to offer consumer credit) in the African reserves meant that most consumer goods and agricultural equipment were purchased in the distant urban areas and mines, forfeiting close contacts between the possible borrowers and the money lenders necessary for the development of an informal money market.[15] Under these circumstances there were no informal money markets in Rhodesia. Thus, Yudelman wrote, 'The only avenue open for the average producer to acquire capital is through the sale of his labour or his cattle or by borrowing from public lending agencies created to meet his needs'.[16]

However, as will be seen, discrimination in the extension of credit from formal sector meant that African farmers were severely constrained in their development. As Giovanni Arrighi noted, 'the extension of credit (which could possibly come only from European sources) to African farmers was hampered and therefore a constant lack of financing was bound to hold back their development'.[17]

In the sub-section below we discuss the supply of formal credit, i.e. institutional facilities of credit in both the European and the African agriculture. As will be seen, dualism and its attendant inequalities in the land market was extended to the provision of credit.

Institutional sources of credit in the European sector

Organised agricultural credit in Rhodesia began with the establishment of the Land Bank in 1912, with a share capital of £250,000. The aim of the Land Bank was to make credit facilities available to persons of European descent only.[18] Bank loans up to £2,000 for the purchase of farms, livestock and other agricultural equipment were made to white farmers.[19] The Land Bank was replaced by the Land and Agricultural Bank of Southern Rhodesia established in 1924.

As can be seen in Table 4.2, the number of loans granted to white farmers increased by 6.5 times from the 1924–30 period up to the 1966–71 period. (The number of white farmers rose from 2,355 in 1921 to 5,700 in

Table 4.2 Loans granted to farmers by the land and agricultural bank, 1924–1971*

Period	*Number*	*Loans granted amount ($)*	*Owing by farmers at last date ($)*
1924–1930	1,765	2,604,414	1,716,874
1931–1935	964	939,800	1,909,974
1936–1940	717	1,055,166	1,716,970
1941–1945	411	806,464	1,054,354
1946–1950	2,407	4,875,106	2,801,538
1951–1955	4,599	11,502,600	6,002,512
1956–1960	6,388	21,568,774	11,598,814
1961–1965	10,302	51,726,884	22,013,132
1966–1971	11,472	73,177,499	31,923,085
(31 March)	39,025	$168,256,707	

Source: Rhodesia – Report of the Operations of the Land and Agricultural Bank, 1971:3.

Note

* The above figures do not include loans granted by the Bank in respect of the various schemes and funds administered on an agency basis.

1965).[20] (The drop in the number of loans during the 1930s and early 1940s can be explained by the depression of the early thirties and the strain in the economy caused by the war in the early forties.) The amounts loaned increased by 28 times from the late twenties to the late sixties. Thus, on its dissolution in 1971, the Bank directors went on record to say, 'the Bank served the agricultural community with the understanding and efficiency, and has done more, probably, than any other organisation to settle men on the land'.[21]

The Land and Agricultural Bank as a statutory organisation reflected government policy and exclusively served European farmers. The first effort to provide credit facilities for African farmers was not made until in 1945, when the Land and Agricultural Bank initiated a scheme of advancing loans to Africans in the African Purchase Areas (APAs). However, these loans were not for the initial purchase of land and capital inputs as was the case with European farmers, but they were limited to permanent improvements and could not exceed two-thirds of the value of the property.

Other public sources providing white agricultural credit included the Agricultural Assistance Board, the Farm Irrigation Fund, and the Agricultural Diversification Fund. The last two were established after the Unilateral Declaration of Independence (UDI) in 1965 in order to assist with diversification of farming activities. But in terms of superseding the Land and Agricultural Bank, the Agricultural Finance Corporation (AFC) was established in 1972. Like the former organisation, the AFC was responsible for the control and administration of all government sponsored credit except some funds made available to African farmers. The primary aim of the AFC was to provide credit to farmers, confining itself mainly to the European farming sector. Thus, apart from an insignificant loan arrangement on some 'water developments' among APA farmers (where tenure system permits to offer some collateral for loans), the AFC did not offer any credit facilities to farmers in the African farmers in the Tribal Trust Lands.[22]

The AFC was the agricultural sector's main source of long-term development loans. The long-term loans provided by the AFC, and prior to its establishment by the Land and Agricultural Bank, rose from R$14.7 million at the end of 1968 to R$24.3 million at the end of 1973.[23] By 1975 the AFC's long-term loans amounted to R$24 million outstanding.[24] The AFC also provided short-term loans along with other institutions especially the private banks.

The commercial banks have been an important source of short-term credit for the white farmers. These credits were supplied either directly by the private banks or through the extension of the suppliers' credit by commercial companies and cooperatives. Short-term credit for farming was mainly in the area of financing cropping activities. Tables 4.3 and 4.4 show relative positions of the three institutions in the provision of short term credit.

As shown in Tables 4.3 and 4.4, the government sponsored short-term credit (AFC) increased its stake in the 1965–1975 period, although there was a clear dominance of private funds, notably from commercial banks. If one takes into consideration that figures advanced through commercial bank overdrafts, and/or discount houses, the declining share of pure bank credit in favour of suppliers' credit probably reflects nothing more than a shift from direct to indirect financing on the part of the banks. Taken together, the commercial banks and discount houses accounted for two thirds to three quarters of all short term credit accruing to the European farming industry.

Table 4.3 Short-term credit extended to white farmers (R$'000)

End of period	*Agricultural Finance Corp. (short-term loans)*[1]	*Commercial banks (advances)*	*Suppliers' credit*[2]	*Total*
1965 December	9,056	27,066	12,636	48,758
1966 December	10,022	23,726	10,926	44,874
1967 December	11,812	20,344	10,942	43,094
1968 December	11,546	25,112	13,550	50,208
1969 December	11,216	24,530	17,105	52,851
1970 December	12,159	28,186	19,235	59,580
1971 December	13,494	32,804	26,603	72,901
1972 December	14,824	33,678	24,238	72,740
1973 December	14,824	36,309	29,003	79,931
1974 December	18,535	45,109	34,415	98,059
1975 December	26,222	51,917	33,014	111,153
1976 December	30,819	54,227	36,338	121,384
1977 December	36,751	47,753	33,264	117,768
1978 December	33,770	51,553	36,218	121,451

Source: Zimbabwe Rhodesia – Supplement to the Monthly Digest of Statistics, January, 1980.

Notes
1 Figures prior to 1 April 1971 relate to Land and Agricultural Bank only.
2 Commercial companies and cooperatives.

Table 4.4 Volume ($ million) and structure (%) by origin of short-term credit to white agriculture 1965, 1971 and 1975

Origin	*1965*		*1971*		*1975*	
	$m	*%*	*$m*	*%*	*$m*	*%*
Agricultural Finance Corp.	9.1	18.6	13.5	18.5	26.2	23.4
Commercial banks	27.1	55.5	32.8	45.0	51.9	46.7
Suppliers' credit	12.6	25.9	26.6	36.5	33.0	29.7
Total	48.8	100.0	72.6	100.0	111.1	100.0

Source: Hume, 1977: Table 11.

Institutional source of credit in the African sector

The scanty sources of credit available to African farmers have been the public financial institutions sponsored by the government. Up to the country's independence from white rule, Rhodesian commercial banks had never had any lending facilities for African farmers.[25] The only exception to this rule was the African Loan and Development Trust (a private commercial finance company), which extended an insignificant amount of loans to APA farmers. As will be seen, only a very small section of the African farmers was reached by this public credit facility and the volume of these loans was low, especially when contrasted with the loans obtained by the white farmers. In the last part of this sub-section we list the reasons for the low volume of credit going to the African farmers.

As shown above, the Land and Agricultural Bank did not advance loans to the APA farmers to start new farms. The 1945 scheme stipulated that the borrower must have completed a three-year probationary period when taking over a new farm. The loans were limited to permanent improvements and could not exceed two-thirds of the value of the property acquired.[26] The size and scope of the programme was very small. In its first ten-year period fewer than 70 farmers received a total sum of less than £6,000.[27]

In 1958, the government initiated a credit program designed to meet the needs of all African producers, i.e. including the peasant farmers in the TTLs. The program was operated with an initial capital of £10,000 supplied by the Native Development Fund, but the area of benefit was restricted to only ten districts and four African Producer Cooperative societies.[28] This fund was augmented in 1959 by £66,000 supplied by the United States International Cooperation Administration. However, the size of the credit program was still inadequate. By the early 1960s, the total amount available for lending to African peasant farmers 'had not exceeded £105,000 amounting to less than a few shillings per family in the African areas'.[29] The additional funds enabled the Native Development Fund to extend its credit facilities, at least in theory, throughout the country but these facilities only reached a few, selected, 'progressive' African farmers.[30]

The African Loan Fund (ALF)[31] was established in 1964 and its operations were put under the control of the Cooperatives and Loans Fund Branch of the Ministry of Agriculture. The APA farmers could obtain short-term loans of up to £50 from the ALF at 7 per cent interest, and long-term loans of up to £300 at 7.25 per cent interest.[32] Peasant farmers in the TTLs could obtain short-term loans of up to £35 at 7 per cent interest, and medium loans of up to £100 at 7.25 per cent interest, but they had no long-term loans.[33] The ALF, in practice, insisted upon an elaborate selection of African farmers, the stated aim being the encouragement of a more rapid advance in the adoption of more modern agricultural techniques. The ALF loans were usually in kind. Cooperative societies were often the most common channels for processing these requisitions.

There were also non-governmental forms of formal credit as well. By 1970, the Catholic Church had established 13 credit unions among peasants in Zimbabwe with a membership of 1,746 and a share capital of £40,769.[34] These unions offered credit to their members for the purchase of seed, fertiliser and capital equipment, notably ploughs, although money could be drawn for the purpose of children's school fees and brides wealth.[35]

The other non-governmental institutions source of credit available to African farmers was the African Loan and Development Trust (ALDT), which extended credit to APA farmers in certain parts of the country. The ALDT. was a private commercial finance company that specialised in a small proportion of APA farmers (only 15.4 per cent of the APA farmers had benefited from the ALDT loans by 1976). During the 1966/77 season, a sum of R$602,623 ALDT loans was outstanding. Of these 1,277 were in Mashonaland, 338 in Midlands and 163 in Manicaland provinces.[36]

The basic conclusion to be drawn from the above data is that the volume of loans going to African farmers in Rhodesia was quite low. Thus, the 680,000 peasant farming households received no more than about R$1 million of credit extended in 1975 (i.e. less than R$2.00 per household) as against some R$111 million extended to some 6,200 white farmers (an average of about R$18,000 per farmer).[37] This inequality in the distribution of agricultural finance is aggravated by the fact that between 1965 and 1974, the government spent R$66 million on black agriculture and R$436 million on European agriculture.[38] Let's now turn to the reasons behind dualism in the agricultural credit market of Rhodesia.

Historically, there were several reasons for the low volume of credit available to the African farmers, namely: (1) the preservation of the traditional tenure system by government policy measures and outright discrimination in the allocation of government credit; (2) lack of collateral, particularly in the African peasant sector; (3) high default rate; (4) lack of interest in repaying loans; (5) lack of ability to repay the loans; (6) lack of inadequate extension services to give information on new opportunities to invest.

From the discussion of dualism in the land market we know that the preservation of the colonial established 'traditional' system of land tenure and legal limitations to the transferability of individually owned land in the APAs generally made credit extension to Africans difficult. This indirect way of checking the spread of credit facilities was further reinforced by discriminatory measures in the allocation of government credit. A low priority was given to the African agricultural sector by those responsible for the allocation of public funds. Thus, only R$270,812 of the ALF loans up to May 1977 was outstanding.[39] This was in sharp contrast to the AFC, which made loans to European farmers, and which distributed about R$30–R$40 million annually, and had R$110 million outstanding at the end of 1977.[40] (The ALF ceased its operations in 1977, leaving virtually no government agency that provided loans to African farmers in the TTLs.)

Given the land tenure system prevailing in the African sector, one of the main reasons for the low level of credit is probably to be found in the tendency towards risk minimisation where loans are extended only to those farmers who are considered safe. The failure of commercial banks and also, to a certain degree, the public institutions, to provide credit is probably exacerbated due to the fact that Africans had no marketable land, or title to land, or other assignable property acceptable as security on mortgages.[41] Thus, as shown above, the Land and Agricultural Bank loans did not apply to African peasant farmers in the TTLs on grounds that the latter lacked collateral. The Rhodesian private banks virtually gave no loans to African farmers as a whole.

Yet another reason for the low level of loans going to the African sector is to be found in the high default rate on loan repayment. With regards to the ALF loans, up to 1965, 9,500 peasants were in arrears with a total of £60,194 and by 1967 13,943 peasants were in arrears to the amount of £236,031.[42] One of the main reasons for this high default rate was connected to the bureaucratic functioning of the public credit programs. In fact, the bureaucratic procedures in giving loans and making arrangements for recovering payments conflicted:

> Applications for loans had to be recommended by the local Agricultural Officer and much of the subsequent administration of these financial operations appears to have fallen on the shoulders of the agricultural extension service. There were, however, no clear cut procedures for the recovery of the outstanding loans. When it came to recovering repayments which were overdue, many members of the agricultural extension service expressed the opinion that this task was incompatible with their role as extension agents.[43]

A similar bottleneck was seen when the ALF channelled its funds via cooperative societies. The ALF ceased to deal with the actual administration of these loans and instead began to grant 'communal loans' to cooperative societies for their individual members. From the ALF point of view, the recovery of funds was now up to the societies as corporate bodies. However, many societies declined the duty of recovering loan payments, and consequently failed to make the necessary repayments if and when such funds were not forthcoming from their members.

The default rate can also be discussed in terms of the responsibility to repay these loans. Many underdeveloped country studies carry reports 'that farmers do not consider the repayment of public loans a compelling moral obligation'.[44] In such a situation, the rate of repayment will be low unless there are enforceable economic sanctions against default. During colonial Zimbabwe, the fourth reason for the low level of credit is connected with the lack of interest in repaying the loans and the fact that the only sanction was that farmers who had defaulted could not get new loans. For example,

ALF simply stipulated that 'expect in very exceptional circumstances, no further loan will be given to the recipient of a previous one, unless an earlier loan has been repaid'.[45]

The lack of interest in repaying loans can also be due to lack of

> efficient ways of creating close working relationship between the lenders and the borrowers. For, instance, to prevent default the government decided in 1969 to brand African cattle so that branded cattle could act as collateral.[46]

This was strongly resented by African peasants who feared that the brand would make the government the owner of their cattle. (Such fears could be justified given the living memories of African cattle looting by the settlers during the early years of colonisation discussed in Chapter 3). As a result, only 21 per cent of all peasants who had taken out loans in 1968 did so in 1969, and the total money paid out in loans dropped from £233,000 to £48,965.[47] In turn, this drop in loans greatly reduced the input of fertiliser; in some APAs crop yields fell by 75 per cent.[48]

Another factor in the list of possible causes of low volumes of credit in the African agricultural sector is directly connected with the consequences of dualism. Because of the falling productivity levels and soil erosion problems in the African rural areas, there was lack of the ability to repay the loans.

There were, finally, the obvious problems connected with the lack of adequate extension service personnel to give information about the new opportunities to invest, adoption of new technologies and convincing the African farmer that the expected yield justifies additional risk. (Evidence from elsewhere indicates that the lack of information and risk aversion often retard innovation among small farmers.[49]) The farmer is only likely to start borrowing increased amounts in the event that his capital requirements increase. This may come about if, say, he starts to clear more land, use more fertiliser or improved seed and so on.

For the reasons given above, the credit programs in colonial Zimbabwe reached only a small section of the African farmers and sooner or later ceased to operate. In a study of Haiti, Mats Lundahl found that formal credit has a sheer physical impossibility of reaching more than a tiny section of peasant farms. The reason usually given for the failure was administrative difficulties and the general lack of trained personnel. The bureaucratic actions of the government in Haiti had caused the lack of necessary extension service personnel, lack of funds as a result of the lack of positive government interest in agriculture, and corruption as well as embezzlement of funds.[50] The dualistic conditions in the land market and direct discrimination in the allocation of credit are the main reasons for dualism in the credit market. As a result, there was a general lack of credit-worthiness in the African sector, which gave rise to problems connected with lack of collateral, high default rates, bureaucratic deficiencies and the lack of adequate extension services. Thus, from the standpoint of credit programs, the principles of good management in terms of recovering their costs and avoiding default, might have compelled them to give loans only to those clients who had collateral and were expected to be solvent when it came to repayment of loans.

Interest rates

The discussion in the above sections shows that while the European agricultural sector received ample amounts of credit from both the private banks and the public financial sources, there was a scarcity in credit to the African farmers. Given that the latter also had a low level of savings, an appropriate tool in analysing the case where interest rates are determined by the element of scarcity in funds as in the Rhodesian African rural sector would have been the role of time preference.[51] In this case, the extreme shortage of funds among the peasant farmers makes them blind to any high interest rates payable later, usually after harvest, because in the slack season they (the peasant families) must get the loans in order to survive.[52] Consequently, their rate of time preference is quite high. Irving Fisher has defined time preference as 'the … excess of the present marginal want of one more unit of future goods'.[53] Thus, the Fisherian theory of time preference can be used to find one of the most important determinants of the rate of interest, though it must be stressed that its application is limited when it comes to a situation where the accessibility to credits and the rate of interest are more or less determined by government regulatory measures. This point will be illustrated by the rather low rate of interest in the Rhodesian rural money market and the fact that these interest rates had remained relatively fixed for several years at a time in spite of the scarcity of credit funds.

The interest rate differentials between European and African loans were not high. Because of its small size, the African Loan and Development Trust overheads were high (high transaction costs) so that it charged 10 per cent interest on its loans. The now defunct African Loan Fund had charged 7.5 per cent annual interest on its short-term loans, and 8 per cent medium and long-term loans.[54] On the other hand, the Agricultural Finance Corporation (the main government agency loaning to white farmers) charged 6.5 per cent on long-term loans, and 7 per cent for short-term loans, fixed for all customers. There was also a category of development loans based on a 5 per cent interest rate. The interest rates for white farmers charged on commercial banks (which can also be taken as minimum for suppliers' credit), range from statutory minimum of 7.5 per cent to 9 per cent depending on the risk factor.[55] The base rates have tended to remain fixed for several years at a time.

When the averages are taken into account, the interest rate prevailing in the European agricultural sector was 7.25 per cent compared with 8.5 per cent in the African sector. However, with a 3.1 per cent per year of inflation rate of agricultural output in the decade up to 1970, these rates would imply real rates of interest of around 4.15 per cent and 5.4 per cent, respectively. Thus, the African farmers paid marginally higher interest rates on both the government and commercial credit markets than white farmers. During the 1970s, lending rates remained virtually unchanged for all lending institutions (commercial banks, building societies, the Agricultural Finance Corporation, etc).[56] But, given that the nominal rates of between 1970 to 1979 remained the same as during the earlier decade whereas the inflation rates between 1970 and 1975 period were around 7.6 per cent per annum,[57] and by 1979 they were around 10–11 per cent, then real interest rates on lending were negative.[58]

In sum, though the African lending rates were slightly higher than those of white farmers, the interest rates were not at all important in the allocation of credit since they were determined by government regulation and remained unchanged for long periods at a time.

In summing up Part I of this chapter, the analysis in the present chapter shows that the savings and demand for agricultural credit in Rhodesia were influenced by dualistic structures in the land market. Thus, assuming that the propensity to save is a function of per capita farm income, the European farmers had better possibilities of savings than the African farmers, because the per capita output levels of the latter were lower than those of the former. In addition, white farmers had a high demand for credit, as demonstrated by the pressure to create institutions to meet this demand. It is probable that there was also a high demand for loans in the African agricultural sector, judging from the needs of these farmers to purchase farm inputs.

The dualistic tendency in the agricultural credit market becomes clearer when we move from the supply of credit to the European farmers on one hand, and to African farmers on the other. Credit extension to the white farmers was made available from 1912 onwards, and its volume increased steadily throughout the colonial period. On the contrary, there were no credit facilities available for African farmers until 1945, when a small section of the APA farmers were given credit for land improvements only. The majority of the African peasant farmers were not considered for loans until the 1960s, when the African Loan Fund was formed. In practice, this scheme also reached just a small fraction of the African farmers.

The reasons for dualism in the agricultural credit market of Rhodesia are closely connected with the preservation of the traditional tenure system for the majority of African farmers in the Tribal Trust Lands. In addition, direct discrimination in the extension of credit facilities in the African sector resulted in a low volume of funds available for development in the African sector. Other reasons for the low level of credit directly follow from the dualistic structure of the land market and discriminatory tendencies. Dualism in the credit market is closely connected and dependent on dualism in the land market.

As the analysis of interest shows, lending rates were not important in the allocation of credit, since they were government controlled and remained fixed for long periods. Thus, like other factor markets in the Rhodesian case, the credit market was also controlled by government policy both in the allocation of the credits and in the determination of the interest rates.

Fast forward to the end of the twentieth century and beginning of the twenty-first century, agriculture would be at the centre of contention in international trade negotiations when access to world markets under the World Trade Organisation's Doha Development Agenda would be a major disservice to many of the world's poorest people, namely those in farm households in developing countries.[59] In this case, Zimbabwean African farmers who had historically been subjected to price and market discrimination under dualism in factor markets would join the rest of the developing countries in the fight for the fair trading system in world markets already from a historical disadvantage.

Though racial discrimination in the allocation and supply of credit had been removed following Zimbabwe's independence in 1980, the remnants of historically embedded dualistic structures still remained in place. Agricultural production had been stimulated in the communal areas, extension services had been greatly expanded from the early 1980s and marketing services had been extended to more remote areas. An important development was Zimbabwe's Economic Structural Adjustment Programme (ESAP) launched in the early 1990s, when the government liberalised the previously tightly controlled economy. Prices and interest rates were unwound, trade was generally liberalised and a few of the public enterprises, including dairy and cotton marketing boards, were commercialised and eventually liberalised.

After more than 60 years, maize was decontrolled in 1994, allowing farmers to sell to whoever they chose. However the decontrol period was short-lived, as government reasserted it by passing a statute that criminalised the sale of most grains to any entity other than the Grain Marketing Board (GMB). Even during this period, low prices of maize and other crops during the liberalisation period, was in part caused by the price policy, but also more fundamentally by the inadequate infrastructure and farm technology particularly in the communal areas.[60]

Part II: agricultural produce market

The produce market in a historical perspective

In the pre-colonial period, Zimbabwe produced a wide variety of both agricultural and non-agricultural products (handcraft products). Although agricultural production was largely geared to subsistence requirements, there also existed a tradable surplus in the pre-colonial economy. Grain, cattle, goats and tobacco were among the products that were frequently exchanged. Existing evidence indicates a quick response by Africans to increase their cash incomes through contact with the Europeans.[61] The African producers and traders immediately seized the opportunity to sell their product as soon as the colonists arrived:

> In September and October 1890 some Shona were already selling a variety of produce, including grain, sweet potatoes, pumpkins and groundnuts to the 'pioneers' – as indeed, villagers had done to earlier white travellers before 1890.[62]

In 1891 Percy Fitzpatrick found that the Shona were very keen on business 'and so quick to perceive an opening, that they have broken up fresh ground and planted double crops this year, in order to supply the rush of white men'.[63] In the same year a white trader acting for Lobengula (the Ndebele king) was anxious to sell cattle and sheep to whites in Mashonaland.[64] There is clear evidence for the production for surplus:

> In Matebeleland at least one district planted a variety of crops 'considerably in excess of their own requirements, with the express intention of trading', while in Mashonaland the price of some peasant produce took cognizance of high transport costs.[65]

The upward trend in the dependence of the African peasants on exchange with the capitalist sector was noticeable around the turn of the century.[66] But soon after the turn of the century, it began to show a tendency to decline. The decline of the participation of the African peasantry in the produce market can be explained by the concept of the effort price. Giovanni Arrighi defined effort price as 'the quantity of labour time of given drudgery necessary to obtain a unit (measured in real terms) of cash income'.[67] In other words, the categories of the effort price of participation in the labour market and the effort price of participation in the produce market indicate the effort price of cash income obtainable through the sale of labour time and through the production and sale of agricultural produce, respectively. Thus, there was an upward tendency in the effort price of African participation in the produce market in the sense that over time a given labour effort in the produce market gave a lower financial return than it had done before. Available official estimates of acreages, yields and population point to three broad trends in African peasant agriculture between 1900 and 1950: a constant grain output per capita of the rural African population and a steady increase of acreage under cultivation, and also to an increase in the rural African population.[68] But the increase in population was more rapid than the expansion of the African areas even though the latter were expanded considerably during this period. 'Available acreage per head declined from around 40 acres to 15 acres.'[69]

The upward trend in the effort price of African participation in the produce market was due to a combination of many factors, ranging from slumps in prices to more fundamental change – in increasing dualism in the land market.

In 1903–1904 and 1911–1912, there was a decline in the price of maize in the order of 30–40 per cent, which by itself must have raised the effort price of participation in the produce market.[70] But the fall in prices received by African peasants was even more drastic than shown by the per centages above, if one takes into account that only 30 per cent of the land assigned to Africans, as against 75 per cent of that alienated to Europeans was within 25 miles of railway line (and therefore from communication with the towns and mines). It was generally recognised that when railway costs were added, grain crops could not bear the costs of more than 15 miles of ox-wagon transport.[71] It is clear that the general movement of the African peasantry into the reserves not only reduced the land resources available both in terms of size and quality, but also their ability to compete on the grain market was progressively reduced.

In Chapter 3, we showed how the capitalist agriculture was promoted at the expense of African peasant agriculture, which formed the basis of the distorted land-tenure system and dualism in the land market. But in the short-run, the growth of white farming sector had some positive effects for the African peasants. Since the stock of European owned cattle was largely built upon cattle purchased from Africans and thereafter upgraded by the use of purchased bulls, the expansion of European mixed farming and cattle ranching generated a demand for African owned cattle, whose price steadily rose from £1–£2 per head around 1905–1906, to £4–£7 in 1909, to £9 in 1918.[72] However, this trend was of a temporary nature as the growth of the European cattle eventually became large enough to supply the entire European market and even compete with African owned cattle.

A deeper slump in cattle and maize prices occurred in 1921–1923. At this time the slump had more far reaching consequences for African farmers than any previous slump. In 1920, African grain sales to European traders was estimated at 198,000 bags at 10s per bag; in 1921 the average price fell approximately 5s per bag, at which price sales of grain became uneconomic in many districts, with the result that, notwithstanding a plentiful harvest, only 43,600 bags were purchased from Africans,[73] i.e. a drop of 78 per cent in sales. A similar reduction was reported for sales of African cattle. From an estimate of at least 20,000 head of cattle sold by Africans in 1919 at prices in the order of £7–£8, in 1921 the demand for African stock declined and by 1922 it had 'practically ceased'.[74] There was slight recovery in 1924 followed by short lived boom that lasted until 1929 on the eve of the 1930s Great Depression when prices collapsed again.

Giovanni Arrighi rightly argues that these trends implied an upward tendency in the effort price of a given quantity of agricultural produce, particularly for the African peasants and that it therefore led to a reversal in the relative importance of sale of produce vis-à-vis wage employment as sources of African cash earnings. Thus, whereas at the beginning of the century, 70 per cent of African total cash earning came from produce sales, by 1932 the figure had fallen to 20 per cent.[75] This change was not just a cyclical phenomenon but rather a 'deep seated' change based on the development of institutional changes that had taken place in the country. The slumps had resulted in the acceleration of the movement of Africans into the reserves. This is because the financial constraint which the slumps had imposed on the Africans made them unable to meet the land rentals, and other charges to which they were subject to outside the reserves. As shown above, there were no loans available to Africans both outside and within the reserves. Thus, peasant production for the marketable surplus was further curtailed, as the forced evictions of Africans into the reserves were aggravated by falling prices in the produce market.

Marketing institutions

In the previous section, we have seen the upward trend in the effort price of African participation in the produce market. As will be shown in this section, this trend was reinforced, when in the 1920s white farmers called on the government to establish statutory marketing agencies in order to stabilise and guarantee producer prices and help find domestic and foreign markets for their produce.[76] As shown above it was the slump in the prices in the wake of great depression of the early 1930s that made the case for statutory marketing institutions even more necessary. Marketing institutions may be defined broadly to include organisations, established by government or by some other public authority, which set the behavioural rules in the marketing of certain products. The first of these institutions in Rhodesia was the Maize Marketing Board, which was established by the Maize Control Act of 1931, and the Maize Control Amendment Act of 1934.

The main reason for the establishment of the Maize Marketing Board was the sudden decline in the price of maize at the beginning of 1931. As shown below, the Board made it compulsory for all maize marketed in the urban areas (except for sales between Africans in the same administrative area) to be sold to the Board. In other words, maize had become a controlled product and the government had established a monopoly in the marketing of maize into urban areas. The Maize Marketing Board functioned up to 1950 when it was replaced by the GMB, which added beans, millet, sorghum and groundnuts to the controlled product list. In the post war period, there was an increase in the list of products marketed through the Marketing Board. However, beans were decontrolled in 1959, bull-rush millet (mhunga) in 1962, and finger millet (rapoko) in 1965,[77] but this did not reduce the tendency towards the greater role of marketing institutions which became more evident in the post Unilateral Declaration of Independence (UDI) period.[78]

Following the UDI in 1965, the government took an even greater role in agricultural marketing. In a major reorganisation of the marketing institutions in 1967, the Agricultural Marketing Authority (AMA) was set up to administer the statutory marketing boards, all of which had been in existence prior to its formation. The four organisations under the AMA were the Grain Marketing Board, the Cold Storage Commission, the Dairy Marketing Board and the Cotton Marketing Board.[79]

The AMA has remained a relatively small parent organisation that coordinates the activities of the Marketing Boards. Its original mandate was to conduct marketing research for different products, study the marketing channels, help coordinate pricing policies and advise the government on other marketing policies. AMA also became a channel for short-term financing of the four Marketing Boards.[80] The AMA also became the principal instrument in stimulating a successful diversification of agriculture, particularly in moving away from a greater dependence on tobacco, but its main activity has been to give the state a stronger influence in agricultural marketing and food supplies.

Thus, in the post UDI period the Marketing Boards handled more products in their marketing list than before. For example, whereas in 1965 only an estimated 35 per cent of agricultural sales were handled by statutory agencies, in 1973 the latter handled over 70 per cent.[81] Since then, further products came under control such that by 1978 soya beans, wheat, coffee, cotton and tobacco have been added to the list of controlled products.[82] The position of the Marketing Boards up to Zimbabwe's independence in 1980 is shown in Table 4.5. In terms of sales, the Grain Marketing Board was the biggest marketing institution accounting for R$93.8 million in 1975–1976 in sales. But in terms of total fixed capital assets and the number of employees, the Cold Storage Commission was the largest organisation. This was because the Cold Storage Commission ran abattoirs and meat plants throughout the country, which usually involved heavier capital investment than was the case with the marketing of grain and other products.

The other marketing agencies in the order of size in sales and total fixed assets were the Dairy Marketing Board and the Cotton Marketing Board. In sum, there has been an expansion in the activities of the Marketing Boards, but as will be seen in the next section on price policy, one main effect of the statutory marketing institutions was to curb competition emanating from the African producers during the colonial period and, therefore, limit the marketing opportunities of the latter.

There were other forms of marketing institutions in the Rhodesian economy, which included Producer Associations. The latter usually regulated those products not under the controlled list of the Marketing Boards. Unlike the Marketing Boards, which marketed both African and European produce, the Producers' Associations almost exclusively handled white agricultural products. The associations had power to levy fees on growers,

Table 4.5 Basic statistics related to the agricultural marketing boards

Boards	*Total fixed assets ($ million)*	*Sales ($ million)*	*Number of employees (1973)*	*Intended capital investment 1979–1983*[d]	*Estimate of government expenditure 1978–1979*
Agriculture Marketing Authority	0.01[b]	n/a	20	5.0	0.05
Cold Storage Commission	26.4[e]	50.1	2,350[f]	38.6	0.75
Cotton Marketing Boards	5.1[a]	33.7[a]	631	8.1	
Dairy Marketing Boards	7.2[b]	25.6[b]	2,330	11.1	
Grain Marketing Boards	6.6[c]	93.8[c]	1,995	27.5	

Source: Tickner, 1977: Table 5.

Notes
a = 1973;
b = 1978;
c = 1975;
d = According to Ministry of finance estimates 1979;
e = 1977;
f = 3,500 in 1979.

regulate prices and set minimum quality standards.[83] Besides setting wholesale prices, the Producers' Associations controlled imports. The most notable of these was the Rhodesian National Farmers Union (RNFU), to which all Producer Associations were members and which wielded powers equal to that of any other statutory body. The Rhodesian Oilseeds Association, the Rhodesian Deciduous Fruit Growers Association and the Rhodesian Tea Growers' Association were all members of the RNFU. One notable effect of these associations is that they improved the prices of crops they were handling. The effect of price discrimination can be depicted in the following statement: 'all the crops in which Africans do not have a share of the market have experienced increasing prices, an indication of the success of Producers' Associations and the RNFU'.[84]

The other forms of marketing institutions were the cooperatives. The European farmers' cooperatives registered under the Cooperatives Companies Act (No. 34 of 1925) were the oldest cooperatives in the country. These cooperatives have always been free from direct government control. However, since the European cooperatives did not concentrate on the marketing of agricultural produce, our discussion will be limited to an examination of the African cooperatives.

In the 1970s, cooperatives became one of the important channels through which African produce was sold. The African cooperative movement in Rhodesia was directly initiated by the government. The number of African farmers cooperatives grew from two in 1956 to 319 in 1976, with a total membership of 41,258 and annual sales turnover of R$5.26 million.[85] Generally, the stated purpose of the cooperatives was to serve as collection agents for controlled products and arrange for their delivery to the Marketing Boards. Some cooperative societies concentrated on the marketing of cotton and the supply of agricultural inputs for cotton growers.[86] Some cooperative societies even supplied general consumer goods, and a few had opened supermarkets for their members. Others supplied inputs to farmers.[87] The significance of African cooperatives in the marketing of agricultural produce can be shown by the following figures: In the 1975/1976 season, 20 per cent of the total sales from African farmers went through the cooperatives, as did some of the maize (17 per cent), coffee (42 per cent), sorghum (49 per cent), wheat (51 per cent) and unshelled nuts (53 per cent).[88]

However, because African cooperatives were required by the government regulation to charge a commission for their services over and above the normal marketing expenses, membership became more costly than direct registration with Marketing Boards. The emphasis on the regulatory role by the government resulted in the impression that the cooperatives were actually not run or even owned by the membership. As a result, the larger African producers who could sell directly to the Marketing Boards invariably did so, thus leaving the cooperative with little volume.[89] In this sense, the African cooperatives were not efficient in the marketing of agricultural produce. However, this did not mean that the cooperative movement had no future in Zimbabwe. On the contrary, with the relaxation of the stringent controls, which were operative under the colonial regime, and the improvement of efficiency in their management, cooperatives could become one of the most important channels in both the marketing of produce and distribution of credits.

The discussion in this section shows that government sponsored marketing institutions exerted an increased influence in the produce market. This trend started in the early 1930s when the Government intervened in the marketing of maize and cattle and by the 1960s almost all the country's major agricultural products had come under the control of the Marketing Boards. Other public marketing agencies, such as the Producer Associations and cooperatives also had direct government involvement as well. While it is true that the marketing institutions described above have had an important role in the development of agriculture in Rhodesia, this development has discriminated against the African producers.

At independence in 1980, the Government continued with control of grain marketing through the colonial established institutions but now with efforts to engage and service smallholder black farmers and consumers. The Grain Marketing Board buying price was now determined by a committee that included the Ministry of Trade and Commerce for the benefit of consumers, as well as representatives of smallholder farmer groups. Producer and retail selling prices were set uniformly throughout the country for the marketing year. Though the system still uses consultative processes in setting producer prices, a lot of questions have been raised as to the level of consultations, with inputs from other interest groups such as farmers not adequately included in the final price decision.

The characteristics of dualism established and entrenched during colonial rule have refused to be obliterated. Under the post-2000 Fast-Track Land Reform Program (FTLRP), land tenure regime remains characterised by the mostly customary communal lands, the Old Resettlement Areas and Model A1s and leasehold in both A2 and small-scale commercial farming areas. The remainder of large-scale commercial farming areas (LSCFA) is still under 'freehold' tenure.

In an effort to ensure food security and price stabilisation under the government's haphazard FTLRP, the Government applied a series of inconsistent market and price interventions. In 2001 market interventions and price control measures (The Grain Marketing Notice Statutory Instrument (SI) number 235A of 16 July 2001, Statutory Instrument 387 in December 2001) were reintroduced. Maize and wheat became controlled products and farmers were ordered to deliver maize to GMB within 14 days after harvest, marking the end of private grain trade and the Zimbabwe Agricultural Commodity Exchange (ZIMACE), and the dissolution of standard grading systems.

However, despite the plethora of agricultural product controls in existence in Zimbabwe since the colonial period, the supreme national law of the land, the Constitution of Zimbabwe passed in 2013, appears to enhance the current status of land marketability (de jure). The Constitution has clear provisions for how land should be dealt with in the national discourse, in terms of the right to own, transfer and hypothecate agricultural land in the country. In Section 72 it defines agricultural land as 'land used for agriculture – a separate piece of land on Deeds Registry' – but excludes communal lands, which is treated under Section 282 where the provisions of traditional leaders are given as to administer communal land and protect the environment, as well as resolve disputes.

Section 289(e) provides for a land tenure system that promotes increased productivity and investment by Zimbabweans in agricultural land, while Section 289(b) provides for real rights to every Zimbabwean regardless of ethnicity or gender. It thus empowers citizens holding agricultural land 'freedom to acquire, hold, occupy, use, transfer, hypothecate, lease, or dispose, of agricultural land'.

As will be argued below, it is important for Zimbabwe to focus attention on this new land distribution pattern to improve agricultural production so as to enhance food security and economic growth, and close the historical unequal land distribution patterns entrenched in dualism. It will be argued in the next section, which deals with price policies under these marketing arrangements, the basic trend was towards discrimination in favour of white produce, a factor that created and sustained dualism in the produce market.

Discriminatory price policies

In the above sections, we have shown how the competitiveness of the African peasantry on the produce market was restricted in a number of ways. Through dualism in the land market, African peasant farmers were confined to the poorer land resources of the country, and as a result of population pressure and overstocking in the reserves, there was a progressively decreasing productivity in African agriculture. In a more direct way segregation and non-competition between whites and blacks in the produce market were achieved through the operation of the marketing institutions. In this section, we turn to the question of how African sales were discouraged through a discriminatory price policy. Discriminatory prices were administered through a series of measures, notably allocation of quotas for maize marketing, marketing levy, the grading system and segregated transport services.

The quota system: The quota system in the sale of maize crop was first administered under the Maize Control Act of 1931. This system was put into action in response to a drastic fall in the export prices of maize in 1931, when the world price of maize had suddenly fallen from around 10s to 12s per bag to one equivalent to 4s 3d per bag, which was less than the cost of production for Rhodesian farmers.[90] The aim was to compel the Rhodesian producer to dispose of his maize crop through the Maize Marketing Board, which fixed a selling price inside Rhodesia at a level sufficiently high in relation to the export price. This provided the local grower with an average return per bag, based on both local and export sales, which was adequate to keep farmers in production. In effect, the government instituted a two-price system, one for the local market and the other for the export pool. The amount of output allocated to the local pool was that amount deemed adequate to meet local demand. The price paid to the local pool was 30 to 50 per cent above world prices.[91] Thus, the local pool constituted a support price scheme for producers. The remaining surplus was sold to the export pool and sold at whatever prices could be realised in the world market.

The small-scale European producers were allocated a quota of up to 80 per cent of all their deliveries to the high priced local market, whereas large-scale European producers were given around 20 per cent of all their deliveries in the internal market. This may be justifiable on grounds of encouraging the small scale European maize growers to remain on the land. The African producers (both APA farmers and TTL peasants) were lumped together and only 20 per cent of their deliveries were allocated a quota in the high priced internal market.[92] Since the African producers were invariably small-scale producers, they were largely excluded from the price incentive enjoyed by the small scale white farmers. If there had not been a discriminatory price policy, the African producers would also have received higher prices for 80 per cent of their deliveries to the internal market instead of only 20 per cent. There can be little doubt that the quota system protected the small-scale European farmers against African competition by restricting African participation in the high price internal market.

The discriminatory price policy through the allocation of quotas was in operation up to 1940. With the Maize Control Amendment Act of 1940, a new price system was instituted whereby the government guaranteed a fixed price to producers, which was based on estimated cost of production plus some profit.[93] In 1943, the government guaranteed a price of 13s 6d, and a bonus of two shillings for all maize delivered to the Maize Control Board provided that 'it was grown under certain conditions of sound farming practice'.[94] The conditions were that the area planted with maize should be protected from soil erosion, and that in the first season one-third of the area (and one half in the following season) under cultivation should be planted with a green manure crop. These conditions obviously excluded the Africans, since the digging of contour ridges for the protection of soil erosion only started seriously after 1951, under the Native Husbandry Act.[95]

If the principal goal of marketing in an underdeveloped economy is to achieve the greatest possible participation by producers in the cash economy – the maximisation of the catchment area[96] – the marketing of produce in Rhodesia under the quota system on maize during the 1930s achieved the opposite, i.e. it narrowed the marketing of agricultural produce by the African majority. This tendency was also reinforced under the marketing levies applied to African products during the 1950s.

The marketing levy: Under the Marketing Board operations a marketing levy was administered on produce sales from African farmers. The levy was directly charged on various types of African agricultural produce marketed through the official channels. The levy charge could be up to 15 per cent of the selling price, but, in practice, it rarely reached this level.[97] The money raised through this source was paid to the Ministry of Internal Affairs' African Development Fund for use in the general development of the TTLs. Like the allocation of maize quotas described above, the levy, as a form of discriminatory tax, tended to reduce the receipts from the sale of African agricultural produce. Therefore, the marketing levy most probably served to widen the gap profitability between the white and the black farming sectors. In this sense economic dualism was further strengthened in the produce market.

The European producers could sell their agricultural output directly to the Marketing Boards so that they did not need to pay the marketing levy. They graded their grain and delivered it in bags to the depots established along the railway line. In the case of maize, the Ministry of Agriculture prescribed producer prices every season. The maize crop delivered to the Grain Marketing Board was then purchased at this price and an 'advance' pay out was made for products delivered at the beginning of the harvest period. The advance was usually less than the prescribed price and the Board paid out an adjustment at the end of the season, based on the market conditions.

The African farmers could also deliver their output directly to the Marketing Boards. The farmer had to be registered with the Board and, in practice, only the APA farmers were large enough to take advantage of this marketing channel. Thus, the bulk of the African farmers who were usually small producers in the TTLs, sold their output through approved buyers,[98] who in turn delivered it in bulk to the Marketing Boards. Under this system a series of levy charges on the African supplies actually resulted in large differentials in the price paid for by the Grain Marketing Board and the actual price received by the producers.

The government fixed the guaranteed price which was paid out by the Board. The guaranteed prices for maize rose from 31s (in 1950) to 36s (in 1960), but dropped 31s 6d in 1961.[99] The prices were fairly stable in these years, but since it is the discriminatory levy that concerns us here, its amount confirms the fact that 'the revenue collecting aspects of the marketing agencies' operations have tended to override their price stabilizing functions'.[100]

As Bulman[101] stated, the deductions constituted a transport levy, a handling fee and a levy paid to the Native Development Fund. The approved buyer retained the handling fee but the transport levy was passed on into a Transport Equalisation Fund, which subsequently reimbursed the approved buyer for his estimated transport costs. In fact, while the approved buyers were reimbursed for the transportation costs incurred, there was no incentive for Africans living near the markets since a uniform price for transportation was charged irrespective of distance from the railway head or depot.

The grading system: The grading system was another form of price discrimination policy that affected the maize crop and livestock marketing, especially cattle. The system of grades had been in operation since the 1940s up to the 1970s in the case of maize, and from the 1940s up to 1956 in the African cattle market. As will be seen, the system was relaxed somewhat in the latter market after 1956.

During the 1940s, maize was classified according to six grades (in a descending order of quality) – A, B, C, D, E and Z. If grades A to D were packed in second-hand bags,[102] they became A_1, B_1, C_1 and D_1. Grades C and C_1 were for yellow maize, which Africans rarely grew. Quantities E and Z were very small. Most African producers sold their maize to approved buyers, who, whatever the grade may have been, almost invariably paid for it as grade D_1. Hence, there was no inducement for the African farmers to improve their crop since the grading and pricing system of the approved buyers, invariably discriminated against them.[103]

The grading system as a price discriminatory policy was introduced in the cattle market when, in 1944, the government set prices for African cattle on weight and grade basis. Of the African cattle graded in 1944, 1.0 per cent were grade A (the highest grade), 24.0 per cent – Good Average Quality, 34.1 per cent – Fair Average Quality, 30.7 per cent – Compound and 10.2 per cent – Inferior.[104]

The Cold Storage Commission held the position of a near monopsony in the buying of African stock. The only other buyers were the African butchers in the TTLs whose market share was insignificant. On the other hand, European livestock were sold at the European cattle auction sales where bargaining or bidding up for prices were practised. It has been estimated in the 1940s that 'the price offered for the three most important African grades were respectively 19% and 16% below comparable prices in the open European market'.[105]

In the Rhodesian white opinion the price difference was based on the curious assumption that since the African costs of production were lower than those of European farmers, the African producer received a very attractive price.[106] A parallel to this assumption was found in the marketing of crops, where maize prices were manipulated so that the well-off European growers were subsidised by the worse-off African growers.[107] The guaranteed producer price for slaughter cattle is translated into a schedule of grade and seasonal prices where the prices of the two top grades were fixed at a level which involved the Commission in losses on both local and export sales, on the other hand, producer prices of the lower grades, comprising all African and part of the European output, were manipulated to allow the Commission to make offsetting profit. Harry Dunlop made the following observation on the impact of pricing arrangements in the cattle market:

Until 1956 the Commission was guaranteed a quota of African slaughter stock at fixed prices, but the changeover to the auction system involved it in competition with private butchers at prices well above the support levels and it was then forced to curtail competition, at a subsequent stage in the marketing process, through its control of abattoirs and other marketing services.[108]

The two top grades fixed at a price that involved the Commission in losses were exclusively European-produced cattle. The government fixed the prices so that the Cold Storage Commission inflated the price of European stock, the loss of which to the Commission was to be made up for by manipulating the grade and price of African produced stock. This dual price system that discriminated against African producers served as a disincentive for the latter's production for the market. This point could not escape even the supporters of discriminatory price policies. As A.F. Hunt reveals in the following statements:

> Africans who sell produce to the Boards are subject to the deduction of a levy for the Ministry of Internal Affairs' African Development Fund. Its deduction from the price is a matter of administrative convenience, however, and is not part of the pricing or marketing system.... These ... charges are certainly disincentives to Africans who wish to sell.[109]

When the marketing system was 'integrated' in 1956, the former grades were reclassified and prices for lower grades were raised. African cattle were sold at auctions in the African areas which were open to all buyers on a competitive basis, with the Cold Storage Commission becoming a residual buyer at government prescribed prices, thus providing a floor price for all slaughter stock.[110] The changeover to auction sales was accompanied by an average increase in prices of about 26 per cent. As a result of this there was a 10 per cent increase in the number of cattle offered for sale between 1955 and 1956.[111] Thereafter, though prices continued to rise steadily, sales dropped. It is probable that the main reason for this lag in sales was connected with the general decline in food production in the African areas, particularly since a ceiling might have been reached in the number of cattle per capita in the TTLs. In 1965, 49 per cent of the latter areas were classified as 'overgrazed' or worse, so that livestock carrying capacity of the land was already exceeded in the Tribal Trust Lands in all but one of the seven provinces of Zimbabwe.[112] Between 1965 and 1977, sales of cattle failed to rise above the low level of 3 per cent of the herd per annum.[113] However, there was an improvement in the quality of African livestock offered for sale. (The TTL sales of fattened cattle for slaughtering increased from an average of 4,800 in 1970–1972 to 14,500 in 1973–1974.[114])

In summary, like the price discriminatory policy under the marketing levy charged on African produce sales, the grading system in both maize and cattle sales was fixed in a way that African producers actually subsidised the

Europeans through a manipulation of price differentials. As we have seen, in the cattle market, grading and prices were fixed in a way that the prices of top grades were inflated so that the Cold Storage Commission actually made losses. These grades were exclusively European stock. The loss to the Commission was made up by under-pricing African cattle. This dual pricing discriminated against African suppliers of livestock. This was aggravated by a levy that was charged on African cattle sold on weight and grade sales, which reduced the real incomes of farmers, with possible disincentive effects on productivity, particularly as the return to labour inputs declined due to the deteriorating land conditions and the market prospects.

Transport services: As a landlocked country, Zimbabwe's railway and roads were created with the aim of assisting transit routes to sea-ports. This was because the commodity composition of the country's exports was primarily made up of heavy bulk minerals and agricultural products, and the greater share of external trade was with countries outside Africa. At the time of the UDI in 1965, efficient transit routes were rail through Umtali (present day Mutare) to the port of Beira and Malvernia (Chicualacuala) to the port of Maputo in Mozambique. Unlike in the post-colonial era, less important routes were the rail via Botswana and by road via Beitbridge to the South African ports. In October, 1974, the Rutenga–Beitbridge rail line linking Rhodesia with South Africa was completed.

When placed in a national context, the Rhodesian transport system discriminated against the African areas. The railway line from South Africa via Botswana runs from Plumtree to Harare through the European areas extending along the high-veld. The line's extension north-west to Sinoia (present day Chinoyi) and the rich farmlands of the Lomagundi and Mazoe districts, as well the Harare to Mutare line run through the European settled areas. This pattern is followed by other spurs to South Africa via Beit Bridge, to Mozambique via Malvernia, and to Zambia via Victoria Falls. During the colonial era the Gweru-Masvingo line also connected the European beef producing region with domestic and foreign markets.

In essence, the railway transport network was concentrated on the high-veld, the area occupied by white farmlands. From the early years of the BSA Company, the policy was to locate European farms within a radius of 25 miles of the railway line so that white farmers had an easy access to the country's transport system. Thus the high-veld primarily became a European area by virtue of its location close to the main railway from Salisbury to Bulawayo. The policy of the provision of a markedly superior infrastructure (roads, power, electricity, irrigation, etc) for Europeans in comparison to those of African producers is clearly illustrated by railway services. For example, in 1970 some 36 per cent of the European areas were within ten miles of a station or siding, while a further 23 per cent were not more than 20 miles from such facilities.[115] Only 6 per cent of the European areas were more than 50 miles away from railway services. On the other hand, two-fifths of the total African areas (both APAs and TTLs) were more than 50 miles from the railway services while only 5 per cent of the African land was within ten miles of the railway.[116] Thus, in contrast to the European areas, the African areas have less access to the railway services, which by 1976 had a network of 3,415 kilometres. The road distribution more or less follows the same pattern as the railways.

The all-weather roads (full mat, narrow mat and strip) were mainly found along the European areas, and the African areas were served almost exclusively by seasonal gravel roads. The Road Motor Service (RMS) which was an adjunct to the railways connects most of the outlying European farming areas with the railway lines. The RMS had a network of 12,000 kilometres of access roads.[117] Like the railway transport, the RMS network was not available to the African areas. Both the railways and the RMS tariff structure was subject to government legislation and has always been designed to stimulate industrial, commercial, and agricultural growth. But the effect was to lower transport costs for the European farmers.

The discussion in this section clearly point to the conclusion that the provisions of railway and road services followed the general pattern of dualism in the economic system. At the same time as they served as an incentive in the marketing of European produce, these services provided a disincentive to the marketing of African produce. Thus, the transport system was a strong factor in the creation of dualism in the produce market in the sense that it made it uneconomic to market produce from those areas that were further away from the railway and road services and also from towns and mines.

Conclusions

In concluding the discussion of the present chapter, evidence presented in the book shows that at the beginning of colonial rule, Africans showed a quick awareness to the opportunity to increase their cash incomes through contact with colonists. This was done through the sale of agricultural surplus produce. However, the era of peasant prosperity generated by the sale of produce to advancing capitalistic sector was short-lived. The African farmers' participation in the produce markets was severely curtailed, mainly as a result of the movement of Africans into the reserves, which reduced their ability to compete on these markets. Further, slumps in the prices of maize and cattle (the main products produced by Africans) inevitably raised the effort price of participation in the produce market. Because of the fall in prices, many African peasant farmers still living as tenants in the European areas or un-alienated lands, could no longer afford to pay their rents and other charges imposed on them in these areas, with the result that there was an increasing movement into the reserves.

The discrimination in the produce and credit markets was reinforced in the further separation of white and black areas as the provision of infrastructural resources (railways, roads, dams, etc.) was biased in favour of white areas, which further widened the productivity gap between the European and African farming sectors. We can clearly conclude that, since transport is a factor input in the marketing of agricultural produce, its inequitable distribution along racial lines has had adverse effects on productivity of African farmers. This is because discrimination in trade, allocation of transport and other infrastructural facilities was directed against African produce suppliers.

Indirect restrictions on the spread of marketing facilities were reinforced by more direct means. Economic dualism in the produce market was further maintained through the statutory marketing institutions and discriminatory price policies administered under the latter. Like the dualism in the land, labour and capital markets, this was bolstered through government legislation and other institutional restrictive practices.

A systematic discrimination policy was administered through the allocation of maize crop quotas, the grading system on the maize output and cattle, various levies that were charged on the African farm output marketed through the Marketing Boards and their agents (approved buyers), including African cooperatives. The levy system and price discrimination practices had the effect of reducing the farm incomes of the African sector. In this sense, dualism in the produce market acted as a disincentive to the growth of agricultural output. This was aggravated by the transport system which also served as a disincentive to the marketing of African produce. Thus, while the European sector had easier access to transport facilities of the railways and all weather roads, African farmers were almost invariably served by 'dirt' roads, and in many remote areas there were no roads at all. Only towards the end of liberation war in the 1970s, as a result of military operations, more gravel roads were opened throughout the country, especially near the borders of Zambia and Mozambique.

Notes

1 Palmer, 1977–1:82.
2 Ibid.
3 Ibid.:147.
4 Ibid., passim.
5 Newly and Rowan, 1954:124–125.
6 Loney, 1975:54, and Tsumba, 1980:398.
7 Hughes, 1974:275.
8 Ibid.
9 Ibid.
10 Nicolle, 1971:3.
11 Lundahl, 1979:508.
12 This is probably characteristic of most poor peasant economies. Lundahl found that the precautionary loans, were 'probably negligible as compared to the volume of actual expense loans' in the Haitian case, ibid.:509.
13 Yudelman, 1964:157.
14 Ibid.

15 For discussion on the effects of the legal environment on the pattern of internal Trade, see Mahlahla, 1980.
16 Yudelman, 1964:157.
17 Arrighi, 1973:347.
18 Palmer, 1977:82.
19 Ibid.
20 Ibid:91.
21 Rhodesia, *Report of the Operations of the Land and Agricultural Bank*, 1971:6.
22 Ibid.
23 Hunt, 1976:86.
24 Hume, 1977:13.
25 Tsumba, 1980:5.
26 UN, 1963:36.
27 Yudelman, 1964:158.
28 UN,1963:36.
29 Yudelman, 1964:158.
30 UN, 1963:36.
31 The African Loan Fund (ALF) is sometimes called the Agricultural Loan Fund. Both names appear frequently in official publications, but we shall use the term African Loan Fund.
32 Weinrich, 1975:32.
33 Ibid.
34 Weinrich, 1975:31–32.
35 Ibid.:32.
36 Nziramasanga, 1980:57.
37 Hume, 1977:14; Riddell, 1980:60.
38 Riddel, 1980:60.
39 Nziramasanga, 1980:57.
40 Ibid.
41 Tsumba, 1980:398.
42 Weinrich, 1975:32–33.
43 Hughes, 1974:276.
44 Long, 1973:83.
45 Hughes, 1974:277.
46 Weinrich, 1975:33.
47 Ibid.
48 Ibid.
49 Long, 1973:82.
50 Lundahl, 1979:547.
51 Lundahl, 1979:513–520.
52 Ibid.:514.
53 Fisher, 1930:62.
54 Hughes, 1974:277.
55 Hume, 1977:15.
56 Zimbabwe Rhodesia – *Supplement to Monthly Digest of Statistics*. Jan:1980 Table 34.
57 Hume, 1977:15.
58 Tsumba, 1980:398.
59 Anderson and Martin, 2006:4, Figure 1.1.
60 For a detailed analysis on 'Distortions in Zimbabwe's Agricultural Incentives see, Ndlela and Robinson, 2007:208–213.
61 Cf. Phimister, 1977; Bhebhe, 1974; Kosmin, 1977, among others.
62 Phimister, 1977:257.
63 Fitzpatrick, 1973:45 in Phimister, ibid.:265.

64 Phimister, ibid.:257.
65 Ibid.
66 Ibid.:255, Arrighi, 1970:212.
67 Arrighi, 1970:229. According to Arrighi, the category effort price is the only possible category of cost for an economy in which there is no social phenomenon of wages (ibid.).
68 Arrighi, 1970:212, Yudelman, 1964:236–237.
69 Yudelman, 1964:237.
70 Arrighi, 1970:215.
71 Ibid.:215–216.
72 Ibid.:216.
73 Ibid.
74 Ibid.
75 Tickner, 1979:26.
76 Nziramasanga, 1980:53.
77 Tickner, 1979:28.
78 The UDI of 11 November 1965 by Ian Douglas Smith the Rhodesian 'rebel' Prime Minister who unilaterally declared Rhodesia independent from the British Crown.
79 Following Zimbabwe's independence in the 1980s the Dairy Marketing Board and the Cotton Marketing Board were commercialised, became public companies and renamed Dairibord Zimbabwe and Cottco respectively. The Cold Storage Commission though remaining under government was renamed the Cold Storage Company.
80 Tickner, 1979:27; Hunt, 1973:189, put the figure of regulated sales at 71 per cent, which is comparable to that of South Africa – 78 per cent.
81 Nziramasanga, 1980:53.
82 Ibid.
83 Ibid.
84 The Farmers' Cooperative (Ltd) – the umbrella organisation of farmers' cooperatives – grants credit to members for the purchase of inputs such as machinery, fencing, fuel, and handles the accounting procedures of member associations.
85 Hughes, 1974:263.
86 For example, in 1972, cooperative purchased for their members R$366,752 worth of seed and fertiliser through societies, and R$505,638 worth of agricultural equipment and general supplies (ibid.:262–63).
87 Nziramasanga, 1980:55.
88 Ibid.:52.
89 Weinrich, 1975:48.
90 Yudelman, 1964:273.
91 Ibid.:179.
92 Ibid.
93 Weinrich, 1975:48.
94 Ibid.
95 For details on soil conservation under the Native Land Husbandry Act of 1951, see Bulman, 1971.
96 Dunlop, 1970.
97 Hughes, 1974:259. See also Hunt, 1973:200.
98 Approved buyers (appointed by Grain Marketing Board) were usually local storekeepers who served as the Board agents for buying the grain from Africans and in turn deliver it to the Grain Marketing Board. By the 1970s transport and handling charges were determined on the basis of distance of the point of sale from the nearest Grain Marketing Board depot. These charges were deducted,

as a form of levy, from the amount actually paid to sellers, who were invariably small-scale African producers. Hughes, 1974:263.

99 Bulman, 1971:Table 4.

100 Yudelman, 1964:177.

101 Ibid.

102 Brand new bags for packing maize were only sold to European farmers while African farmers had access only to second hand bags which when used lowered the grade of maize and hence the price fetched in the market.

103 Yudelman, 1964:179.

104 Report of Native Production and Trade Commission, 1945:29.

105 Yudelman, 1964:190.

106 The African in Southern Rhodesia, 1952:9.

107 Report of Native Production and Trade Commission, 1950:15.

108 Dunlop, 1970:15.

109 Hunt, 1973:200.

110 The non-slaughter stock were placed in agreement with white farmers and in some cases APAs, who were later required to deliver them to the Commission's abattoirs, the white farmer or the APA farmer taking a profit on improved condition of the animals and/or progeny.

111 Yudelman, 1964:191.

112 Yudelman, 1964:10.

113 Ibid.:9. Also, according to a report of the Secretary of Internal Affairs, from 1971 to 1972 the increase in the number of cattle owned by Africans in the TTLs was put at 3.56 per cent while sales through weight and grade channel dropped from 95,306 in 1971, to 70,904 in 1972, a decrease of over 24,000 head. Hughes, 1974:264.

114 The increased number of fattened cattle offered in the market was partly due to the removal of levy charged on the price received by sellers of livestock at the weight and grade sales and partly because of the direct sales to the Cold Storage Commission.

115 International Labour Office, 1978.

116 Ibid.

117 Ibid.

References

Anderson, Kym and Martin, Will. 2006. 'Agriculture, Trade Reform and the Doha Agenda', in Kym Anderson and Will Martin (eds), *Agricultural Trade Reform & the Doha Development Agenda*. Washington, DC: A co-publication of Palgrave Macmillan and the World Bank, The International Bank of Reconstruction and Development/World Bank.

Arrighi, Giovanni. 1970. 'Labour Supplies in Historical Perspective: A Study of the Prelotarianization of the African Peasantry in Rhodesia', *The Journal of Development Studies*, Vol. 6, No. 3:197–234.

Arrighi, Giovanni. 1973. 'The Political Economy of Rhodesia', in Giovanni Arrighi and John Saul. *Essays on the Political Economy of Africa*. New York and London: Monthly Review Press.

Bhebhe, Ngwabi M.B. 1974. 'Ndebele Trade in the Nineteenth Century', *Journal of African Studies*, Vol. 1, No. 1:87–100.

Bulman, Mary Elizabeth. 1971. *The Native Land Husbandry Act of Southern Rhodesia*. MSc thesis, University of London.

Dunlop, H. 1970. 'Efficiency Criteria in Primary Marketing: An Analysis of African Marketing Policies in Rhodesia', *Rhodesian Journal of Economics*, Vol. 4, No. 3:10–20.

Hughes, A.J.B. 1974. *Development in Rhodesian Tribal Areas: An Overview*. Salisbury: Tribal Areas of Rhodesia Research Foundation.

Hume, Ian M. 1977. *Agriculture in Rhodesia* (unpublished paper), Salisbury.

Hunt, A.F. 1973. 'Agricultural Pricing in Rhodesia', *The Rhodesia Journal of Economics*, Vol. l. 7, No. 4:189.

Hunt, A.F. 1976. 'European Agriculture', in G.M.E. Leistner (ed.), *Rhodesia: Economic Structure and Change*. Pretoria: Africa Institute of South Africa.

IDAF 1977. *International Defence and Aid Fund. Zimbabwe: The Facts about Rhodesia*. London, Pretoria: The Human Sciences Research Council (HSRC) Press.

International Labour Office (ILO). 1978. *Labour Conditions and Discrimination in Southern Rhodesia (Zimbabwe)*. Geneva: United Nations, UNCTAD.

Kosmin, Barry. 1977. 'The Inyoka Tobacco of the Shangwe People. The Displacement of a Pre-Colonial Economy in Southern Rhodesia, 1898–1938', in Robin Palmer and Neil Parsons (eds), *The Roots of Rural Poverty in Central and Southern Africa*. London: Heineman.

Loney, Martin. 1975. *White Racism and Imperial Response*. Harmondsworth: Penguin African Library.

Long, Millard F. 1973. 'Conditions for Success of Public credit Programs for Small Farmers', *AID Spring Review of Small Farmer Credit: Small Farm Credit*, Analytical Papers, Vol. 19, Washington DC.

Lundahl, Mats. 1979. *Peasants and Poverty. A Study of Haiti*. London: Groom Helm.

Mahlahla, S. 1980. 'A Survey of the Distribution Industry in Zimbabwe', in UN – United Nations. *Zimbabwe, Towards a New Order: An Economic and Social Study*. Working Paper, Vol. 1, United Nations.

Ndlela, D.B. 1981. 'Dualism in the Rhodesian Colonial Economy', *Lund Economic Studies*, Department of Economics, University of Lund.

Ndlela, D. and Robinson, P. 2007. 'Zimbabwe', in Kym Anderson and William Masters (eds), *Distortions to Agricultural Incentives in Africa*. Washington, DC: The World Bank.

Newly, W. and Rowan, D.C. 1954. *Money and Banking in British Colonial Africa*. Oxford: Oxford University Press.

Nicolle, W.H.H. 1971. 'The Development of the Subsistence Sector: What is Being Done in Rhodesia', *Rhodesian Economic Journal*, Vol. 5, No. 4:3.

Nziramasanga, M. 1980. 'The Agricultural Sector in Zimbabwe: Prospects for Change and Development', in UN – United Nations. *Zimbabwe, Towards a New Order: An Economic and Social Survey*. Working Papers, Vol. 1, United Nations.

Palmer, Robin. 1977. *Land and Racial Discrimination in Rhodesia*. London: Heinemann.

Phimister, I.R. 1977. 'The Shamva Mine Strike of 1977: An Emerging African Proletariat', *Rhodesian History*, Vol. 2:29.

Report on Native Production and Trade Commission. 1945. C.S.R. No. 2, Salisbury.

Report of Native Production and Trade Commission. 1950. Salisbury: Government Printer.

Rhodesia. 1971. *Report of the Operations of the Land and Agricultural Bank of Southern Rhodesia for the Period of the Fifteen Months ended 31 March, 1971*. Salisbury: Government Printers.

Riddell, R. 1980. 'Before and after Liberation of Zimbabwe: A New Nation with Old Problems', *IDS Sussex, Southern Africa: The Political Economy of Inequality*, Vol. 2, No. 4:60.

The African in Southern Rhodesia. 1952. *Yearbook of Southern Rhodesia*, No. 3.

Tickner, Vincent. 1979. *From Rhodesia to Zimbabwe, No. 8: The Food Problem*. London: Catholic Institute for International Relations.

Tsumba, L. 1980. 'Money, Credit and Financial Flows in Zimbabwe', in UN – United Nations. *Zimbabwe, Towards a New Order: An Economic and Social Survey*. Working Papers, Vol. 1, United Nations.

UN (United Nations). 1963. *Economic and Social Consequences of Racial Discriminatory Practices*. New York: United Nations, UNCTAD.

Weinrich, A.K.H. 1975. *African Farmers in Rhodesia: Old and New Peasant Communities in Karangaland*. London: Oxford University Press.

Yudelman, Montague. 1964. *Africans on the Land: Economic Problems of African Agricultural Development in Southern, Central and East Africa, with Special Reference to Southern Rhodesia*. Cambridge, MA: Harvard University Press.

Zimbabwe Rhodesia. 1980. *Supplement to the Monthly Digest of Statistics*. Salisbury: Central Statistical Office.

5 Economic dualism in the labour market

Introduction

This chapter discusses the development of dualism in the labour market of Zimbabwe, a dualism that is closely connected and consequent on dualism in the land market. A specific structural feature of economic dualism in the labour market of developing economies, typical of the Zimbabwean situation, is the existence of two distinct parts in the economy. On the one hand, is the modern or formal segment employing a small segment of the labour force, on the other is a large traditional or non-formal segment employing the bulk of the labour force. Our analysis in this chapter is based on three foundations. First, a cheap labour policy was historically promoted in which workers were being supplied both through the importation of African foreign labourers from the neighbouring territories, as well as eventual creation of an internal labour supply from the steadily impoverished African reserves. In the long term, labour supplies to the modern economy were to be generated out of increasing impoverishment of the peasant farming sector.

Second, the assumption that contrary to the belief that Rhodesia's colonial economy had moved from a situation of labour surplus at the beginning of colonisation towards an eventual elimination of this surplus during the 1950s is both flawed and incorrect. Empirical evidence suggests that the labour supply actually moved from conditions of labour shortage towards one of a labour surplus, i.e. 'unlimited' supply of labour in the Lewis sense.[1] As already has been shown in Chapter 3, the conditions of rural overpopulation had become serious economic problems of the early 1940s and 1950s.

Emphasis is put on the connection of dualism in the land market, as described in Chapter 3, and the 'discriminatory' dualism in the labour market. Third, the conditions for the creation of an 'unlimited' supply of labour are analysed in a formal model. In order to carry out a rigorous analysis of the theory, Figures 5.1 and 5.2 have been used for explanatory and illustrative purposes.

Finally, the discussion of wages and employment is connected with the problem of labour migration. The literature of development economics has accepted that labour migration in most developing countries is a function of earning gaps between 'traditional' agricultural work and urban employment, hence the great deal of evidence to support this hypothesis. William J. Barber shows that, that the percentage of the male population in Northern Rhodesia (Zambia) and Rhodesia that migrated to find employment during the 1940s and 1950s was inversely related to the cash crop potential of their home region.[2] It has also been established that the time spent on cash crop production by Malawian tobacco farmers was inversely and significantly related to wage rates in the Rhodesian and South African labour markets where migrants could find work.[3] In a well-known model developed by Michael P. Todaro, migration decisions depend first on the gap in earnings between agricultural wage and modern sector urban wage, and second on the probability of getting a job in the modern sector, for which the existing level of urban unemployment might serve as a proxy, i.e. that an increase in the modern sector wage will induce more rural labour to migrate.[4] The trends and policy of labour migration in the Rhodesian labour market, however, has depended on a number of features that are not dealt with in these models.

Our emphasis in the sections below will be seen to be dependent on one basic condition – land alienation of the African lands which laid the foundations on an 'unlimited' supply of unskilled labour. Finally, the conditions for the creation of an 'unlimited' supply of labour are analysed in a formal model.

Development of dualism in the labour market

In this section our analysis begins with the state of labour market at the beginning of the colonisation process when employers experienced a severe labour shortage. The discussion focuses on the origins of the labour shortage and the measures resorted to by employers and the BSA Company government in order to secure their required labour supplies. As will be seen, the foundations of dualism in the labour market of Rhodesia were laid in the dualistic development of land tenure system and in the colonial methods of recruiting indigenous and foreign African labour.

The basic connection between the dualism in the land and labour markets is illustrated by evidence of the causes of shifts in the labour supply curve to the right as shown in Figure 5.1 below. As a result of dualism in the land tenure system, an 'unlimited' supply of labour was created in the economy, and through discriminatory laws in the labour market, Africans were relegated to holding unskilled jobs only.

The initial shortage of the indigenous labour

There is abundant evidence to show that one of the most pressing economic problems of the colonialists in the early days of Rhodesia was the initial labour deficit. This general shortage of labour occupied a central place in policy making[5] from the early period of the country's colonisation up to the end of the Company administration in 1923. Acute shortages of labour were recorded in 1896–1903, 1905–1911 and 1916.[6]

There are several reasons why the indigenous African labourers avoided mine labour during the early years of colonisation. The low wages and appalling conditions in the mines were important in influencing the Africans to stay away from the modern sector employment. Charles van Onselen observed that:

> in the most general terms these problems derived from the functioning of the industry itself, from economic conditions within Rhodesia, and the situation of the colony's premier industry within the regional economic system that embraced the whole of Southern Africa.[7]

Due to certain crucial limitations, the mining industry was unable to attract sufficient labour. Gold mining in Rhodesia was usually found in a series of smaller quartz reefs, which meant that the industry could not take advantage of the economies of scale that were possible in the Witwatersrand, or benefit from centralisation that existed in the Johannesburg area in South Africa.[8] Furthermore, the ore was often scattered around and of an unknown quantity, which also contrasted sharply with extremely consistent, although low grade, ore in the Rand mines.[9]

In addition, the Rhodesian mining industry was constrained by the fact that it had to operate within a regional economic system in which the powerful Rand mines dominated. 'The output of a "large" Rhodesian mines was only about one tenth of that of an average Witwatersrand mines.'[10] In this circumstance, if the Rhodesian mines were to develop despite their geological limitations, it meant that they had to attract capital on the basis of profits that could match what the shareholders were receiving in the Rand area in South Africa. This was particularly difficult at the turn of the twentieth century – between 1901 and 1912, the average output of the Rand mines increased by 14.2 per cent per year.[11] It was invariably the case, especially during this period, that the Rhodesian industry was in need of reconstruction.

In the face of these uncertainties and lack of profitability, the Rhodesian industry reduced its costs of production, and this was achieved at the expense of the African workers' wages. As a result of this process black mine wages were lower in 1922 than they had been in 1904.[12] Further, the industry cut down on indirect expenditure, which made for miserable conditions in the mine compounds. The Africans were aware of this and took steps to avoid jobs in the mines if possible.[13]

As already shown above, the African workers had two alternatives open to them to increase their cash incomes: sale of labour power and sale of agricultural products. The latter alternative was the most preferred one. The Africans actively took to selling agricultural surplus products to the mines so that it appears that the opportunity cost of their entry into the 'modern' employment sector was high. This was probably because many Africans, though deprived of their former land rights, still remained on some convenient part of their ancestral lands, earning the necessary cash income through sales of surplus agricultural produce. This was still a period of peasant development because surplus land was available, and conditions in the product markets were favourable as there existed a growing demand for peasant produce in the mines and urban centres.

Thus, in 1903 agricultural sales comprised 70 per cent of total African cash earnings.[14] The African peasantry supplied the bulk of the food stuffs required by the mines until after the end of the first decade of the nineteenth century. This is because European farming before 1914 was still insignificant.[15]

In response to the problems of labour shortage, forced labour became the first expedient adopted by the colonialists. Only two years after the occupation of Mashonaland a pioneer wrote 'we have great trouble in getting native labour here, the only way we can do is to go and catch them at dawn and compel them to work'.[16] Native Commissioners also resorted to forced labour.[17] For example, in 1895 the Native Commissioner for Hartley (present day Chegutu) noted, 'I am at present forcing the natives of this district to work solely against their will, using such methods as I think is desirable'.[18] However, after the African uprisings in 1896, the presence of a Residence Commissioner representing the Colonial Office somewhat reduced the open forms of compulsion. From now on, forced labour was carried out through compelling Chiefs to turn out certain numbers of young men. Conditions of work were, however, appalling. Both employers and Native Commissioners had frequent recourse to the sjambok, the hide whip. The Native Commissioner for Mazoe 'had a reputation of flogging Africans indiscriminately'.[19] The Native Commissioner for Lomagundi observed in 1899 that employers 'also interfere in other ways with natives thinking that because they came with the pioneers, or in the early days, they are entitled to treat natives as they please, and as apparently they have done nothing hitherto'.[20] An African chief who failed to deliver his expected quota of labourers was given 50 lashes, fined six goats and three herd of cattle and his rifle confiscated.[21] As more severe punishment was meted out, African labourers tended to flee with the result that labour became increasingly scarcer.

A second means used to coerce or furnish labour was taxation. The tax was collected in cash, cattle, grain or alluvial gold or in labour, usually for two months.[22] In 1895 alone, £8,000 worth of tax was collected and 'in some districts as much as one third of Shona cattle, sheep and goats were rounded up often by force'.[23] This was undoubtedly one of the causes of the 1893–1896 African resistance against the white settlers. In 1904 the hut tax was raised from 10s to a £1 poll tax for each male African. Taxation, however, did not prove to be an efficient means of supplying labourers to the employment sector, since it was possible for the Africans to pay taxes with cash raised in their participation in the produce market.

But as in South Africa, the Rhodesian African peasantry soon lost its ability to produce for the markets.[24] The end came with the realisation by the BSA Company and settlers that Zimbabwe had no gold reef to be compared with that of the Rand. As seen in Chapter 3, this was realised by further land alienation. In order to raise the value of the country's land resources through commercial farming, the Company government launched an attack on the African reserves in the years 1908–1914 with the intention of recovering the best land and making it available for European settlement.[25] African peasants were increasingly evicted from the more fertile lands and from the lands within easy reach of the markets. In this way the growth of the peasantry was severely curtailed, so that an increasing number of African workers were left with the alternative of looking for jobs in the modern sector. However, other means of increasing the supply of African labour were tied from the beginning of the century.

Imported African labour

During the 1890s the BSA Company introduced schemes to bring in foreign African labour. At first this took the form of encouraging neighbouring and even far away peoples to come and settle in Rhodesia on a permanent basis, e.g. the Fingoes of Eastern Cape who were invited by Cecil John Rhodes himself. People from Mozambique, from Northern Transvaal, and from Bechuanaland (Botswana) 'were encouraged, sometimes in secrecy, to cross the border into Rhodesia'.[26] The Chamber of Mines put up extraordinary attempts to recruit labour as far away as Somalia, Abyssinia, Saudi Arabia and Yemen.[27]

The rather uncoordinated attempts to recruit extra-territorial labour during the first decade of the Company administration were replaced by the establishment in 1903 of the Rhodesian Native Labour Bureau (RNLB), which was government sponsored and funded, and had the express purpose of the recruiting foreign African labour. The aim was to channel this labour to the mines where desperate attempts were made to stabilise labour within the confines of a low wage policy. From about 1914 onwards, the white plantation sector also came to be served by foreign African labour recruits. The RNLB was termed 'Chibaro', which means 'slave' or 'forced labour' by the Africans.[28] Because of its exploitative wage structure, the RNLB enabled the mining industry to embark on a programme of wage reductions between 1903 and 1908, and thereby overcome the bargaining power of the indigenous Africans in the labour market.[29] The RNLB had many elements of forced labour. Duncan G. Clarke has noted that 'forced labour "contracts" were also secured with the purpose of illegally indenturing workers, the administrative agencies of the Company government of the time being complicit in these labour practices'.[30]

The mine owners had earlier acted independently of each other, but by the formation of the RNLB, they attempted to act in concert, like in the typical case of a monopsony.[31] The RNLB set up contact labour bureaus both inside Rhodesia and in recruiting countries, in order to transport, finance and 'distribute' labour to Rhodesian employers who had previously paid the purchase price.[32] It acted as a single buyer of labour for the Rhodesian employers in the neighbouring countries. However, in the Rhodesian case monopsony did not succeed. This was unlike in the South African experience, where monopsony was finally successfully established in the form of Native Recruiting Corporation which subsequently managed to secure a reduction in the cost of unskilled labour.[33] In the markets for foreign labour the RNLB competed with Witwatersrand Native Labour Association (WNLA), which supplied labour to the Rand, in South Africa. Arrangements were made for cooperation between the two organisations but they did not prove effective.[34] In the local labour market the WNLA was not granted rights to recruit labour. Thus, the conditions for effective monopsony were not present.

However, the RNLB was not without success in its specific purpose of providing cheap labour in large amounts. There was a preponderance of alien African labour in the Rhodesian mines and farms from the end of the first decade of this century up to the 1950s.[35] Between 1906 and 1912 alone, the RNLB recruits comprised, on average over 36 per cent of the mining industry's labour requirements. In 1907 and 1908 it provided 54 per cent and 48 per cent respectively.[36]

From the demand side the largest employers of the African labour (mines and farms) opted for contract labour because its supply price was lower than that of local labour. However, from the supply side earnings might have played a significant role in attracting labour. It would seem that during most of the colonial period contract workers came largely from areas of relatively poor peasant communities, where there was a relative lack of opportunities to fully participate and benefit from trade transactions in the agricultural produce market in their own countries. This behaviour of labour seems supported by Barber's conclusion that during the 1940s and 1950s, the percentage of the male population that migrated to find employment was inversely related to the cash crop potential of their region.[37] If this is true, it only encouraged employers to increase the supply of labour through RNLB contractees because it was an important means of maintaining low wage levels for domestic labour as well. As van Onselen noted:

> Between 1906 and 1911 a growing number of RNLB labourers worked at consistently lower rates than those paid to 'voluntary' (i.e. non bureau) labourers. Besides the savings which this fact itself constituted it also placed the employers in a position to make reductions in wages of other black workers. With supply relatively well assured, a general reduction in wages was effected in 1906, and when the recession set in

> 1908, employers used the opportunity to lower African wages once more. It was thus the RNLB and wage reductions between 1904 and 1908 which made the largest contribution to cost minimisation during reconstruction.[38]

In sum, the Rhodesian labour market started off from a position of labour shortage at the beginning of colonisation. Most probably, the low wages and conditions of labour in the mines did not attract African labour into wage employment. Second, from the indigenous African point of view, the opportunity cost of selling surplus agricultural produce to the urban markets was lower than that of going into wage employment in the mines. Thus, in order to increase the requisite supply of labour the BSA Company tried many schemes to provide forced labour. The most successful of these schemes (as will be demonstrated further below) were the land alienation policies for local labour and importation of foreign labourers from neighbouring territories. These policies also had the effect of lowering the wage level obtained by unskilled (African) labour in the modern sector.

A shift in the labour supply curve

In this section we shall distinguish a change in labour supply involving shifts in the whole curve, from a movement along the same curve as a result of a change in the wages of labour. This will be illustrated with the aid of Figure 5.1 in which we measure the actual numbers in employment on the horizontal axis while the vertical axis denotes the wage level.

Let us suppose that the wage rises from w_1 to w_2 (everything else remaining unchanged), the number of workers who prefer to enter employment will rise from L_1 to L_2. This is, however, not an increase in the labour supply. Rather, it is a movement to another point on the same supply schedule.[39] Since our interest lies with the shift in the whole supply schedule and the causes of such a shift, we shall go on to the case where the whole schedule is shifted outwards.

An increase in the supply of labour means that the whole schedule has shifted e.g. from S_1 to S_2 so that at every possible wage more labour is supplied than before the shift in the curve, for instance, at wage $0w_1$ the number of labourers supplied before the change in the supply schedule is $0L_1$, but after the shift $0L_3$ labourers would be supplied. An outward shift of the supply curve also means that a given quantity of labour would be offered at a lower wage than previously. Thus e.g. with the supply curve S_2, it is sufficient to offer $0w_3$. In a market characterised by free choice of labour, i.e. a voluntary relationship of labour with respect to other available income opportunities, an outward shift of the supply curve may indicate an increased willingness on the part of labourers to seek employment in the labour market. But, as will be seen, in the long run, the shift can be caused by reasons not necessarily reflecting the voluntary relationship of

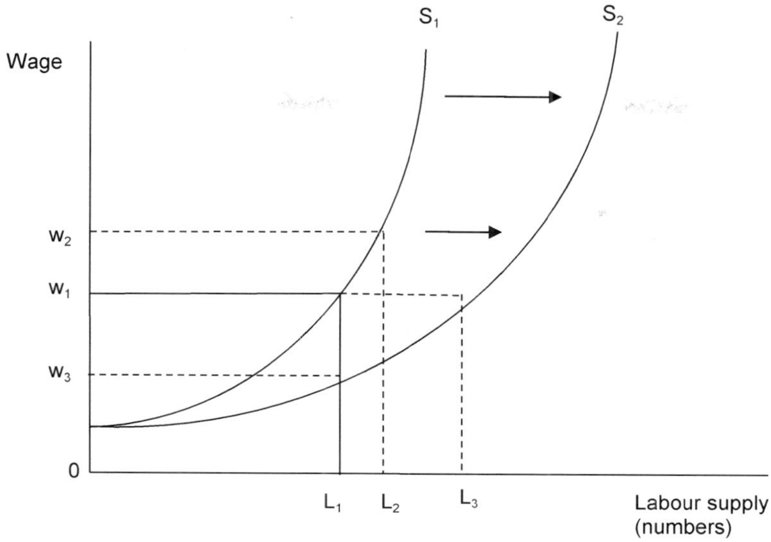

Figure 5.1 A shift in the labour supply curve.
Source: Ndlela, 1981:108.

labour choice with respect to other income opportunities. Thus, the historical experience of the Rhodesian labour market points to the following causes of the shift in the labour supply curve: land alienation, foreign labour recruitment and discrimination as well as other stringent labour controls that redirected the unskilled labour to areas of low wages where it was most needed.

Between 1906 and 1910, the number of blacks employed in the Rhodesian mining industry rose from 17,381 to 37,826, and the proportion supplied by the RNLB increased from 28.27 per cent to 40.65 per cent.[40] Thereafter, the total number of black employees remained more or less stable, reaching a peak of 41,286 in 1924. However, the percentage of the RNLB recruits dropped from 40.65 per cent in 1910 to a figure of 3.80 per cent in 1924.[41] This may be interpreted as arise in the number of local Africans (including 'voluntary' foreign recruits) taking up jobs in the mines.

Once an increase in the supply of labour shifted the supply curve to the right and employers were relatively assured of a systemic flow of labour from both local and foreign labourers, the wage level could be continually reduced. This occurred between 1912 and 1933.[42] In 1931, some Rhodesian mining districts reduced wages by 12.5 to 20 per cent. By 1934, these continual reductions in the wage level were causing considerable concern to some native commissioners.[43] Barber has noted that because of the extra-territorial labour in the period 1929–1945, real wages showed a tendency to decline, while the volume of African employment continued to expand.[44] These wage cuts were, however, officially justified on the grounds of minimising costs and hence enhancing the mining industry's profitability.[45] In this context, it became necessary to crush once and for all the indigenous peasantry's ability to rely on producing agricultural marketable surplus in order to gain cash incomes.

Hence developments in the land market became crucial for obtaining an 'unlimited' supply of cheap labour for Rhodesian mining and agricultural sectors. This 'unlimited' supply of labour could then be further increased by discrimination and the introduction of the colour bar, i.e. a social system in which blacks or people of different races were discriminated.

Dualism, discrimination and the colour bar

The discussion above demonstrates that the Rhodesian economy exhibited characteristics of economic dualism in the general sense of the 'classical' model associated with Lewis. The national economy may be (roughly) divided into one 'traditional' and one 'modern' sector. The latter is dynamic, relatively capital intensive, and is based on a highly developed, monetised exchange economy, whereas the former is stagnant, labour intensive (i.e. lacking capital), and based on activities which are often of a predominantly subsistence nature (see Chapter 2). A distinguishing feature of this type of economic dualism has continued to be the availability of labour surplus in the non-formal segment of the economy, implying that a substantial portion of the workers in the non-formal sector are underemployed. This dualistic structure was historically created by land annexations which had the effect of increasing the supply of low-cost, unskilled labour in the modern sector thereby destroying the alternative, preferred livelihood – that of the traditional African economy.

In this section it will be demonstrated that dualism in the land market and 'discriminatory' dualism in the labour market are not independent of each other, but that they are based on the same condition – that of the land alienation from the African majority by the white minority.[46] As shown in Chapter 3, what may be identified as 'traditional' sector in the contemporary economy was created as result of a policy where the whites gradually took over African lands, thereby drastically changing the production conditions in the original 'traditional' economy to the point where it is almost appropriate to speak of destruction. This policy, in turn, made it possible to call forth an 'unlimited' supply of African labour which, by means of discriminatory legislation, has been confined to unskilled jobs in the 'modern' sector. As a result, from this moment African incomes and working conditions began to appear grossly inadequate, both when the 'traditional' and the modern sector are considered separately, and when they are taken as a single entity.

In Zimbabwe, the attitude of white unions towards the advancement of African workers into skilled and semi-skilled positions, was one of hostility.

Inspectors of Mines Inquiries in 1912 showed that skilled Africans were only made use of in the smaller mines,[47] and that the white workers of the Shanva Mine had threatened to strike in 1913 if Africans were employed as skilled labour.[48] Thus, in practice the skilled jobs were reserved for whites for a long time, but the onset of the Depression in the early 1930s brought pressure to bear on the government to give a *de jure* sanction as well.

The Industrial Conciliation Act of 1934, modelled on its South African pattern (the South African Industrial Conciliation Act of 1924 denied the African workers the right to organise in trade unions).[49] The Industrial Conciliation Act defined an employee as 'any person engaged by employer to perform ... work ... but shall not include a native'.[50] The Africans, therefore, could not be members of recognised trade unions, but instead remained under the Masters and Servants Act of 1901,[51] which regulated the duties and rights of employers and employees by contracts arrived at individually by the contracting parties, i.e. according to the bargaining powers of each. This generally placed the Africans in an inferior position regarding the determination of wages and conditions of work. More importantly, the Industrial Conciliation Act also contained a clause that directly established a colour bar, by giving the Industrial Councils (consisting of white employers and employees) power to regulate apprenticeships – which were reserved for whites. In this way, the white workers entrenched a non-competitive wage structure in each industry by influencing the rate at which workers acquired skills and entered the industry.

Thus, once an 'unlimited' labour supply was assured through land alienation policies, discriminatory legislation confined it to unskilled jobs in the 'modern' sector. Further, discriminatory legislation placed African workers in an inferior and non-bargaining position in comparison with white workers. For instance, the Industrial Conciliation Act of 1934 laid down strict regulations and control over African labour, in contradistinction to free bargaining found in the white labour force. These measures led to African incomes being grossly inadequate in both the 'traditional' and the 'modern' sector. It became obvious, therefore, that these developments led to large differentials in wages and salaries between white and black workers on the one hand, and within different sectors of black labour on the other.

Thus, while discrimination through law and practice can cause dualism in the labour market, creating a situation in which workers of similar abilities are paid substantially different wages, the colour bar reinforces this tendency by controlling the entry into skilled jobs, and excluding a section of workers from the latter on the basis of colour. During Zimbabwe's colonial period, the Industrial Conciliation Act 1934 had excluded Africans from the definition of 'an employee'. However, unlike in South Africa, where the colour bar was legalised in the 1920s and not relaxed subsequently,[52] the Rhodesian state considered it necessary to respond to African union formation in the 1940s and to agree to institutionalise some, but not all African unions. In addition, the need for stabilised labour following the emergence of manufacturing industry also led to a relaxation of the colour bar during the period up to the advent of the Rhodesia Front government in 1962, and the Unilateral Declaration of Independence in 1965. Although labour unionisation was allowed, the official point of view remained that the African unions should be subject to close control.

In a statement on the provisions of the Industrial Conciliation Act of 1959, the Minister of Labour recorded in the introduction to the Act that 'it could be argued that to provide for these associations is nothing more than a control measure, and let me be frank, it is'.[53] The 1959 Act, it was felt, should only formally recognise African unions and give them limited rights, provided 'this form of conciliation (was) without repercussions occurring to the existing European organisations'.[54]

The provisions of the Act covered all employers except those engaged in domestic service, agriculture and Rhodesia Railways. Public Service employees 'negotiated' directly with their employers, and were subject to special provisions which, given the weight of employee influence in the civil service, guaranteed that white preferences were met with regard to wage policy. Employees of the Rhodesia Railways were regulated by the Rhodesia Railways Act, but were later assimilated under the Industrial Conciliation Act. Those Africans employed in domestic service and agriculture who accounted for 51.6 per cent of all wage employed Africans in 1959[55] had their employment conditions regulated under the Masters and Servants Act (1901), which denied them union formation and collective bargaining.

White unions were regarded as automatically 'registered' under the Industrial Conciliation Act of 1959, but could be allowed to renegotiate their status in order to take African workers into their fold, while African unions were to apply and qualify for registration. Thus, a certain degree of 'multi-racial' unionism was allowed under the system of strict regulation and control. These 'multi-racial' unions were actually more multiracial in theory than in practice. Their recognition was along hierarchical lines in which power within the unions lay with the skilled (white) workers. This was ensured by section 47 of the Industrial Conciliation Act (Chapter 246) of 1959, where section 47 (1) (a) provides for 'the equitable representation on the governing body of the trade unions or the employers' organisations of any different branches of employees and employers and, in particular, the adequate representation of the skilled and minority interests'. The constitution of the unions did not allow an applicant to be excluded from the union on the basis of colour, but the union could differentiate on racial grounds between its members. Thus section 47 (3) provides:

> (a) for the establishment of a branch of the union or its organisation; and (b) for its membership to be divided into branches on the basis of class of work or enterprise or the place of work or business or the sex or the *race or colour* of the members or otherwise.

The registrar also regulated and protected the voting rights of the skilled and minority interests.[56] As a result of these discriminatory and control measures, Africans who are in the main in unskilled and semi-skilled classes of work, had very little collective voting strength within the 'multi-racial' unions.

In sum, the existence of dualism in the land market and 'discriminatory' dualism in the labour market reinforced each other and they were based on the same condition – that of land alienation from the African majority by the white minority. This policy, in turn, made it possible to call forth an 'unlimited' supply of African labour which 'discriminatory' legislation subsequently confined to unskilled jobs in the modern sector. These developments created grossly inadequate African incomes both in relation to the 'traditional' sector and the 'modern' sector viewed separately, and also when they are considered jointly. In the next section we shall make an analysis of the creation of an 'unlimited 'supply of labour in the Zimbabwean economy.

Creation of an unlimited supply of labour

The historical experience of Zimbabwe's labour market presented in the preceding sections of this chapter can be summarised in a formal model. The model seeks to explain how an 'unlimited' labour supply is created, and the behaviour of wages under conditions of a continued presence or maintenance of 'unlimited' supply of labour in the economy. In this model it is assumed that the economy can be divided into one 'modern' (white) and one 'traditional' (African) sector. The characteristics of these sectors are discussed in detail in Chapters 2 and 3, and in the preceding sections of the present chapter. Both sectors employ land and unskilled labour, and in addition the modern sector uses skilled labour. The 'traditional' sector produces mostly food products and to a limited degree some raw materials while the output of the modern sector consists of food, minerals, agricultural raw materials and industrial products. In the case of colonial Zimbabwe (Rhodesia), whites were employed in skilled jobs, while Africans could (at the outset) do both skilled (when having the necessary education) and mainly unskilled labour. However, since, the model focuses mainly on the conditions which shift the labour supply curve of the predominantly unskilled labour to the right, we shall concentrate for the most part on the behaviour of unskilled labour.

In Figure 5.2 the first quadrant represents the market for unskilled labour in the modern sector. The supply curve s_1 begins on the vertical axis at a wage that may be defined as the subsistence wage (the wage needed to keep a single person alive and working in the sector) and extends north-eastwards to a maximum level of employment (not shown in the figure) where all unskilled labourers are working in this sector. The total supply of unskilled labour is assumed to be given. The first quadrant also contains

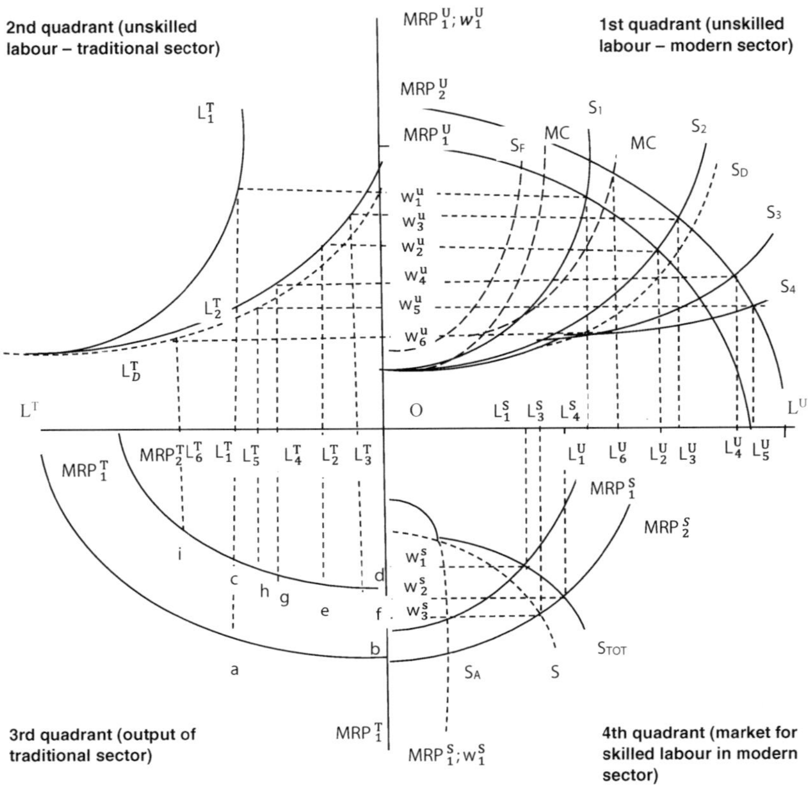

Figure 5.2 Labour market behaviour in segmented economic sectors.
Source: Ndlela, 1981:116.

the marginal revenue product (demand) curve for unskilled labour in the modern sector MRP^U_1. The equilibrium of this labour market, assumed to be competitive at the outset, is given by wage level of w^U_1 and a corresponding employment of L^U_1.

The second quadrant represents the employment of unskilled labour in the 'traditional' sector. The unskilled labour curve L^T_1 is identical with curve s_1 in the first quadrant. The alternative to working in the modern sector for unskilled labour is to fall back into the 'traditional' peasant sector. The L^T curve measures leftwards how much labour can be employed in the traditional economy given the wage (and conditions) for unskilled labour in the modern sector. The traditional sector acts as a 'sink' where all labourers not used in the modern sector of the economy are absorbed. In a dual economic model, employment in the traditional sector reaches a maximum when employment (unskilled) in the modern sector is minimised, and vice versa.

In the third quadrant we have the output of the traditional sector. The marginal revenue product curve in the traditional sector (MRP_1^T) corresponds to L^T curve in the second quadrant. With a level of unskilled employment corresponding to L_1^U in the modern sector and to L_1^T in the traditional sector, the output of the latter is given by $0L_1^Tab$, which is divided among those working and using land in the sector.

This leaves us with the fourth quadrant, where we find the market for skilled labour in the modern sector. Let us assume that at the outset the labour supply is divided into one African and one white component. It is assumed that all Africans are prepared to work at lower wage than the whites and that after a certain point (corresponding to a wage lower than the one where the first whites will enter the market) the supply for skilled African labour will be exhausted, i.e. completely inelastic. This is the case because no further training possibilities are offered the Africans. ('The vast majority of black workers in colonial Rhodesia remained in unskilled or semi-skilled occupations and opportunities for higher training were restricted. White employees and white workers together formed a powerful block to African advancement.'[57]) Horizontal addition of the S_A and S_W gives the total supply curve of skilled labour, S_{TOT}. The intersection of this curve with the marginal revenue product (demand) curve under competitive conditions yields the equilibrium wage w_1^S and the equilibrium employment L_1^S, i.e. the number of Africans and whites employed is given by S_A and S_W at wage w_1^S.

Thus we have the initial situation characterised by competitive equilibria in all the three markets. But let us see what happens after discriminatory measures of all kinds are introduced in the labour market. In the analysis we shall assume that all product prices are given and that no technological change takes place. For the sake of simplicity we also assume that the influence of changes in employment of unskilled labour on the employment of skilled workers and vice versa is so small as to be negligible. (Our main interest lies in unskilled rather than in skilled labour).

The initial effect of land alienation in the traditional sector is to shift the MRP_1^T curve upwards in the diagram to MRP_2^T. We assume that the production function of the traditional sector has positive second cross derivatives with respect to land and labour, so that a reduction in the amount of land should reduce the marginal revenue product of labour at all levels of employment in the traditional sector.[58] Thus, at a given employment level, L_1^T, the total output of the sector is reduced to $0L_1^Tcd$. This, in turn, leads to a decline in the per capita income in the sector.

The decline in the per capita income in the traditional sector should make it comparatively more rewarding at the margin to seek wage employment in the modern sector. As the analysis of Chapter 2 shows, the literature of economic development has examples of economic behavioural models of the rural-urban labour migration, ranging from simple wage differential approaches of Lewis (1954), Ranis and Fei (1961), Jorgenson (1961), to the later models of Todaro type.[59] All these assume that the rural labour migration is a function of a combination of the prevailing real income differentials and rural–urban 'expected' income differentials, that is, income differential adjusted for the probability of finding an urban job.[60] In the present model, because of the decline in income per capita in the African rural sector, unskilled labour is forced out of that sector in order to seek alternative incomes in the modern sector albeit at falling wage rates in the latter sector. This is because of massive land alienations, which prevented the traditional sector from providing sufficient incomes for everybody, and consequently these incomes have to be supplemented with wage incomes in the modern sector. As a result, the supply curve of unskilled labour shifts, e.g. in the manner shown in Figure 5.2 (from S_1 to S_2). The L^T curve also shifts in a corresponding manner. As both curves are flattened out, the traditional sector will now be emptied of labour at a lower wage than before.

The increased supply of unskilled labour in the modern sector will shift employment to L^U_2 and depress the wage to w^U_2. The employment level in the traditional sector, in turn will fall to L^T_2 and the output of the latter decreases to $0L^T_2ed$. This output is shared among fewer persons than before, but if substantial amounts of land were alienated, as was actually the case in Zimbabwe, the output per capita of those active in the traditional sector should fall. Together with a fall in the wage level of unskilled labourers in the modern sector, this leads to a decline in the per capita income of the African population as a whole.[61]

However, the alienated land is put to work in the modern sector on the white farms. This has the effect of raising the marginal productivity schedules of both skilled (downwards as shown in the diagram) and unskilled labour. More skilled and unskilled labourers are hired and wages increase as well (to the levels indicated by w^U_3 and w^S_2). In the meantime, employment in the traditional sector decreases, but output per labourer increases there (assuming diminishing returns to labour to prevail). Thus, to a certain extent, increased unskilled wages and increased per capita production in the traditional sector compensate for negative effects of land alienation. The value of output in the traditional sector comes from both land and labour. With large parts of land lost for the Africans through massive alienation of land to the Europeans, the only way to compensate for the incomes lost is for large numbers to leave to seek jobs in the modern sector. In the actual experience it is hard to believe that the net effect of land alienation would be other than a decline in the overall standard of living of the Africans.[62]

But presumably due to population growth, while unskilled labour was pushed out of the traditional sector, actual numbers of the persons remaining there did not decrease much. In the typical Rhodesian experience the majority of the economically active men spend their active lives as wage earners in the modern sector, but their dependents remain in the traditional sector.[63]

As shown in the above sections, the second most important means of providing labour for the modern sector was through the import of foreign

African labour from abroad. The immediate effect of this was felt in the market for unskilled labour in the modern sector. To the supply curve S_2, we now add another curve for foreign labour, S_F, assumed to begin at some stage above the subsistence level. If we add this curve horizontally to S_2 we get new, flatter, supply curve S_3.Total employment of unskilled labour increases to L_4^U and the wage decreases to w_4^U. But at this stage the effect of the increased supply of domestic labourers and foreign labourers eventually creates an 'unlimited' supply of labour in the modern sector. Employment of domestic labourers, therefore, falls back to the level indicated by S_2 in the diagram. These workers are now pushed into the traditional sector where, due to diminishing returns to labour, output per capita will again fall. In sum, this leads to a decline in African (domestic) per capita income.

Finally, when the colour bar is introduced in the modern sector, we first have to move from S_{TOT} curve to the S_W curve to determine the new wage and employment levels for skilled labour. Because of the colour bar in the market for skilled labour, S_W now represents the total supply of skilled labour. As shown in the diagram, the total level of employment (skilled) is reduced and the wage level increases (to L_3^S and w_2^S, respectively). White employment increases as a result of the wage increase while at the same time all Africans are being removed from the market for unskilled labour.

The skilled African labour will have to be employed elsewhere. Let us assume that they are transferred to the traditional sector even though their special skills are not applicable in the sector. At the margin, it will pay for some people to leave the sector and take up unskilled jobs in the modern sector instead. In this case, the supply curve for domestic labour, S_2, shifts to S_D and L_2^T shifts to L_D^T, beginning further to the left, and the new total supply curve of unskilled labour is S_4, which is further to the right and flatter than S_3. Again, the wage level declines (to w_S^U), due to the increased supply of labour. Employment also increases in the traditional sector (to L_S^T and per capita output declines. Once more, the overall standard of living of the Africans declines.[64]

The cumulative process of economic dualism illustrated

The process analysed above contains a cumulative element. When the land area at the disposal of the 'traditional' sector is reduced or when too many people are packed into given area, overgrazing, soil degradation and erosion, as demonstrated above, sooner or later take their toll. As the natural resources are successively destroyed, the supply curve for unskilled labour shifts once more to the right. More people will then be pushed into the modern sector holding unskilled jobs at falling wages. Provided that the African population grows, it will be difficult to stop the land degradation and soil erosion process, and an increasing number of people will be compelled to leave the sector. The model analysis is mainly built on the situation of Zimbabwe's colonial era where dualistic policies based on land alienation, labour policies and outright colour bar held sway.

The irony of Zimbabwe's post-independence development of the labour market, is that it kept virtually all the characteristics of the colonial era labour market economic dualism. The current labour market in Zimbabwe was shaped during the colonial period where the ideology of white supremacy resulted in a distorted dual and enclave economy, where a modern white settler economy existed side-by-side with a pre-capitalist impoverished African peasant sector. In the post-independence period, the distinguishing feature of dualism continued to be the availability of surplus labour now piling in the non-formal segment of the economy, implying the continued existence of labour surplus in the non-formal sector. As in the Lewis (1954) model, a substantial proportion of workers in this segment could be withdrawn into the formal sector without affecting the labour input used in production.

The applicability of the model may be marred by the question as to whether it is realistic to assume that product prices do not change. In practice, we would not expect the adjustment to be such as to leave commodity prices unaltered. What the model indicates is that given that changes in commodity prices are sufficiently small, the measures analysed have a tendency to create an 'unlimited', i.e. infinitely elastic supply of labour in the modern sector. The case of gold for a long period comes closer to reality, as Charles van Onselen noted that 'The industry (gold) had … to contend with the fact for long periods the price of the product was fixed'.[65]

When it comes to other commodities, the assumption is, of course, more dubious, but commodity price changes cannot be advantageously handled in the present simple model. For that we should need a complete general equilibrium structure, simplifying not only the supply side but the demand for different products as well. However, within the limitations of the present analysis and assuming that movements in commodity prices are either small or exogenous, we conclude that the elements included in the land alienation cum discrimination process tend to create an 'unlimited' supply of labour by gradually shifting the supply curve to the right, i.e. towards the subsistence level. The existence of such an 'unlimited' supply of labour has been noted in the case for colonial Zimbabwe, where the real wages appear to have fallen from 1929 to 1945.[66]

As the above analysis illustrates, the concrete case of the 'unlimited' supply of labour has its basis in the land alienation process. Land alienation does not only have an impact on the supply of labour in that it forces people out of the traditional sector. It is also a prerequisite for establishing the uneven power relations in the market for unskilled labour. The discriminatory laws in the labour market and the colour bar that finally restricted Africans to unskilled and menial jobs might also have been created without annexation of African land, but they would not have been effective, since the Africans would then always have had the alternative of going back to a traditional economy, allowing for a much higher standard of living than has actually been the case. If the Africans had been backed by a substantial amount of landed wealth, they could have used it against white monopolisation of skilled jobs, as well as against discrimination laws forbidding unionisation. Since the white economy depended on the large supplies of unskilled labour, the strike weapon could have been used to force rises in the wages and demolition of the job reservation policy.

In conclusion, this chapter demonstrates that the development of dualism in the labour market of Zimbabwe was closely connected and consequent on the development of dualism in the land market. During the early years of colonisation there was a labour deficit in the modern sector. African labour avoided wage employment because of low wages and bad conditions in the mines, and instead took to selling agricultural surplus products in order to increase their cash incomes. This was possible because surplus land was available and conditions in the product markets were favourable, since there existed a growing demand for peasant produce in the mines and urban centres.

As the above analysis shows, a shift in the unskilled labour supply curve to the right was eventually caused by a combination of forced labour, recruitment of African foreign labour and land annexations. The latter was the most important cause of the outward shift in the unskilled labour supply curve. It was also the basis for dualism in the labour market, since historically, land alienations had the effect of increasing the supply of low-cost, unskilled labour in the modern sector by destroying the alternative, preferred livelihood – that of the traditional African economy. Thus one important conclusion of the analysis is that dualism in the land market and discriminatory dualism in the labour market were not independent of each other, but were based on the same condition – that of the land alienation from the African majority by the white minority. This led to an 'unlimited' supply of labour, which by means of discriminatory legislation and the colour bar was confined to unskilled jobs in the modern sector.

Notes

1 For details, see Chapter 6.
2 Barber, 1960:241–242.
3 Dean, 1965.
4 Todaro, 1969.
5 Several aspects of the Rhodesian labour supply problem have been documented by historians, geographers and economists alike. See Arrighi, 1970; Mackenzie, 1970; Scott, 1954; van Onselen, 1976, 1978; Phimister, 1977; Mason, 1958.
6 Arrighi, 1970:200.
7 Van Onselen, 1976:74.
8 Ibid.:17.
9 Ibid.:18.
10 Ibid.
11 Ibid.
12 Ibid.

13 Ibid.:74.
14 Arrighi, 1970:216; Palmer, 1977:229.
15 van Onselen, 1976:74.
16 Mackenzie, 1970:46.
17 Ibid.:50.
18 Palmer, 1977:143.
19 Ibid.
20 Ibid.
21 Ibid.
22 Ibid.:44.
23 Ibid.
24 Lundahl and Ndlela, 1980:11.
25 Palmer,1977:80.
26 Mackenzie, 1970:43.
27 Ibid.
28 Van Onselen, 1976:99; 1978:89.
29 Van Onselen, 1978:89.
30 Clarke, 1974:9.
31 This is a market structure in which only one buyer interacts with many would-be sellers of a particular product, that is having a market power over the terms of offer to its sellers as the only purchaser of goods and services.
32 Ibid.:8.
33 Jeeves, 1975:28; Horwitz, 1967:190–93; Wilson, 1972:3–5.
34 Van Onselen, 1976:85–86.
35 Scott, 1954:31; Phimister, 1977:87.
36 Van Onselen, 1976:114.
37 Barber, 1961:244.
38 Van Onselen, 1976:25–26.
39 Reynolds, 1978:92–94; Douglas, 1934:237.
40 Van Onselen, 1976:114.
41 Ibid.
42 Ibid.:33.
43 Ibid.
44 Barber, 1961:208.
45 In 1933 an official government publication recorded: 'the cost of living for natives is and will remain in depreciated sterling exactly what it was in the sterling of 1930. There is, therefore, no need for native wages to rise – a big factor in mining costs', van Onselen, 1976:33.
46 A similar case is that of South Africa, see Lundahl and Ndlela, 1980.
47 Phimister, 1971:69.
48 Ibid.
49 Horwitz, 1967:193.
50 Sprack, 1974:19.
51 For details see ILO, 1978:76–77; Clarke, 1974:1, Chapter 5.
52 Lundahl and Ndlela, 1980:115.
53 ILO, 1978:65.
54 Ibid.
55 Ibid.
56 Ibid:69, See also Harris, 1974:55.
57 International Defence and Aid Fund. IDAF, 1977:15.
58 If say the production function of the traditional sector is $Q=g(T, L)$, where T is land or terrain and L is labour, and we have $\frac{\partial^2 g}{T\partial L}>0$, an increase of T implies and increase of $\frac{\partial g}{\partial L}$ and a reduction of T also implies a reduction in $\frac{\partial g}{\partial L}$.

59 Well documented from these authors. Lewis, 1954; Ranis and Fei, 1961; Jorgenson, 1961.

60 Todaro, 1969.

61 To maintain fixed product prices when the supply of unskilled labour shifts from S1 to S2, the price of land must rise. When more unskilled labour is employed in the modern sector as the unskilled wage falls, the change in profits in this sector equals

$$d\Pi = \acute{P}\frac{\partial Q}{\partial L^U}\partial L^U - L^U dw^U - w^U \partial L^U - \hat{J}dr \tag{1}$$

Where J stands for land and r for rent, given the supply of land, given the product price, $\acute{P}$, and given that changes in the level of unskilled wages have no repercussions in the market for skilled labour. Temporarily, these profits are positive, but as firms compete, profits again fall to zero. For this we must have that

$$\acute{P}\frac{\partial Q}{\partial L^U}\partial L^U - L^U dw^U - w^U \partial L^U - \hat{J}dr \tag{2}$$

At the outset, the marginal revenue of employing more unskilled labour must be equal to the marginal cost of doing so, given product and factor prices, for each firm, and hence also for the industry as a whole:

$$\acute{P}\frac{\partial Q}{\partial L^U} = w^U \tag{3}$$

Thus, for zero profits if follows that

$$-L^U dw^U = \hat{J}dr \tag{4}$$

With the fall in unskilled wages, rent must increase, but with a given commodity price, firms compete for the given resource, land, so as to make its price increase until profits are wiped out.

62 When more land in put to use in the modern sector, profits are again increased this time by

$$d\Pi = \acute{P}\left(\frac{\partial Q}{\partial L}\partial J + \frac{\partial Q}{\partial L^U}\partial L^U\, \partial Q \backslash \partial L^S\right) - rdJ - Jdr - L^U dw^U - w^U \partial L^U -$$
$$L^S dw^S - w^S dL^S \tag{5}$$

and at the outset, in addition to (3) we have

$$\acute{P}\frac{\partial Q}{\partial J} = r \tag{6}$$

and

$$\acute{P}\frac{\partial Q}{\partial L^S} = w^S \tag{7}$$

so that for profits to fall to zero we must have

$$-L^U dw^U - L^S dw^S = Jdr \tag{8}$$

This time, however, rents have fallen due to the increased supply of land. With positive profits, firms bid for more labour (both skilled and unskilled) to add to the new land and hence there is a rise in both wage levels.

63 Mswaka, 1974:60, and Weinrich, 1975:60.

64 The change in profits in the economy is

$$d? = \acute{P}\left(\frac{\partial Q}{\partial L^S}\partial L^S + \frac{\partial Q}{\partial L^U}\partial L^U\right) - w^S dL^S - L^S dw^S - w^U \partial L^U - L^U dw^U - \hat{J}dr \qquad (9)$$

and for profits to be wiped out wiped we must have, with skilled wages rising and unskilled wages falling, that

$$L^S dw^S - L^U dw^U - \hat{J}dr \qquad (10)$$

i.e. that the effect on rents is indeterminate.

65 Van Onselen, 1976:18.

66 Arrighi, 1970:205.

References

Arrighi, Giovanni 1970. 'Labour Supplies in Historical Perspective: A Study of the Prelotarianization of the African Peasantry in Rhodesia', *The Journal of Development Studies*, Vol. 6, No. 3:200.

Barber, William J. 1961. *The British Economy of Central Africa: A Case Study of Economic Development in a Dualistic Society*. London: Oxford University Press.

Clarke, Duncan G. 1974. *Contract Workers and Underdevelopment in Rhodesia*. Mambo Occasional Papers, Socio-Economic Series No. 3, Gwelo.

Dean, E.R. 1965. 'Economic Analysis and African Response to Price', *Journal of Farm Economics*, Vol. 47:402–409.

Douglas, Paul H. 1934. *The Theory of Wages*. New York: Macmillan.

Harris, Peter S. 1974. *Black Industrial Workers in Rhodesia: The General Problems of Low Pay*. Mambo Occasional Papers, Socio-Economic Series No. 2, Gwelo.

Horwitz, R. 1967. *The Political Economy of South Africa*. London: Weidenfeld and Nicholson.

ILO (International Labour Office). 1978. *Labour Conditions and Discrimination in Southern Rhodesia (Zimbabwe)*. Geneva: United Nations.

IDAF (International Defence and Aid Fund). 1977. *Zimbabwe: The Facts About Rhodesia I.D.A.F.* London: Research Department. Defence and Aid Fund for Southern Africa.

Jeeves, A. 1975. 'The Control of Migratory Labour on the South African Gold Mines in the Era of Krugger and Milner', *Journal of Southern African Studies*, Vol. 2:28.

Jorgenson, Dale W. 1961. 'The Development of Dual Economy', *Economic Journal*, Vol. 71:312.

Lewis, W. Arthur. 1954. 'Economic Development with Unlimited Supplies of Labour', *Manchester School*, Vol. 22:196–210.

Lundahl, Mats and Ndlela, Daniel B. 1980. 'Land Alienation. Dualism, and Economic Discrimination: South Africa and Rhodesia', *Economy and History*, University of Lund, Sweden, Vol. 23, No. 2:106–132.

Mackenzie, J.M. 1970. 'African Labour in the Chartered Company Period', *Rhodesian History*, Vol. 1:46.

Mason, P. 1958. *Birth of a Dilemma: The Conquest and Settlement of Rhodesia*. Oxford: Oxford University Press.

Mswaka, T.E. 1974. 'African Employment and the Rural Areas of Rhodesia', *Rural Africans in Social Sciences*, African Studies Centre, Michigan State University, No. 24.

Ndlela, D.B. 1981. 'Dualism in the Rhodesian Colonial Economy', *Lund Economic Studies*, Department of Economics, University of Lund.

Palmer, Robin. 1977. *Land and Racial Discrimination in Rhodesia*. London, Ibadan, Nairobi, Lusaka: Heinemann.

Phimister, I.R. 1971. 'The Shamwa Mine Strike in 1937: An Emerging African Proletariat', *Rhodesian History*, Vol. 2:69.

Phimister, I.R. 1977. 'Peasant Production and Underdevelopment in Southern Rhodesia, 1890–1914, with Particular Reference to the Victoria District', in Robin Palmer and Neil Parsons (eds), *The Roots of Rural Poverty in Central and Southern Africa*. London, Ibadan, Nairobi and Lusaka: Heinemann.

Ranis, Gustav and Fei, John, C.H. 1961. 'A Theory of Economic Development', *The American Economic Review*, Vol. 51, No. 4:533–565.

Reynolds, Lloyd G. 1978. *Labour Economics and Labour Relations*. 7th Edition, New Jersey: Prentice-Hall.

Scott, Peter. 1954. 'Migrant Labour in Southern Africa', *The Geographical Review*, Vol. 44:31.

Sprack, J. 1974. *Rhodesia, South Africa's Sixth Province*. London: IDAF.

Todaro, Michael P. 1969. 'A Model of Labour Migration and Urban Unemployment in Less Developed Countries', *American Economic Review*, Vol. 59, No. 1:143.

Van Onselen, C. 1976. *Chibaro: African Mine Labour in Southern Rhodesia 1900–1933*. London: Pluto Press.

Van Onselen, C. 1978. 'Black Workers in Central African Industry: A Critical Essay on the Historiography and Sociology of Rhodesia', in I.R. Phimister and C. van Onselen (eds), *Studies in the History of African Mine Labour in Colonial Zimbabwe*. Gwelo: Mambo Press.

Weinrich, A.K.H. 1975. *African Farmers in Rhodesia: Old and New Peasant Communities in Karangaland*. London, Nairobi and Cape Town: Oxford University Press.

Wilson, Francis. 1972. *Labour in the South African Gold Mines 1911–1960*. Cambridge: Cambridge University Press.

6 The theory of economic dualism

Theoretical foundations of economic dualism

This chapter presents the theoretical and empirical foundations of dualism, with the emphasis being put on the main body of the theory – represented by the 'classical' model of dualism associated with W. Arthur Lewis. The Lewis model divides the economy into one capitalist sector and one subsistence sector, and goes on to demonstrate that under the classical assumption labour is inelastic supply to the capitalist sector, and that the path of accumulation becomes different from the one that is based on the neo-classical assumption that supply of labour is less than perfectly elastic.[1]

In the Lewis model, economic development is generated in the capitalist sector where reinvestment of the surplus over wages provides savings and the stock of capital increases over time. With further growth of the capitalistic sector also invariably called the modern sector, the profit share in the national income may vary over time, depending on the nature of technical change, but given the constant real wage, it will increase. The Lewis model is mainly concerned with the accumulation of capital in the modern sector and forms the basis for contributions to an analysis of the function and expansion of the modern sector in undeveloped countries. The subsistence sector is treated as a backlog in the development process, with a function of providing 'surplus' labour at a more or less constant wage to the modern sector.

Space is also given to the sociological, technological and the neo-classical variants of dualism and a criticism of these theories. The Lewis dualism theory's main criticism is directed against the skewed distribution of income which results from the specification of the classical model, since the latter does not necessarily involve an equalising of the existing distribution of income. The rise in capitalist incomes may be accompanied by a declining share going to the members of the subsistence sector. The criticism of the Lewis model is also directed against the relative neglect of the subsistence sector, as well as against the assumption that the dualistic structure of the economy is given and that the theory conveniently ignores the forces that stood to gain from dualism – the metropolitan enterprise and the privileged minority classes operating in these underdeveloped countries. There is also a criticism of the policy implications of the Lewis model, which seeks to industrialise without the need to divert extra resources to the lower income agricultural sector so that rising inequalities are inevitable in the process.

In the current economic structure of underdeveloped countries, the Lewis dualism theory can easily be reformulated to shift emphasis towards addressing the policies and institutions that create and benefit from the existence of dualism. In the case under study, this analytical perspective can be used to distinguish between dualism in general and the specific case of the Zimbabwean colonial experience. At the general level, Zimbabwe's colonial dualistic structure was mainly caused by the low wage policies of the mines and plantations as well as by discrimination in the provision of infrastructure by government. Land concentration and growing inequalities in the allocation of factors of production also constituted one of the major causes of dualism. The discussion stresses the view that the general shortage of land and those resources that are complementary to land, leads to an artificial population pressure, land degradation, 'unlimited' supply of labour and skewed distribution of income. This framework of dualism is applicable to the Rhodesian case. In the latter, the analysis of dualism is based on a historical perspective, i.e. from the standpoint of the policies of the colonial governments and in particular their land alienation policies. As will be shown below, instead of striving to end the spectre of dualism, the post-colonial state maintained the status quo and in fact deepened dualism.

Definitions

In the literature, most writers define dualism as the co-existence of the capitalist sector and the subsistence sector (largely a 'traditional' agricultural economy) within the framework of an underdeveloped economy. The capitalist sector is that sector which uses reproducible capital from which the operating capitalists derive a surplus or profit, part of which is reinvested in the production cycle. The subsistence sector may include everything else. but is largely identified with traditional agriculture. Thus, while the subsistence sector is often identified empirically with the traditional agricultural sector, the surplus labour that is often located in the traditional agriculture may also be found in petty trade, the often over-manned domestic service and other service occupations.[2] As will be shown in the chapters below, this is now referred to as the non-formal sector, which consists of the informal and communal sectors. It is, however, clear that, in a certain sense, this definition deals with the problem of dualism at superficial level, taking the dualistic structure as given. Our focus will be on the origin and initial conditions for creation and maintenance of dualism. In this sense dualism (social and economic) is also defined as including the creation of initial conditions by the entry of foreign capital or colonialism into the 'original' pre-capitalistic indigenous economy. In the case of Zimbabwe, land alienation policies and the low wage policies of mines and plantations were the initial forms of exploitation that later became institutionalised as the creation of a distinct 'modern' economy came to co-exist and thrive by the maintenance of the low productivity and relatively stagnant 'traditional' sector.

The advantage of the above analysis over the 'conventional' theories that were in vogue during the 1950s and early 1960s is that it does not overlook the initial conditions that create dualism. Our definition does not take the dualistic structures of the economy as given, but instead it proposes to investigate the principal causes of dualism in order to suggest the restructuring of an economy that suffers from stagnation that is to a large extent caused by dualism. Our analysis will focus on the influence of government policy, institutions and the monopoly elements that affect factor markets in order to understand the crucial links between economic sectors.

The chapter reviews the main theories of dualism in development economics, namely sociological, classical, technological and so called neoclassical dualism. The theories are discussed in order to examine their hypothetical propositions and to assess their relevance in relation to conditions of actual underdeveloped economies. Our criticism of the theories of dualism, especially the main variant of classical dualism, is focussed particularly on the relative neglect of the traditional or subsistence sector in the analysis.

While the rest of the analysis relies on the main foundations of the theory of dualism, we also put forward an alternative approach to the theory. In the latter, the intention is to build on a theory originated by Keith Griffin that focuses attention on the binding relations of dualism in the factor markets as well as its possible consequences.[3] The remaining chapters of the study are concerned with an analysis that focuses not only on the initial conditions for the creation of dualism in the Zimbabwean economy, but its further entrenchment in the country's post-independence economy.

The methodology used relies on the use of such macroeconomic concepts as the standard of living, per capita incomes, aggregate production and average output levels. Microeconomic analysis will be limited to the sectoral level of the economy. This is because a discussion of economic dualism at the national level assumes that the more significant variables pertain to society, and individuals are affected as their standard of living thereby become influenced in one way or another. In addition, our methodology benefits from the assumption that economic analysis of undeveloped countries concedes the fundamental significance of the distinction between 'growth' and 'development' and therefore permits the explicit incorporation of social and particularly political economy issues. In the literature dealing with development economics there has long been a growing realisation that economic issues cannot be scientifically considered in isolation, especially from political and social issues such as class and organisation, which lie at the heart of the production relations underlying the economic and social structure. This proposition is by no means limited to development economies as for example Nicholas Georgescu-Roegen has observed:

> It is … understandable for physics to treat as fiction and view with mistrust the un-observables it had to invent in order to unify into one picture disparate observables and thus simplify its logical foundation. But there is absolutely no reason for economics to treat as fiction the very springs of economic action – wants, beliefs, expectations, institutional attitudes, etc. For these elements are known to us by immediate acquaintance, that is, more intimately than any of the economic 'observables' – prices, sales, production and so forth.[4]

Theories of dualism

The modern theory of dualism came into being during the 1950s when economists focused on how capital accumulation could occur under the conditions facing the underdeveloped countries. As shown in the definition of dualism above, one of the well-known and influential exponents of dualism theory is W. Arthur Lewis. In this section we shall review the main body of dualism theory and emphasis will be put on the main variant of this theory that is represented by the model of classical dualism originated by Lewis.[5] The other variants of the theory are: the sociological, the technological and the neoclassical approaches to dualism theory. However, as Harold Brookfield has shown, the idea of dualism at least goes back to Malthus and Marx, with the peasant economy as a special type of an economy with the analytical properties of dualism.[6]

Sociological dualism

Development economics in the 1950s and 1960s started off as an unusual mixture of classical economic propositions and the prevailing economic and social theory of western countries tailored with assumption thought to be appropriate to the institutional framework of underdeveloped countries. Development economics sought to forge a distinctive theory that was applicable to the latter. Before Lewis came to grips with dualism, J.H. Boeke, a Dutch economist, had already developed the idea of social dualism. Boeke is perhaps the leading exponent of the attempt to develop a distinctive theory that may be applicable to underdeveloped countries. His theory of sociological dualism was formulated on the basis of his experiences in Indonesia, and was duly presented as a theory of 'eastern societies'.[7] The underlying assumption of Boeke's theory is that the traditional sector is more or less given, and that the penetration and spread of modern capitalist thinking and ideas will be ineffective there. 'We shall do well', writes Boeke, 'not to try to transplant the tender, delicate hot-house plants of western theory to tropical soil, where an early death awaits them'.[8]

Business and entrepreneurship had been in the hands of Dutch and Chinese for so long that many Dutch officials and economists were convinced that the Indonesians were not business-minded. Boeke writes that 'Capitalism can only be realized by capitalist-minded individuals.... There is no question of the eastern producer adapting himself to the western example technologically, economically, or socially'.[9]

Boeke defines dualism as the clashing of an imported social system with an indigenous traditional system of another style. Most frequently the imported social system is capitalism, but it may be socialism or communism or a mixture of them both.[10] Thus, dualism is a direct result of the introduction of capitalism into pre-capitalistic society. Social dualism is a lasting formation and is always the result of the penetration of the imported, foreign social system. As the two societies are diametrically opposed in character, 'neither of them becomes general and characteristic of the society as a whole'; therefore 'as a rule one policy for the whole country is not possible ... and what is more beneficial for one section of the society may be harmful for the other'.[11]

The main characteristic of the pre-capitalistic sector is the 'limited' needs, in sharp contrast with the 'unlimited' needs of the western society. The members of the former sector are supposed not to respond to economic incentives. Thus, writes Boeke,

> When the price of coconut is high, the chances are that less of the commodities will be offered for sale; when wages are raised the manager of the estates risks that less work will be done; if three acres are enough to supply the needs of a household a cultivator will not fix six; when rubber prices fall the owner of the grove may decide to tap more intensively, whereas high prices may mean that he leaves a larger or smaller proportion of tapable trees untapped.[12]

Because of the 'limited' needs, according to Boeke, eastern society (in contrast to the unlimited needs of a western society) is characterised by backward–sloping supply curves of effort and risk-taking, so that the supply of labour and that of the entrepreneurial efforts after a certain point diminish as the wage level and the level of expected profits, respectively rise. Boeke assumes an almost complete absence of profit seeking (with the exception of speculative profits). There is a total lack of that continuity in profit seeking which characterises a regular income. Hence there is no professional trading in the eastern society.[13]

In many respects, Boeke's thesis has not only proved to be incorrect, but incoherent and borders on mistrust and racial prejudice. A great deal of research evidence points out that the difference between the developed and underdeveloped countries are not as sharp as Boeke believed them to be. The main criticism of Boeke's thesis is found in Benjamin Higgins' work.[14] The notion of the 'inert peasant' bound by custom and tradition, unresponsive to production and consumption possibilities or the 'satisficing peasant' who will provide the effort needed to achieve a fixed income target has been criticised by many writers. The existence of the Boeke type of economic insulation of pure subsistence societies was obviously a very rare phenomenon (which was at best on its way out) in underdeveloped countries.

The idea of 'limited wants' was strongly rejected by Higgins.[15] While there may be an element of truth in saying that the people of the under-developed countries may have trouble in finding efficient ways of raising their standard of living by their own efforts or enterprise, Higgins argues that it is definitely not true for example in Indonesia that the people cannot envisage a standard of living higher than their own or that they could think of no satisfactory ways of spending increases in income.[16] In his criticism of the theories of dualism, Keith Griffin may be right in suspecting that the lack of empirical evidence to justify the argument that labour works less when paid more suggests that the Boeke thesis might be drawn from former colonial times when local people were forced to raise money only in order to pay taxes to the colonial regime. In such a situation, if the tax bundle could be raised by less effort there remained no need to work hard in raising more funds.[17] In the literature there is considerable evidence of allocative efficiency in input combination and output choices shown by peasants in underdeveloped countries.[18] We shall return to the criticism of Boeke in the following section.

Classical dualism

'Classical' dualism à la W. Arthur Lewis was introduced by the latter's path-breaking paper 'Economic Development with Unlimited Supplies of Labour' in 1954.[19] The Lewis model draws on the historical experience of Western industrialised countries and on the ideas of the classical economists to derive a general picture of the development process. The model is in the classical tradition in the sense that the classics had addressed themselves to the problem of growth in a largely agrarian economy where an 'unlimited' supply of labour was available at subsistence wages. Lewis shows how the classical assumption that labour is in perfectly elastic supply to the capitalist sector leads to conclusions different from those based on the neo-classical assumption that the supply of labour is less than perfectly elastic. The author believes that a model couched in the classical assumptions illuminates several problems of economic growth which modern economics cannot solve. Lewis divides the economy into one capitalist and one subsistence sector.[20] The capitalist sector is 'that part of the economy which uses reproducible capital and pays capitalists for the use thereof', or that sector of the economy in which labour is employed for wages for profit-making purposes.[21] The subsistence sector is that part of the economy outside the capitalistic sector. While the subsistence sector is often identified empirically with traditional agriculture sector, Lewis notes that surplus labour may also be found, e.g. in petty trade, the often over-manned domestic service and other service occupations. Because of this composite nature of Lewis's subsistence sector some writers have aptly argued that even today's informal sector of underdeveloped economies can be satisfactorily analysed under the Lewis assumption of a dual economy.[22]

Functionally, the model assumes the existence of 'unlimited' supplies of labour in some, though not all countries in the early stage of development process, so that the labour supply to the capitalist sector will exceed demand at a wage that can remain constant during a prolonged period of development with labour transfer from subsistence to the capitalist sector. The purpose is 'to provide a mechanism explaining the rapid growth of the proportion of domestic savings in the national income in the early stages of an economy whose growth is due to expansion of capitalist forms of production'.[23] In other words, the non-capitalist sector is postulated to be a temporary reservoir from which the capitalist sector draws labour. The key features in the process of capitalist accumulation are illustrated in Figure 6.1. On the horizontal axis we have the quantity of labour, while on the vertical axis there is the wage and the value of the marginal product of labour.

Given the fixed amount of capital at the initial stage, the demand for labour may be represented by the marginal productivity schedule for labour $N_1D'_1$ in Figure 6.1. With employment in the capitalist sector determined by ordinary profit maximising principles, labour will be applied to the point where the current wage equals the value of the marginal product of labour. When the latter is N_1D_1 and the wage is OW, WD_1 workers will be hired. The capitalist profit share becomes N_1D_1W, and Lewis assumes that this share will be reinvested. In this sense, the system is dynamic, since savings occur, and the stock of capital will increase over time.[24] As a result this

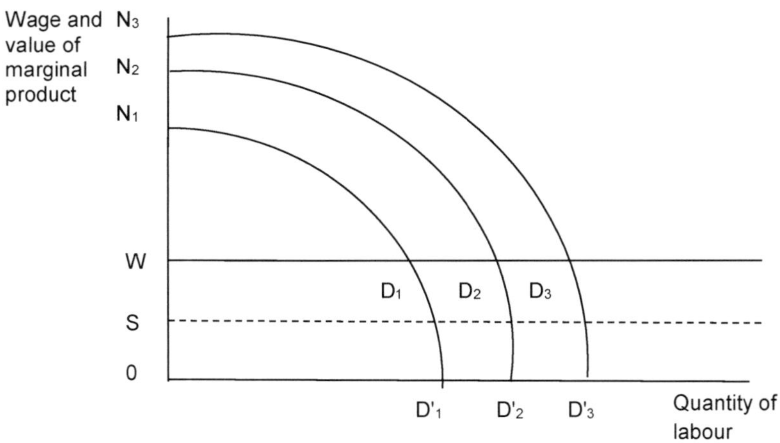

Figure 6.1 Key features in the process of capitalist accumulation.
Source: Ndlela, 1981:30.

raises the marginal productivity schedule to $N_2D'_2$ and employment increases, etc. As the development of the capitalist sector proceeds, the share of profits in the national income might vary over time, depending on the nature of technical change but given the constant real wage, it will almost certainly rise. Even if the profit share remains constant, the growth of the capitalist sector relative to the subsistence sector will lead to a growing share of profits in the national income.[25] Lewis assumes that capitalists save and invest a large part of their income than in the case with other forms of income. Thus, the savings ratio will increase and with it the capital accumulation on which economic development depends. (This process is illustrated by an outward shift of the marginal productivity schedule of labour as more capital per unit of labour is applied.) Capital accumulation is certainly ensured as the labour supply to the capitalist sector is infinitely elastic at a constant real wage OW. Labour supply is unlimited in the sense that if capitalists offered additional employment at the existing wage, there will be more candidates than they require.[26]

An important part of the Lewis model is the question of what determines the wage in the capitalist sector. Lewis says that the capitalist wage is determined by the alternative available to those entering capitalist employment, i.e. by the standards of living in the subsistence sector or what people earn there, as shown by the following quotation:

> in economics where the majority of the people are peasant farmers working on their own land, we have a more objective index, for the minimum at which labour can be had is now set by the average product of the farmers; men will not leave the family farm to seek employment if the wage is worth less than they would be able to consume if they remained home.[27]

In Figure 6.1, OS represents an income received by workers in the subsistence sector. The wage in the capitalist sector is OW, and must be somewhat above the average income in the non-capitalist sector. In practice the wage will have to be above the minimum subsistence wage by a margin which is necessary to induce labour transfer. It is suggested by Lewis that the margin may be 30 per cent or more, though the exact size of the gap is not important to his argument. The reasons for this higher wage include higher costs of living in the towns, the psychological cost of transferring from the much easier life style connected with traditional activities to the much tighter discipline of industry, and also perhaps higher conventional standards of life in the urban areas.

The wage gap view seems supported by the fact that employers in the modern sector of the underdeveloped countries rarely have any difficulty in recruiting labour force. But this does not demonstrate that the labour supply curve is horizontal, for it is quite possible that, for one reason or another, employers could pay neither more or less than the supply price of labour. In the former case, industrial wages may be forced upward by the minimum wage legislation, trade union pressure or other institutional forces. On the other hand, wages may also be forced down by institutional controls and discrimination. The supposed link between the level of rural incomes and urban wages has not followed Lewis predictions, but the gap has widened enormously for reasons not connected with the level of wages in the subsistence sector.[28] We shall return to this later on in the section below.

The Lewis model could also imply a general disguised unemployment in the subsistence sector (both the rural peasant sector and the urban informal sector). There may be zero marginal productivity of labour so that the labour transfer can take place without loss of output in the subsistence sector. Thus, if the marginal productivity rises as labour transfer takes place, the wage level ought to rise too.[29]

As already noted above the growth of the capitalist sector must accelerate as long as the share of profits in the national income is increasing. This phase comes to an end when labour surplus has been absorbed and wages begin to rise. There exist circumstances, however, when the wage level might increase and eat into the capitalist surplus when a labour surplus still exists. This may come about for the following reasons: (a) rising living standards in the subsistence sector might exercise an effect on the real wage; (b) where trade between the capitalist and subsistence sectors exist and the former buys the wage goods (such as food, fuel and clothing) from the latter, worsened terms of trade might cause even a constant real wage to take a larger share of the capitalist product; (c) the workers in the capitalist sector might by trade union action or by government minimum legislation manage to widen the gap between their wage and the subsistence sector standards. Any of these reasons may be sufficient cause to end the expansion of the capitalist sector even though there is still surplus labour available at the constant wage. Otherwise, the expansion ultimately leads to the exhaustion of the labour surplus, that is, it makes the supply curve for labour turn upwards.

Lewis could not give a satisfactory analysis of the conditions for the turning point. The model does not discuss the conditions of the expansion of development of the subsistence sector. There are statements in the Lewis texts describing the stagnant conditions of the earnings and productivity of the subsistence workers,[30] but the Lewis model treats the subsistence sector as a backlog in the development process of the modern capitalist sector and makes no effort to describe any development process of the peasant agricultural sector. Therefore, the model sheds little light on the subsistence sector, though it does perhaps recognise the plight of the latter.[31] In his reply to the criticism about why he said very little on the preponderant subsistence sector he claims to transform, Lewis says that all his

> model needs is the fact that supply exceeds demand at the current wage (thus) it was not necessary to say anything about productivity of the

> marginal units of labour in the reservoir, beyond noting that it must be less than the wage offered by capitalists.[32]

The task of analysing the conditions of the turning point in some more detail was left to Ranis and Fei.[33]

The Fei–Ranis model of economic growth is a dualism model which retains the Lewis's postulate of 'disguised unemployment' in the traditional agricultural sector. In addition, the Fei–Ranis model attempts to introduce technological change both in the agricultural and in the industrial sector. The authors recognise the presence of a dual economy comprising both the modern and the backward agricultural sector and take the economic situation of unemployment and underemployment of resources into account. Both sectors co-exist in the economy, wherein lies the core of the development problem. In their argument, development can be brought about only by a complete shift in the focal point of progress from the agricultural to the industrial economy, such that there is augmentation of industrial output. This is done by the transfer of labour from the agricultural to the industrial sector. At the same time, growth of the agricultural sector must not be negligible and its output should be sufficient to support the whole economy with food and raw materials. In many ways this is likened to the Harrod–Domar model, where saving and investment become the driving forces when it comes to economic development of underdeveloped countries.

Fei and Ranis also draw on the classic problem of population pressure on the land but unlike the classics they handle it in conjunction with the reallocation of the surplus labour from the agricultural to the industrial sector. In their model economic surpluses can be generated as profits in the industrial and the agricultural sectors; and 'the inter-sectoral channelization of the savings fund constitutes an essential ingredient of the dualistic framework of thinking'.[34]

In the long run, the problem of successful development requires that the rate of reallocation of the disguisedly unemployed members of the initial agricultural labour force be in excess of the population growth which is continuously augmenting the agricultural reserve army. But for the sake of simplicity the analysis is carried out under the assumption of a static population.

Fei and Ranis explain the turning point with the aid of the concepts of redundant labour, disguised unemployment and institutional wage.[35] In Figure 6.2 the vertical axis represents the total output of the agricultural sector measured downwards. On the horizontal axis we have the agricultural labour force which is measured from right to left. The XQZG curve describes the total physical productivity of labour (TPPL) of the agricultural sector of the dualistic economy. This curve is assumed to have a concave portion XQZ, which shows a gradual diminishing marginal productivity of agricultural labour force as we move from right to left, and a horizontal

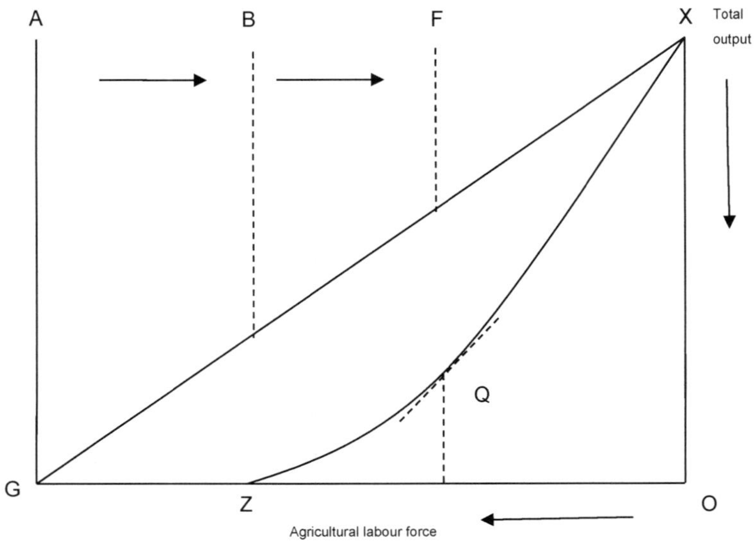

Figure 6.2 Labour-force behaviour in the agricultural sector.
Source: Ndlela, 1981:34.

portion of GZ where the marginal productivity of labour equals zero. Any agricultural labour force in excess of XB units is thus considered redundant in the sense that its withdrawal would not affect agricultural output. The non-redundancy portion equals XB/XA.

In Figure 6.3, the vertical axis measures the agricultural output per worker i.e. the average output. The horizontal axis measures the agricultural labour force from the right to the left. Let the DCAP curve represent the MPPL curve in the agricultural sector, with the negatively sloped portion DCA and the horizontal portion AP. If we mark off the CIW on the vertical axis as PS (corresponding to the slope of XG in Figure 6.2), we are able to distinguish three regions or phases in the labour reallocation process: phase one is the range PA for which labour is redundant, i.e. MPPL = 0; phase two is the range for which MPPL is less than the institutional wage (phase one and two together mark off disguised unemployment labour force PR); phase three (RO) is the range for which the MPPL is greater than the CIW.

The concept of constant institutional wage CIW is represented (as a first approximation) by the slope of the straight line XG. This is equal to the average product of agricultural labour. If Q on the total output curve represents the point at which the marginal physical productivity MPPL is equal to CIW, and since the dotted tangential line at Q is parallel to XG, we can define AF workers as the total disguised unemployed in this sector, i.e. all those workers whose wage income (CIW) is in excess of their contribution to

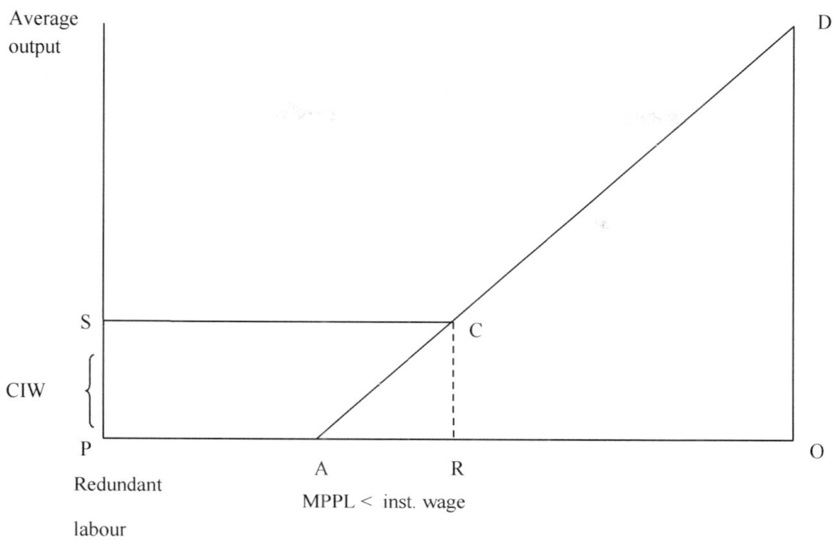

Figure 6.3 Absorption of disguisedly unemployed labour.
Source: Ndlela, 1983:36.

output (MPPL). The disguised unemployment include those with a zero marginal product – the redundant labour force – and those with a low but positive marginal product below the CIW. Fei and Ranis take the view that redundancy is thus seen to constitute a technological phenomenon, determined by the production function and the economy's endowment ratio. Disguised unemployment, on the other hand, constitutes an economic concept, depending on the wage level as well. In other words, the institutional wage is sustained by non-market forces as under competitive conditions the real wage could fall to zero to equate with marginal physical productivity.[36]

Fei and Ranis have assumed that the institutionally determined wage level PS continues to prevail as long as some disguised unemployed workers remain in agriculture, but a wage rate equal to the marginal productivity of labour begins to operate once all the disguisedly unemployed workers have been reallocated. At point C, the MPPL surpasses the institutional wage rate and the real wage rate curve begins to turn up following the MPPL curve along CD. In this phase, labour's marginal contribution is greater than the socially determined institutional wage level PS. As a result, it is to the advantage of the landlords to compete actively with industrial sector for labour rather than encourage its departure.

This is the turning point that comes with the final absorption of the disguisedly unemployed labour and when the agricultural sector is commercialised and the institutional wage is abandoned. The competitive market forces yield the commonly accepted equilibrium conditions. The agricultural real wage in terms of agricultural goods is defined by the curve SCD, the supply-price curve of agricultural labour.

The turning point may also be explained by a shortage of agricultural goods measured in the average agricultural surplus which may spark off deterioration in the terms of trade of the industrial sector and a rise in the industrial real wage measured in terms of industrial goods. This is in line with Lewis's 'worsening terms of trade'[37] for the industrial sector that occurs as a result of a shortage of agricultural commodities exchanged for industrial goods in the market. Because of the 'exhaustion of the labour surplus' (interpreted as a market phenomenon rather than as a physical shortage of manpower), an increase in the real wage ensues at the source of the supply. For the simplicity of their exposition Fei and Ranis assume equality of the real wage rates of industrial and agricultural sectors. Under this assumption there is tendency for the industrial supply curve of labour to turn up after point C. Lewis, on the other hand, says that because of urbanisation, transfer costs, etc, there may be need to maintain an industrial real wage (about 30 per cent) above the institutional wage in agriculture.

As the description of the 'classical' dualism theory shows, the Lewis model made contributions to the analysis of the functioning and expansion of the modern industrial sector in undeveloped countries. Economic development was to be generated in the modern capitalist sector where reinvestment of the surplus over wages is the main fuel of the modern sector expansion. The subsistence sector was treated as a backlog in the economic system, providing 'surplus' labour at more or less constant wage to the modern sector. Thus, while the Lewis model gives a substantial positive contribution regarding the possible behaviour of the modern sector, given certain assumptions, this contribution was, however, in a sense short-circuited by its neglect of the very sector that is at the centre of anxieties about the distributional consequences of dualism. The Ranis and Fei model attempted to close this gap by assuming for economic development to take place in the context of dualistic economy, the agricultural sector must produce a large enough surplus, so that together with profits simultaneously generated in the industrial sector, the expansion of the later can adequately be fuelled. By focusing more closely on the conditions of the expansion of the agricultural sector, Ranis and Fei were thus able to describe satisfactorily the conditions of the turning point. (Given our purposes, the discussion of the Fei and Ranis dualistic model is limited to their contribution regarding the conditions of the turning point in the economic development of a dualistic economy.)

The Lewis model is criticised on the grounds that it neglects agriculture. The Fei–Ranis model goes a step beyond and states that agriculture has a very major role to play in the expansion of the industrial sector. In fact, it says that the rate of growth of the industrial sector depends on the amount of total agricultural surplus and on the amount of profits that are earned in the industrial sector. In other words, the larger the amount of agricultural surplus put into productive investment and the larger the amount of industrial profits earned, the larger will be the rate of growth of the industrial economy. As the model focuses on the shifting of the focal point of progress from the agricultural to the industrial sector, Fei and Ranis believe that the ideal shifting takes place when the investment funds from agricultural surplus and industrial profits are sufficiently large so as to purchase industrial capital goods like plants and machinery.

The success of the industrial accumulation depends on the connectivity between these two sectors. In driving this point home, Fei and Ranis took the example of Japan's dualistic economy in the nineteenth century and said that connectivity between the two sectors of Japan was heightened due to the presence of a decentralised rural industry which was often linked to urban production. In this sense, in dualistic economies of underdeveloped countries economic progress is achieved through the work of a small number of entrepreneurs who have access to land and decision-making powers and use industrial capital and consumer goods for agricultural practices. Capital goods are needed for the creation of employment opportunities. Hence, the condition put by Fei and Ranis for a successful transformation is that the Rate of increase of capital stock and rate of employment opportunities > Rate of population growth. The point at which a transformation or transition occurs from an underdeveloped economy set-up to industrialising is the point where the economy becomes completely commercialised and there is the absence of disguised unemployment. Economic literature abounds with the argument that only if the rate at which labour is shifted from the agricultural to the industrial sector is greater than the rate of growth of population, at this point the economy will be able to lift itself up from the Malthusian population trap.[38]

The argument of indispensability of labour reallocation is pertinent. As an underdeveloped country goes through its development process, labour is reallocated from the agricultural to the industrial sector. The more the rate of reallocation, the faster is the growth of that economy. The economic rationale behind the idea of labour reallocation is that it paves the path for faster economic development. The essence of labour reallocation lies in Engel's Law, which states that the proportion of income being spent on food decreases with increase in the income-level of an individual, even if there is a rise in the actual expenditure on food. For example, in the case of Zimbabwe the agricultural sector provides employment for some 70 per cent of the population, and about 60 per cent of all raw materials for the industry. Employment in agriculture (as percentage of total employment) was reported at 67.23 per cent in 2014, according to the World Bank collection of development indicators, compiled from officially recognised sources. In a purely agriculture-industrial sector dichotomy, this leaves only 30 per cent of the population in the industrial sector. But in the case of Zimbabwe where as a result of persistent de-industrialisation and decline, the economy has increasingly informalised, the percentage of the population involved in the formal industrial sector has progressively declined over time. The share of Zimbabwe's informal employment in total employment increased from 80 per cent in 2004 to 84.2 per cent in 2011 and 94.5 per cent in 2014.[39] The 2014 Labour Force Survey reveals that as much as 98 per cent of the currently employed youth aged 15–24 years and 96 per cent of currently employed youth aged 15–34 years were in informal employment. In terms of enterprises, the FinScope survey of 2012 highlighted that 85 per cent of the 3.4 million Micro, Small and Medium Enterprises (MSMEs) were unregistered. Such levels of informalisation are profound considering that 5.7 million people were working in MSMEs in 2012, 2.8 million were business owners while 2.9 million were employees. This adds to the truism that it is the failure of the state that leads people to spontaneously enter informal sector activities in order to survive. Under these circumstances, instead of decreasing dualism of the economy has increased.

There is, therefore, urgent need for labour reallocation from both the agricultural sector and informal sector activities since consumers begin to want more of industrial goods than agricultural goods in relative terms. This is because the growth process observes a slow-paced increase in the consumer purchasing power, as dualistic economies follow the path of natural austerity, which is characterised by more demand and hence importance of capital good industries as compared to consumer good ones. However, investment in capital goods comes with a long gestation period, which drives the private entrepreneurs away. This suggests that in order to enable growth, the government must step in and play a major role, especially in the initial few stages of growth on the social and economic overheads by investing in infrastructure such as the construction of roads, railways, bridges, educational institutions, health care facilities and so on.

Technological dualism

A second important variant of economic dualism within conventional economic theory is known as technological dualism. This variant represented mainly by Richard Eckaus and Benjamin Higgins is illustrated as shown in Figure 6.4 below. Curve Y_1 in Figure 6.4 denotes an isoquant representing a certain level of output. Output Y_1 (as drawn) can only be produced with a unique combination of factors at point a. Curves Y_2, Y_3, and so on stand for higher levels of output with expansion taking place along the line OE. Output can only be increased by increasing the use capital and labour in the constant proportions given by this ray.[40] Eckaus and Benjamin postulated that western economic theory was applicable to underdeveloped countries provided that certain assumptions were properly adapted to the institutional framework of these countries.[41] This school of thought treated the old problem of disguised unemployment or redundancy as 'technological

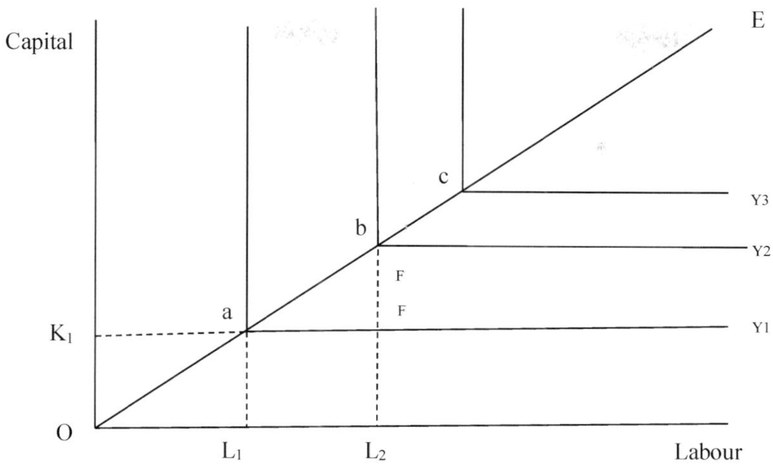

Figure 6.4 A production function with fixed technical coefficients.
Source: Ndlela, 1981:38.

unemployment', which they saw as a consequence of 'technological dualism', where different production functions were used in the capitalist and subsistence sectors, respectively.

Higgins argued that productive employment opportunities in underdeveloped countries may be limited not by lack of effective demand but because of limitations of resources and technology in the two sectors.[42] His analysis begins with the simplified and abstract case represented in Figure 6.4. In the first case, he considers that only one good is produced in the economy, national product, which requires two factors, capital and labour. Capital is measured on the vertical axis and the labour units on the horizontal axis.

Let us assume for the first case that only one process can be used to produce the national product and that the factors of production must be combined in fixed proportions. Points a, b, c, etc. in Figure 6.4 denote the fixed combinations of factors of capital and labour that that would be used to produce outputs Y_1, Y_2, Y_3, etc., irrespective of what the relative factor prices might be,[43] and the slope of the line joining these points is equal to the constant, capital–labour ratio.

Full utilisation of the factors of production become possible only when they are available in proportions equal to the fixed capital-labour ratio. If the actual factor endowment is given by a point which lies to the right of the line OE, unemployment inevitably occurs because in order to produce output Y_1, OK_1 units of capital and OL_1 units of labour will be used be used even though OL_2 units of labour exist. In the latter case, L_1L_2 (excess labour) will be unemployed, regardless of the relative factor prices of labour and capital. Only if capital could be increased by the amount denoted by FF' could the unemployed labour be absorbed in this sector.

Eckaus believes that technological unemployment may be aggravated if government policy or trade union activity keeps wages artificially high, if there is restriction of innovation to types favouring the capital intensive sector, and if the rate of population growth exceeds the rate of capital accumulation in the labour-intensive sector. The same results may occur if businessmen in underdeveloped countries believe that they face production functions with constant input coefficients, i.e. with no possibility of factor substitution.

Eckaus, however, introduces a second, relatively more labour-intensive process for production of the single 'good' (national product). He shows that structural unemployment of the relatively abundant factor will still occur, unless the proportions in which factors are available (factor endowment) fall within a certain limited range. But with labour–capital ratios as high as they are in the subsistence sector of underdeveloped countries, structural unemployment of labour would be extremely likely under technical conditions assumed. Finally, the effects of adding more processes are considered. Eckaus concludes that if more processes are available to the economy, there may be full employment as long as the proportions of the country's factor endowments 'fall on or within the limits set by the processes as can be seen in the following statement:

> Suppose that the respective demands of output are such that a large part of the available capital is drawn into the capital intensive and fixed coefficient sector. The amount of labour which can be absorbed in these sectors is dependent on the amount of the capital available. Since capital is a scarce factor, labour employment opportunities in this sector are limited by its availability rather than by demand for output. The relatively plentiful labour is then pushed into the variable.[44]

A similar view of technological dualism due to the interrelationship between factor endowments and techniques of production was put forward by Higgins, who analysed production function in an economy with two sectors, two factors of production, and two goods. Although such a model is simplified, it is argued that it approximates reality closely enough to provide significant results.[45] The two sectors are the industrial sector (plantations, mines, oil fields, refineries, etc.) and a rural sector engaged in the production of foodstuffs and other very small industries. As in the Eckaus model, the former sector is characterised by relatively fixed technical coefficients (fixed proportions in which factors of production must be combined), or is assumed by entrepreneurs to be so. The rural sector is characterised by variable technical coefficients where the products can be produced with a wide range of factor proportions. The two factors of production are labour, on one hand, and capital (including improved land) on the other. The two products are industrial raw materials for export and necessities for domestic consumption.

The production function in the industrial sector can be represented by Figure 6.5. Capital units are measured on the vertical axis, labour units on the horizontal axis. Points e_1, e_2, e_3, etc. represent fixed combinations of capital and labour that would be used to produce outputs z_1, z_2, z_3, etc. Solid line curves z_1, z_2, z_3, etc. denote a movement up the 'hill' of production to higher and higher levels of output. Line BS is the expansion path of this industrial sector. Output can be increased only by proportionately increasing the amounts used of both factors of production so as to maintain these proportions. Higgins states that some production processes such as petroleum refining, actually come very close to having fixed technical coefficients.[46] The industrial sector of underdeveloped countries is also characterised by a high capital intensity. Relatively large amounts of capital and relatively small amounts of labour are used. Thus to produce an output z_1 this sector will use $0c_1$ units of capital and 01_1 units of labour. If the actual labour units in this sector were at 01_2, $1_1 1_2$ labour units would remain unemployed or would have to seek employment in the rural sector irrespective of the relation of wage rates to capital costs. As more capital is made available through time, more labour will be employed and output will be increased.

However, employment increases relatively little as investment and output in the industrial sector expand along the expansion path (BS). As in the Eckaus model, technical coefficients are thought to be fixed by entrepreneurs. Perhaps the coefficients are actually less than entrepreneurs think, but

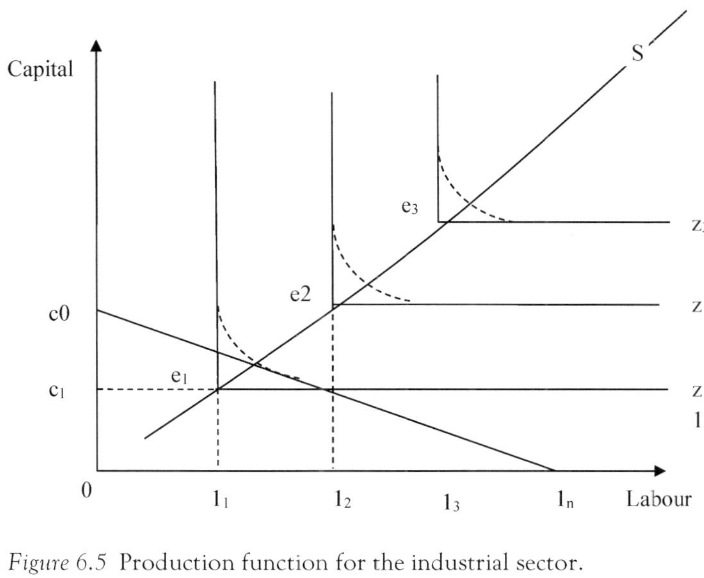

Figure 6.5 Production function for the industrial sector.

Source: Ndlela, 1981:41.

if the latter do not look for alternative techniques which are more suited to the factor endowment, the effect may be the same as if coefficients were technologically fixed. The dotted lines in Figure 6.5 denote a situation in which there is actually some flexibility in factor–proportions. But the diagram shows small changes in factor endowments (and in relative prices of factors of production) would not bring much change in technique even if entrepreneurs learned that production function resembled the dotted lines rather than the solid ones. Only if large differences in factor endowments (and prices), such as that indicated by line $c_0 1_n$ existed and were recognised by policy makers could a more labour-intensive technique be used.

Figure 6.6 represents a production function for the rural sector. The vertical and horizontal axes are the same as in Figure 6.5. The rural sector coefficients are variable i.e. a wide range of techniques and combinations of labour and capital will produce the same output. The proportions actually used will be in accordance with factor endowments (and the relative prices of labour and capital). In this case capital includes improved land.

Let us imagine that we begin with production at $z_1$both in the industrial and rural sectors. In time capital flows into the industrial sector, mostly from abroad. But in some countries and at some periods the rate of population growth considerably exceeded the rate at which capital accumulated in the industrial sector,[47] thereby giving rise to population explosion.

Because of the actual or accepted technical coefficients in the industrial sector, the rate at which employment opportunities occurred was slower than that at which population grew. Thus Higgins concludes 'Far from bringing a shift of population from rural to the industrial sector, industrialisation, after

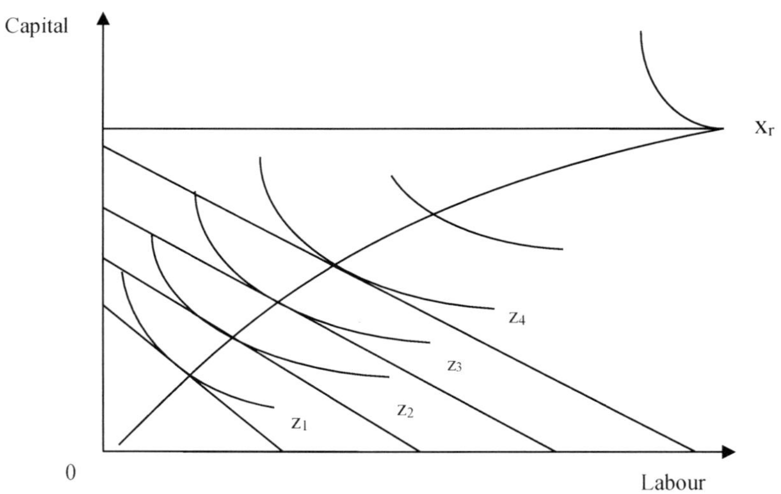

Figure 6.6 Production function for the rural sector.

Source: Ndlela, 1981:42.

its first impact, may even have brought a relative decline in the proportion of total employment in that sector'.[48] This meant that the increased population had to seek a livelihood in the variable-coefficient sector. At the beginning of the expansion process factors of production were more or less equal to one another. Thus, for a while the response to population growth was to bring additional land under cultivation, so that the ratio of labour to land could be kept relatively constant. Lack of other forms of capital in the rural sector made for relatively limited amounts of land to be effectively worked by family–farm units. The increase in output from z_1 to z_3 can be assumed to have taken place during the early period of expansion when an 'optimal' combination of labour and capital (mostly improved land) could be maintained. But as good land became scarce the ratio of labour to capital rose steadily and since technical coefficients were variable, techniques in that sector became increasingly labour intensive. The rising labour–land ratio culminated at point x_r, when all land was already 'cultivated by highly labour-intensive techniques and the marginal productivity of labour fell below zero even with the most labour intensive techniques available; with continuing population growth, disguised unemployment began to appear'.[49]

The tendency toward disguised unemployment in the rural sector is enhanced if technological progress in the economy is labour saving. Second, this tendency can be aggravated if wage rates are kept artificially high by trade union activities or government policy. If industrial wages are high in relation to labour productivity, labour-saving devices will be encouraged and these will in turn diminish the capacity of modern sector to absorb the increasing labour force. A high man–land ratio in the rural sector is virtually a sign of 'unlimited' labour supplies in the economy. Dualism also manifests itself in the often advanced techniques and high productivity trends in the industrial sector, while agriculture techniques are labour-intensive and simple and productivity is extremely low. The exponents of technological dualism propose that 'the only way to overcome redundancy of labour in the rural sector is to increase the supply of the scarce factor'.[50] Higgins concludes that industrialisation has to be stepped up simultaneously with a program of agricultural revolution, a conclusion reached independently in the Fei–Ranis model. Higgins says that the immediate scarce factor is land. The marginal productivity of capital can only be raised if the ratio of land to capital is increased a great deal.[51] But since the labour force in the rural areas will have to be displaced and attracted into the modern sector, large amounts of capital will be needed as well.

Neo-classical dualism

The neo-classical approach to the development of economic dualism was originated by Dale Jorgensen.[52] His version of economic dualism approach also assumes the existence of an advanced or modern sector alongside a traditional sector which may be (suggestively) denoted by agriculture.

Production in each of the sectors may be characterised by a function relating output to land, labour and capital, but as in classical dualistic theory, Jorgensen asserts that a special characteristic of the theory of economic dualism is the asymmetry of the production functions. Output in the traditional sector is a function of land and labour alone. There is no capital accumulation except where investment takes the form of land reclamation. Output in the modern sector is a function of labour and capital.

However, as we have seen, a fundamental assumption in classical dualism theory is that there is a point at which the marginal productivity of labour in the traditional agriculture is zero. Lewis, Ranis and Fei[53] used this assumption to explain the notion of disguised unemployment where if the labour force exceeds the quantity at which the marginal productivity of labour is zero, labour is available to the modern sector without loss of agricultural output. In Jorgensen's neo-classical theory of development of economic dualism this classical assumption is dropped, and instead it is assumed that the marginal productivity in the agricultural sector is always positive, and that labour is not redundant. The neo-classical theory is characterised by the assumption that production in agriculture and manufacturing industries shift over time so that a given bundle of factors will generate a higher level of output at a given time than at an earlier date.[54] The autonomous shifts in the production functions corresponding to technological changes are assumed to be neutral.[55]

However, Jorgensen's theory hardly succeeds in breaking away from the classical assumption of the existence of a labour surplus and consequent subsistence wages. His neo-classical dualism theory seems to be caught up in the Malthusian population thesis and low level equilibrium trap.[56] A standard explanation of the low level equilibrium trap focuses upon the rate of the increase of population up to a certain point as per capita income rises in relation to a given rate of technological progress. Given some rate of technical progress and population responsiveness to income level, there is a level of income per capita at which it is necessary for the economy to pass for the growth of output to exceed the rate of population increase. The analysis also borrows from Malthus' 'progressive state' in which production per capita is somehow raised above bare subsistence,[57] and where if agriculture output per head exceeds that level above which there is surplus for sale, withdrawal of part of the agricultural labour force to the production of manufactured goods is possible without a reduction in the rate of growth of the population. Jorgenson accepts the Malthusian population thesis rather explicitly: 'The net rate of reproduction in the minimum of the physiological maximum rate and gross reproduction rate which corresponds to the output of food per capita for the total population less the force of mortality'.[58] The Jorgensen theory will only be discussed briefly because, as will be seen, it is not quite relevant to our case.

Criticism of the conventional dualism theory

As the preceding discussion shows, the dual economy models have a wide range of specifications since different writers have made use of different assumptions. Thus, any criticism of the theory cannot be of much benefit if levelled against the dual economic theory as a whole. Such as, e.g. the handling of theories of dualism by Keith Griffin, in which the dualistic models of growth were lumped together and criticised.[59] For our purpose we shall look into these theories individually, paying more attention to the classical theory since it forms the central and most surviving part of dualism theory in economic development.

The earlier model of sociological dualism originated by Boeke has been criticised extensively in the literature. The most comprehensive criticism of Boeke's social dualism was advanced by Higgins,[60] who strongly refuted Boeke's main idea that economic development of any kind is hampered by limited wants. Higgins argues that while there may be an element of truth in saying that the people of underdeveloped countries may not have efficient ways of raising their standards of living by their own efforts or enterprise, it is definitely not true that people cannot envisage a standard of living higher than their own or that they could think of no satisfactory ways of spending increases in income.[61] The notion of the 'satisficing peasant' who does not respond to economic incentives so that he is characterised by backward sloping supply curve of effort and risk taking has been conclusively refuted by empirical evidence reflected in the literature.[62]

Boeke's analysis may also lend itself to defeatism. He concluded, e.g. that the process of social disintegration in dual societies cannot be reversed because it is not possible to transform the operating forces into opposite of what they are. Boeke suggested that dualism has to be accepted as an irretrievable fact,[63] as he also suggested that any industrialisation or agricultural improvement must be 'a slow process' and that it must be adapted to a dualistic framework. It is thus clear that the obvious policy conclusion from such a suggestion is the perpetuation of dualism. Boeke's insistence on 'slow evolution' and 'village restoration' is not only defeatist but also dangerous because it is precisely 'slow' evolution that cannot succeed in the face of all obstacles.[64] In contrast to Boeke's conclusion that the eastern society cannot be changed by western society theory, Higgins argues that dualism is not essentially social, but economic and technical, and that the economic problems of dualism can be solved by economic and technical assistance of the kind the West can provide.[65] It is said that sufficient and large amounts of technical and capital assistance in combination with technological progress of a non-labour-saving type can provide a solution to the problem of underdevelopment, and that there is a good chance that social and cultural obstacles may disappear without necessarily being attacked directly. This result will be attained only if large amounts of assistance are provided which can turn the disguised unemployed labour into an asset.

However, given the resource endowment pattern in the underdeveloped countries and the policies often pursued, there is greater likelihood that the flow of capital would favour the relatively capital-intensive modern sector. Therefore, dualism could be enhanced if capital inflows cannot absorb all labour force in the modern sector such that some of it is forced to remain in the subsistence sector with some permeating into the sprawling informal sector where there are variable technical coefficients. However, the Eckaus–Higgins models could not affect the disguised unemployed labour that is largely located in the subsistence sector. The massive capital amounts envisaged in Higgins' model for deployment in the agricultural sector, have not been forthcoming at least for most underdeveloped countries.

The remaining part of the criticism will be devoted to the Lewis model of classical dualism, and, to a lesser extent, also to the neo-classical model. Though relatively little space will be devoted to the Fei–Ranis model, their focus on the conditions of the turning point deserves comments from this writer. Our main interest lies in discussing the conditions at which transformation or transition from an underdeveloped economy set-up to industrialising occurs and the point where the economy becomes commercialised and there is the absence of disguised unemployment.

Since the publication of Lewis's celebrated paper in 1954, the economies of many underdeveloped countries have been transformed more or less along the following lines: first, the distribution of income has tended to become more unequal with the share of wages in the national income falling, while the combined share of profits and rents has risen.[66] Given the level of inequitable distribution in ownership of productive assets, this pattern of the distribution of income has led to increased inequality in the household distribution of income. Second, the share of national income devoted to savings has gone up, and with it the rate of capital formation.[67] Third, in the majority of undeveloped countries there has been a sharp acceleration in the rate of growth of output. Fourth, there has been little improvement in the standard of living of the people remaining in what Lewis called subsistence sector of the economy.

As Keith Griffin and Jeffrey James stated, all four of these tendencies can be understood, at least in part, in terms of the Lewis model.[68] Other contributors to *The Manchester School* journal of September 1979, commemorating the 25th anniversary of the publication of the original Lewis paper, were also in agreement that the Lewis model has retained its place in the literature in spite of massive criticism. Most of the criticism has been a mixture of policy prescriptions with historical analysis of the type which is wide-spread in development economics has been succinctly summarised by P.F. Leeson as follows:

> progress in the particular subject has not been such that the Lewis model has ever dropped out of discussion, nor has it quite been elevated to the status of respected, but superseded, founding contribution

> though it sometimes seems to have suffered the fate of such contributions in being read only in secondary and not always accurate accounts.[69]

As seen above, on the general level, the optimistic outlook of the Lewis model assumed that the constancy of wages will lead to high and possibly rising rates of the profits in the national income as capitalists' savings are reinvested and further capital accumulation takes place. There has been a sharp rise in the rate of growth of output in some underdeveloped countries, but the distribution of income has tended to be more unequal with the share of wages in the national income falling. This may be interpreted as exactly what the Lewis model predicts, since the model does not necessarily involve an equalisation of the existing distribution of income as the rising capitalist incomes can be explained by a declining share going to the landowning class.[70] Thus, there has been little improvement in the standard of living of the people in the subsistence sector of the economy. Lewis has argued that his model is not normative: it describes what has happened. However, this negative distributional consequence for the subsistence sector remains the bone of contention in the model. Most of the critics of the dualism theory attack the state of mind present in most of this theory, particularly the encouragement of large-scale enterprise and the neglect and lack of adequate goals for the small family enterprise in the subsistence sector. The critics are also at variance with interpretations which take the dualistic structure of the economy as given, and 'conveniently ignore the forces which stood to gain from dualism – the metropolitan enterprise and a privileged minority ... the exploitative characteristics of dualism are quite insufficiently stressed in the literature'.[71]

The policy implication of the model appears to be that industrialisation could be accomplished without the need to pump extra resources to the agricultural sector so that rising inequalities are inevitable in the process. On the contrary, Lewis's main criticism is that, it is urgent that priority should be given to agriculture and small-scale enterprise, thus leading to greater equality and more speedy eradication of poverty. The criticism seems vindicated by the evidence from overwhelmingly stagnant and economically irrational traditional sector indicating that there exist great possibilities for increasing rural output if farmers are given cheap inputs, better prices for output, and appropriate institutional reforms. However, it ought to be mentioned in this context that Lewis himself noticed the unfavourable distributional consequences of the forces that stood to benefit from dualism, but his model all the same neglects the subsistence sector, relatively speaking and focuses mainly on the behaviour of the modern sector.

Lewis made several qualifications and challenged his critics to go back and study his model with greater care,[72] but despite this the persuasive force of the model itself, as far as policy is concerned, the predictions are along the lines asserted by the critics.[73] However, Lewis was fully aware of the need to improve the lot of the peasant farmer and 'has written extensively about the need for this, and the fact that industrial revolutions have often depended on a simultaneous or prior agrarian revolution'.[74]

In addition to the criticism of the policy implications of the model, there is some criticism as to the functioning of the model. This criticism focuses on the assumption of zero marginal productivity of labour so that the labour transfer can take place without loss of output in the subsistence sector. Lewis has in mind that the marginal product per man could be zero, while the marginal product per man-hour is positive.[75] Thus, if the marginal productivity of labour rose as labour transfers took place, then the wage level ought to rise too. But since according to Lewis population growth in the traditional sector helps to negate the rise in incomes; and the link between the subsistence income and capitalist sector wage is flexible, a small wage rise in the subsistence sector need not automatically cause an upward movement in the latter.[76]

The link between the industrial wage and the subsistence sector income has always been a major difficulty in the Lewis model. Thus, in his most recent article *The Dual Economy Revisited*, Lewis agrees that his model shed little light on the question of great size of wage gap in some countries in the face of large numbers of job seekers – one of the pull factors attracting migrant labour.

> The flow to towns – growing at about 5 to 10 per cent per annum – is everywhere larger than it needs to be because development is (wrongly) concentrated in the towns at the expense of the countryside, and because the wage differentials are too wide.[77]

In spite of this criticism, Lewis's contribution was that the conventional wage was not based directly on subsistence needs but rather on the alternative standard of living available in the subsistence sector. Admittedly, the modern sector wage is also determined by productivity, by minimum wage laws or by trade union action.

The Lewis model can also be criticised from the standpoint that it portrays a smooth transfer of labour from disguised unemployment in the rural sector to full employment in the modern sector. Admittedly, the original Lewis model did not anticipate a growing un- and underemployment in the modern sector to the extent of the contemporary expansion of the informal sector in urban areas of the underdeveloped countries. To those who argue that the model is capable of analysing the Lewis composite subsistence sector (both the traditional agriculture, and the informal sector), the answer is that in the original optimistic economic dualism model there was hardly any mention of a potential piling up of the informal sector. Undoubtedly the experience of the reservoir of cheap labour filling instead of emptying as a major experience of the present situation was not anticipated in the model.

Finally, let us briefly turn to the criticism of the neo-classical dual model associated with Dale Jorgenson. As seen in the description of the model, the latter seems to rely on unrealistic and rather restrictive assumptions. First, Jorgenson retained the classical assumption of the asymmetry in the production functions, i.e. output of the traditional sector is a function of land and labour alone (there in no capital),[78] and that in the manufacturing sector 'output is a function of capital and labour alone'.[79] Therefore, the only link between the two sectors is a flow of unemployed labour from peasant agriculture to industry, since the model permits no flows of capital or savings between the sectors. Jorgenson also assumes that 'savings is equal to total profits in the industrial sector'.[80]

In the neo-classical model the marginal productivity of labour in agriculture is always positive, so that labour is never available to the industrial sector at a constant real wage. In this sense, the real wage rises continuously with development. Further, Jorgenson assumes that the entire increase in the agricultural surplus is used for consumption by farm labour, which is highly unrealistic given the land-ownership and tenure arrangements in most of the underdeveloped economies.

Third, the acceptance of the Malthusian population theory may be subject to doubtful, at least according to much of modern demographic evidence. Jorgenson assumes a constant death rate and a birth rate that rises with *per capita* income. In actual experience, we find that the rate behaves unpredictably and that it is the decline in the death rate – related to preventive and public health facilities (and not to per capita income) – which causes the rise in population growth. Thus, though Jorgenson claims to be neo-classical, his acceptance of the consumption adjustment and Malthusian population thesis in this aspect renders his framework a rather distinctly classical cast.

Fourth, Jorgenson assumes that technological change in agriculture takes place at a constant rate and that all changes are neutral. For instance, that 'so long as there is disguised unemployment population expands at the same rate as the growth of agriculture',[81] is also not realistic. As Fei and Ranis have remarked, 'It rules out an important and perhaps more realistic alternative to the consumption – population adjustment mechanism as a method of disposing of the economy's agricultural slack'.[82]

The shortcomings of the theory of dualism seem to be corrected somewhat in the more recent literature. In the latter, there is a tendency to shift from mainly resources framework[83] to be more concerned about the mutual interaction between the economy's human agents and the institutional framework within which these agents organise themselves.[84]

In the late 1970s the literature observed that there was an increasing evidence, in most parts of Sub-Saharan Africa where the proportion of population living in poverty, at least in the rural areas, may have risen and their standard of living fallen.[85] This trend was confirmed in the recent Economic Commission for Africa (ECA) papers that, unlike the other developing regions of the world where poverty has been on the decline, the proportion of people living below the poverty line in Africa increased from 44.1 per cent in 1990 to 45.7 per cent in 2003.

Poverty in Africa is still spatial, and highly prevalent in rural areas. The non-inclusive nature of economic growth and the more specific sectoral challenges – of poor rural infrastructure, failure to modernise rural livelihoods, little jobs diversification (for rural youth especially), limited access to education and pervasive child labour – are key drivers of rural poverty.[86]

These hard facts must certainly tilt the focus of development economics from its earlier preoccupation with lagging development indices, and the so-called development processes in low income countries to the core issue of the continued and deepening structural disintegration of these economies. Consequently, an increasing number of Africans have suffered from insufficient income and capacity to access food and other basic amenities such as potable water, minimum health care and education. Indeed, estimates from FAO show that although the proportion of total population suffering from hunger fell slightly from 35 per cent in 1990 to 32 per cent in 2003, some 215 million people in Africa are undernourished, a number up by 26 per cent from 171 million in 1990–1992.[87]

In Chapter 7 we revisit the theory of dualism and propose to look into the policies and institutions that create, sustain and benefit from maintenance of a dual economic structure. It was through such policies and institutions that dualistic structures appear to defy the original logic that this was merely an era of the cradle of western capitalist penetration into the undeveloped and pre-capitalist economies. A framework for the initial conditions for the creation of the dualism will be laid for ensuing discussion in the remaining chapters.

Notes

1 Lewis, 1954, 1958.
2 Lewis, ibid.; Ranis and Fei, 1961; Fei and Ranis, 1964.
3 Griffin, 1972, 1974, 1976.
4 Georgescu-Roegen, 1971:336.
5 Lewis, 1954.
6 Brookfield, 1975:55–56 and Chayanov, 1966.
7 Boekes' main work in Boeke, 1953, but this can be compared with Boeke, 1942, 1946 and 1954.
8 Boeke, 1953:143.
9 Ibid.
10 Ibid.:1953:4.
11 Ibid.
12 Ibid.:40.
13 Ibid.:41.
14 Higgins, 1956, 1968. See also Griffin, 1969 and van Marle, 1961.
15 Higgins, 1956:104.
16 It is demonstrated that the marginal propensity to consume and the marginal propensity to import were actually high in Indonesia. This demonstrable

limitlessness of wants drove the authorities to cut down on imports of semi-luxuries by rigorous import and exchange controls, ibid.

17 Griffin, 1969:22.
18 Schultz, 1974; Wharton, 1969; Hayami and Ruttan, 1971; Reynolds, 1975:5–7; Helleiner, 1975.
19 Lewis, 1954.
20 Lewis, 1954, 1958, 1972. However, in the recent article commemorating the 25th anniversary of the publication of his 1954 pioneer paper, Lewis, 1979, while retaining all the major assumptions adopted earlier has renamed his two sectors 'modern' and 'traditional'.
21 Lewis, 1954:146, 1958:8.
22 Godfrey, 1979; Leeson, 1979:204.
23 Lewis, 1972:75.
24 Lewis, 1958:3.
25 Ibid.:18. See also Leeson, 1979.
26 Lewis, 1972:77.
27 Lewis, 1954:148–149.
28 Leeson, 1979:204.
29 Ibid.:198.
30 See Lewis, 1954:149; 1958:22–23.
31 Lewis, 1953:23; see also Lewis 1972:7.
32 Lewis, 1972:7.
33 Ranis and Fei, 1961; Fei and Ranis, 1964, 1966.
34 Fei and Ranis, 1966:6–7.
35 Fei and Ranis, 1964:201–205; ibid.:203.
36 See Ranis and Fei, 1961:537.
37 Lewis, 1958:19–26.
38 See, Galor, 2005; Tisdell, 2015.
39 See ILO 2011, 2014, the Labour Force Surveys of 2011 and 2014 respectively.
40 Cf. of Eckaus, 1955 and Higgins, 1956.
41 Ibid.
42 Higgins, 1956, 1959.
43 Eckaus, 1955:540.
44 Eckaus, 1955:559–560.
45 Higgins, 1959:326.
46 Ibid.:327.
47 Ibid.:328.
48 Ibid.:328–329.
49 Ibid.:329.
50 Ibid.:343.
51 Ibid. The production function is highly discontinuous in this context, so that it is not enough to raise the acreage from two to three acres, instead the size must be raised to 20 or 200 acres so that mechanisation becomes possible.
52 Jorgenson, 1961, 1967.
53 Lewis, 1954:141; Ranis and Fei, 1961:30.
54 Jorgenson, 1961:312.
55 Under a 'neutral' technological change the marginal rate of substitution between factors for a given output will not be affected by change. Jorgenson, 1961:312.
56 Nelson, 1956.
57 For details on the Malthusian population theory and the 'progressive state' see Baumol, 1951:13.
58 Jorgenson, 1961:320.
59 Griffin, 1969:19–31.
60 Higgins, 1956.

61 Ibid.:104.
62 Hayami and Ruttan, 1971; Helleiner, 1975; Reynolds, 1975:5–7; Lipton, 1968 for a different notion of the 'satisficing' peasant.
63 Boeke, 1954:289.
64 Ibid.:293.
65 Higgins, 1956:114.
66 Griffin and James, 1979:248.
67 Ibid.
68 Griffin and James, 1979:248.
69 Leeson, 1979:196.
70 Ibid.:200.
71 Brookfield, 1975:69.
72 Lewis, 1972.
73 Leeson, 1979:200.
74 Ibid.
75 Lewis, 1972:79–82.
76 Leeson, 1979:200.
77 Lewis, 1979:220–221.
78 Jorgenson, 1967:291.
79 Ibid.:292.
80 Ibid.
81 Jorgenson, 1967:293.
82 Fei and Ranis, 1966:14–22.
83 The emphasis on the factor disproportionalities and technological rigidities is essentially a resource allocation framework approach. Thus, it is said that technological dualism can be broken by an 'infusion' of large amounts of capital investment. Higgins, 1956:113–115.
84 Myint, 1954, 1973; Lipton, 1977; and Griffin, 1976.
85 Griffin, 1978; ILO, 1977; Griffin and James, 1979.
86 FAO *et al.*, 2010 quoted in ECA, 2013.
87 Ibid.

References

Baumol, William J. 1951. *Economic Dynamics: An Introduction*. New York: Institute of Pacific Relations.

Boeke, J.H. 1942. *The Structure of the Netherlands Indian Economy*. New York: Institute of Pacific Relations.

Boeke, J.H. 1946. *The Evolution of the Netherlands Indies Economy*. New York: Institute of Pacific Relations.

Boeke, J.H. 1953. *Economics and Economic Policy of Dual Societies*. New York: Institute of Pacific Relations.

Boeke, J.H. 1954. *Three Forms of Disintegration in the Dual Societies*. Indonesia: Institute of Pacific Relations.

Brookfield, Harrold. (ed.) 1975. *Interdependent Development: Perspectives on Development*. London: Oxford University Press.

Chayanov, Alexander V. 1966. 'The Theory of Peasant Economy', in Daniel Thorner, R.E.F Smith and Basile Kerblay (eds), *Homewood*. Homewood, IL: Richard D. Irwin, Inc.

Eckaus, Richard S. 1955. 'The Factor Proportions Problem in Underdeveloped Areas', *American Economic Review*, Vol. 45:559–560.

ECA. 2013. *Making the Most of Africa's Commodities: Industrializing for Growth, Jobs and Economic Transformation*. Economic Report on Africa, Economic Commission for Africa, Addis Ababa, Ethiopia.

Fei, J.C.H. and Ranis, Gustav. 1964. *Development of the Labor Surplus Economy: Theory and Policy*. New Haven, CT: The Economic Growth Center, Yale University.

Fei, J.C.H. and Ranis, Gustav. 1966. *Agrarianism, Dualism and Economic Development*, Center Discussion Paper, No. 2, Yale University.

Galor, O. 2005. *From Stagnation to Growth: Unified Growth Theory*. Amsterdam: Elsevier B.V., Brown University and Hebrew University.

Georgescu-Roegen, Nicholas. 1971. *The Entropy Law and the Economic Process*. Cambridge, MA: Harvard University Press.

Godfrey, Martin. 1979. 'Rural Urban Migration in a "Lewis–Model" Context' *Manchester School*, Vol. 47:230–231.

Griffin, K. 1969. *Underdevelopment in Spanish America*. London: George Allen and Unwin Ltd.

Griffin, K. 1972. *The Green Revolution: An Economic Analysis*. Geneva: United Nations Institute for Social Development.

Griffin, K. 1974. *The Political Economy of Agrarian Change: An Essay on the Green Revolution*. Cambridge, MA: Harvard University Press.

Griffin, K. 1976. *Land Concentration and Rural Poverty*. London: Macmillan.

Griffin, K. 1978. *International Inequality and National Poverty*. London: Macmillan.

Griffin, Keith and James, Jeffrey. 1979. 'Problems of Transition to Egalitarian Development', *Manchester School*, Vol. 47:248.

Hayami, Y. and Ruttan, V.W. 1971. *Agricultural Development: An International Perspective*. Baltimore, MD: Johns Hopkins Press.

Helleiner, Gerald, K.1975. 'Smallholder Decision Making: Tropical African Evidence', in Lloyd G. Reynolds (ed.), *Agriculture in Development Theory*. New Haven and London: Yale University Press.

Higgins, B. 1956. 'The Dualistic Theory of Underdeveloped Areas', *Economic Development and Cultural Change*, Vol. 4:104.

Higgins, B. 1959. *Economic Development: Principles, Problems and Policies*. London Amazon.

Higgins, B. 1968. *Economic Development*. Revised Edition. New York: W.W. Norton.

International Labour Office (ILO). 1977:2. *Employment Growth and Basic Needs: A One World Problem*: Tripartite World Conference on Employment Income Distribution and Social Progress and ILO: Meeting Basic Needs – Strategies for Eradicating Mass Poverty and Unemployment. Geneva.

International Labour Office (ILO). 2011. *Zimbabwe Labour Force Surveys*. Harare. Zimbabwe: Zimstat.

Jorgenson, Dale W. 1961. 'The Development of Dual Economy', *Economic Journal*, Vol. 71:312.

Jorgenson, Dale. 1966. 'Testing Alternative Theories of the Economic Development of A Dual Economy', in I. Adelman and E. Thorbecke (eds), *The Theory and Design of Economic Development*. Baltimore: Johns Hopkins Press.

Jorgenson, Dale W. 1967. 'Surplus Agricultural Labour and the Development of a Dual Economy', *Oxford Economic Papers*, Vol. 19:288–312.

Leeson, P.F. 1979. 'The Lewis Model and Development Theory', *Manchester School*. Vol. 47:196–210.

Lewis, W. Arthur. 1953. *Report on industrialisation and the Gold Coast*. Accra: Government Printing Department.

Lewis, W. Arthur. 1954. 'Economic Development with Unlimited Supplies of Labour', *Manchester School*, Vol. 22:139–191.

Lewis, W. Arthur. 1958. 'Unlimited Labour Supplies: Further Notes', *Manchester School*, Vol. 26:1–32.

Lewis, W. Arthur. 1972. 'Reflections on Unlimited Labour', in *Essays in Honour of Raul Prebish* (ed.). Luis Di Marco, New York and London: Luisa Di Marco.

Lewis, W. Arthur. 1979. 'The Dual Economy Revisited', *Manchester School*, Vol. 47:220–221.

Lipton, M. 1968. 'The Theory of the Optimising Peasant', *The Journal of Development Studies*, Vol. 4, No. 2:327–351.

Lipton, M. 1977. *Why Poor People Stay Poor: Urban Bias in World Development*. London and Canberra: Temple Smith and Australian National University Press.

Myint, Hla. 1971. 'Dualism and Internal Integration of Underdeveloped Economies', *Banca Nazionale del Lavora. Quarterly Review*, Vol. 23, 1970:15–17.

Myint, Hla. 1973. *The Economics of Developing Countries*. 4th (revised) edition, London: Hutchinson.

Ndlela, D.B. 1981. 'Dualism in the Rhodesian Colonial Economy', *Lund Economic Studies*, Department of Economics, University of Lund.

Nelson, Richard R. 1956. 'A Theory of the Low – Level Equilibrium Trap in Underdeveloped Economies', *American Economic Review*, Vol. 46:894–908.

Ranis, G. and Fei, J.C.H. 1961. 'A Theory of Economic Development', *The American Economic Review*, Vol. 51: 533–565.

Reynolds, Lloyd G. 1975. (ed.) *Agriculture in Development Theory*. New Haven and London: Yale University Press.

Schultz, Theodore W. 1974. *Transforming Traditional Agriculture*. Chicago, IL: University of Chicago Press.

Tisdell, Clem. 2015. *Handbook of Economic Growth*. Amsterdam: Elsevier, University of Queensland.

Van Marle, A. 1961. *Indonesian Economics: The Concept of Dualism in Theory and Policy*. The Hague: W. van Hoeve.

Wharton, C.R. 1969. (ed.). *Subsistence Agriculture and Economic Development*. Chicago, IL: Aldine Pub. Co.

7 Dualism theory revisited

Dualism theory reformulated

The present chapter looks at the later empirical development of the institutions and classes that has made the post-colonial regimes fail to shift their countries' focal point of progress from the rural agricultural activities to industrial transformation. The issue is why has this gridlock failed to take-off in the sense of Fei and Ranis who believed 'that the ideal shifting takes place when the investment funds from agricultural surplus and industrial profits are sufficiently large so as to purchase industrial capital goods like plants and machinery'.[1] The underdeveloped country's post independent state has also failed to provide the legal and political environment that supports the majority of the population's assets to transform into the formal property system, thus becoming effective and dynamic capital.

The present chapter goes further than the review and criticism of the classical and neo-classical dualism models, to look at the latest empirical development of the institutions and classes that stand to sustain and benefit from this lopsided nature and mode of development largely caused by and associated with economic dualism. The discussion of the dualism theories in the preceding chapters highlights that the main feature of these theories – viewed from the classical approach formulated by Lewis – was the availability of labour at a constant real wage to the dynamic capitalist sector and the consequent generation of surplus in the form of profits in the latter sector.

With the assumption that profits are re-invested in the capitalist sector, Lewis drew a picture of a steady process of capitalistic expansion, constrained finally by a rise in wages or prices of wage goods so that the terms of trade turned against the capitalist sector. This stylised view of growth provided the framework of those 'dual economy' models that largely focus on the distribution of income inside the modern sector and on the rate of growth of that sector, treating the traditional sector more or less as a backlog in the system.

However, in the real experience of the underdeveloped countries, while output growth and capital formation have increased according to predictions of the dual model, the distributional consequences, especially in the traditional sector, have been a source of much disillusionment. In reply to this disillusionment expressed by many writers, Lewis advises us that

> there is no reason to expect the traditional sector to always benefit from the expansion of the modern. There are forces working for the benefit and forces working for the loss; the net result will vary from case to case.[2]

The Lewis argument not only defends a theory that fails to incorporate the development of the traditional sector, it is also inappropriate if we assume that it is unrealistic to expect a 'trickle down' from modern to traditional sector but that a simultaneous development of both sectors should take place in the economy. In this case the effects of one sector on the other will be of mutual benefit. As noted above, Lewis is himself aware of the fact that industrial revolutions have often depended on a simultaneous or prior agrarian revolution.[3]

In this section we represent the discussion of dualism along the lines indicated by the recent contributions to the theory of dualism by writers such as Myint, Griffin and Lipton.[4] The discussion will be focused on the general level of the theory and its relevance to the actual experience of underdeveloped countries. The aim is to highlight the contribution of this theory in general as well as some of its weaknesses. An attempt will be made to distinguish between the discussions of dualism in general, i.e. along lines reflected in the literature, and the case of dualism represented by the Zimbabwean colonial and post-colonial experience. My aim is to reformulate the approach of dualism theory so that the emphasis is focused on the historical causes and initial conditions of dualism in the economic system. It is hoped that this approach will help policy makers, researchers and/or any other social scientist in reformulating development priorities with a view to bring the traditional agricultural sector into the rhythm of growth and development taking place in the modern sector.

As will be shown below, it is inconceivable to think of the post 1990s and twenty-first-century development without putting at the centre, emphasis to address poverty challenges as well as sustain poverty reduction efforts. This calls for development policies to address market failures that contribute to the continued poverty trap, environmental pollution, land degradation and climate change challenges. The chapter advocates and calls for structural transformation of the hitherto 'peasant-cum informal sector' of the African economy into a rapid, sustained and inclusive growth and its integration with the large-scale formal enterprise of the modern sector of the economy.

One of the usual formulations of economic dualism has been to depart from its existence during the colonial era. Under the latter, dualistic structure was caused by the low wage policies, and the initial forms of exploitation which later became institutionalised. Thus, Myint analyses two variants in which dualism shows up: the gap in interest rates between the often small-scale production units of the traditional sector and the large-scale enterprise of the modern sector, and discrimination in the provision of infrastructure by government agencies.[5]

Under the typical colonial regime, the extent of unequal access to economic resources was frequently described in terms of the gap in the interest rates between the modern and traditional sectors. A form of financial dualism manifested itself by a markedly higher level of interest rates and a lower level of wages in the traditional sector when contrasted with the modern sector. This pattern of resources allocation mechanism is not only responsible for the large part of differences in factor proportions used in the two sectors, but may also provide reasonable explanation of the differences in factor proportions used in the two sectors, without the need to introduce special assumptions of sociological and technological rigidities.

Traditionally, financial dualism was often explained by the following two main factors: first, because of the higher risks and costs in lending money on a retail basis to small borrowers in the traditional sector than of lending to well organised larger economic units in the modern sector, one would expect the rate of interest facing the 'unorganised' small borrowers (mostly placed in the traditional rural sector) to be higher than that facing the 'organised' borrowers of the modern sector. Second, the gap in interest rates is most likely to be larger the greater the underdevelopment of the domestic credit markets and financial institutions.

Under the colonial regime, dualism was also due to discrimination in the provision of infrastructure: public funds in overhead capital were often directed towards urban centres or those selected areas of large-scale economic activity.[6] In the post-colonial period, dualism was a result of discrimination against the small economic units of the traditional sector and direct government policy in most of underdeveloped countries.

Confronted with a disequilibrium situation of the type described above, governments react by setting up a network of direct controls for rationing the scarce capital and foreign exchange resources between different economic units. This rationing process does adversely affect the small economic units outside the modern sector. Even if the government policy is neutral, the established large firms would still be better placed than the small economic units in terms of obtaining resources, given the ability of the former to deal more effectively and in close proximity with the government bureaucracy. But there is substantial evidence that many governments do not exhibit a neutral policy but often encourage large scale economic units and public sector. Thus, government industrialisation policies may directly contribute to the state of unequal accessibility of economic resources and thereby enhance economic dualism.

The notion of skewing of resources away from the traditional sector has been forcefully asserted as urban bias in Michael Lipton's book *Why Poor*

People Stay Poor.[7] Central to Lipton's argument was that the struggle for resources is between the urban and the rural sector, and that the former exploits the latter in a variety of ways. Lipton argues that urban bias rest on convergent interests between the urban workers, urban employers and big farmers. All these interest groups are supposed to benefit if agriculture gets squeezed as long as its resources are taken care of by subsidising the big capitalist farmers in order to produce cheap food and raw materials for the cities. In this way, the urban elite is able to 'buy off' the rural elite of big farmers largely by means of subsidised inputs.[8] This steering of resources, subsidies and legal advantage towards the big farmers – who alone produce substantial surplus – is frequently done at the cost of the small farmers.[9]

It can be further argued that this rural-urban misallocation has a devastating impact on efficiency and equity, since for the majority of agricultural crops including horticulture, the small farmers are more efficient than big farmers. This is because the small farmers have little land and much underused family labour so that they tend to complement any extra development resources received, particularly foreign aid, with much more extra labour than big farmers. Thus, the small farmers in yielding a given product, use less land resources and more of the increasingly plentiful labour, than do big farmers.[10]

The Lipton rural–urban bias is presented as a general case explaining almost all forms of inequality, from regional inequality between East and West Pakistan (before the emergence of Bangladesh) to inequality in Brazil, racial inequality in South Africa,[11] and inter-generational inequality, in as much as adult males are more heavily represented in the urban areas. However, this sweeping statement in explaining inequality is quite unsatisfactory. In a review of Lipton's book, T.J. Byres noted that in an endeavour to find a general applicable statement of urban bias, Lipton flashes many underdeveloped countries, often with comparatively different experiences in the extent of urban bias and reduction of inequality.[12] In this sense Lipton ends up ignoring the necessity to explore the historical roots of urban bias, to identify the reasons for its relative strength in some societies and weaknesses in others so as to examine the conditions necessary for its eradication. In an unconvincing fashion Lipton also dismisses the argument that differences in the nature of development of capitalistic structure or the impact of colonialism or neo-colonialism influence urban bias.[13] Byres corrects this view in the following observation:

> The nature of the mode of production and the impact of colonialism and neo-colonialism do matter. A comparison of inequality and its treatment in say, India and China shows this only too clearly.[14]

The lack of finding the root causes of urban bias in the Lipton's analysis can be seen in his proposal to eliminate this state of inequality through 'outside education' so that urban politicians, students and thinkers as long as they are sympathetic to the cause of rural development should to some extent detach themselves from their tendency towards urban bias and involve themselves directly in the problems of rural life by visiting, learning and explaining. This should be reinforced by a programme of 'ruralising' politicians, planners, bureaucrats, professors and visiting experts, especially from the United Nations and the World Bank who should spend some few weeks a year in the field acquainting themselves to the problems of the poor.[15] Urban trade unions should be persuaded to adopt an expansionist strategy and open their membership to the low wage strata. Urban firms should be persuaded to buy up land and let it out at reasonable rents in small plots to highly productive poor peasants.[16]

Looking specifically at the problem of efficient utilisation of underemployed labour, Michal Kalecki emphasises that it is necessary to expand agricultural production rapidly as this is a prerequisite for a larger transfer of labour to other occupations.[17] A shift of resources to the rural sector, and within the latter, to the rural poor, would tend to raise productivity per hectare, which in turn raises productivity per man and contributes to overall solution of the problem of employment.

Techniques that merely raise productivity per man may contribute to a higher surplus of agricultural products being available to the urban areas, which would make it possible to augment employment there, but at the same time would increase unemployment in the rural areas. Such would be the consequences of establishing large-scale mechanised farms.[18] But it does not seem that this can be done within the generalised Lipton framework because of a lack of understanding of the specific historical causes of urban bias in his analysis. Elimination of dualism at the national level must take into account the specific conditions of the development of dualism. The latter methodology can be seen in the works of Griffin, who has written quite extensively on conditions for the creation of dualism due to land concentration and imperfection in other factor markets.[19]

Land concentration prevails in countries where population densities are not high. Cases can be found where 5 per cent of those active in agriculture possess 60 per cent or more of usable land.[20] In addition to pointing to land concentration Griffin also suggests that growing inequalities in development could be traced to other factor markets. As shown in Chapters 8, this affects the allocation of resources, especially the agricultural methods of production, the readiness to innovate and the distribution of income. The high degree of market imperfection is usually explained by immobility of resources, poor means of communication and sparseness of information. But probably the two most important causes of inequality are government policies that are systematically biased in favour of certain groups and monopoly power in the hands of the relatively wealthy and prosperous, members of the farming community.

Under conditions of land concentration and general shortage of resources there is usually a high correlation between monopoly over land

and higher productivity on the one hand, and a shortage of land and low productivity on the other. This in turn increases inequality and allows large land owners to exert influence over the labour market as well. In this sense, 'monopoly of material resources may give the landlords monopsony power over labour',[21] which enables landlords to exploit labour by fixing the wage rate below what it would have been in a fully competitive market. In other words, an unequal distribution of land ownership, a defective tenure system, and privileged access to the market may combine to give big landowners monopsony power over labour, and where this occurs the result would be lower wages and less employment than would otherwise be the case.[22] As argued above and in the chapters below, an unlimited labour supply is a result of land tenure and an imperfect market structure rather than, as is often believed, a result of high population densities.

Enhanced dualism in the African economy

As the representation of the theories of mainly classical and neoclassical dualism has shown above, the two most important reasons behind the creation and sustenance of economic dualism are government policies that historically set up the prevailing institutions and monopoly power in the hands of both the urban elites and wealthy farmers. This resulted in the little improvement in the standard of living of the people in the subsistence sector of the economy. The theory of dualism has also taught us to look into the policies and institutions that create, sustain and benefit from maintenance of a dual economic structure.

The battle still needs to be fought to change the current duality of the formal sector of the economy on one hand, and the large peasant farming sector and informal sector on the other hand. As long as the majority of the population is involved in informal, communal/subsistence sector (60–80 per cent), there will be little if any traction from the majority of economic actors in participating in the nation's or regional industrial plans. However, recently, development economists have expanded the discourse of the intractability of unlocking economic resources at the hands of the poor to include the legal systems governing property rights.

By and large, most of Africa's post-independence industrial strategies or plans, though well-crafted on paper, have failed to have traction on the ground. Second, the countries in the region, including Zimbabwe, have not succeeded to make effective use of the vast natural and human resources endowment at their disposal. In fact, this may not have come as a surprise to many development economic thinkers. It may simply be a matter of a wish or desire to postulate what we wish to achieve, but without a deep understanding of the political economy and structure of the economies of the region, this will remain a pie in the sky. The conventional understanding of Africa's economy is succinctly captured in Thandika Mkandawire's note that:

> Colonial powers discouraged local industrial production for the domestic market of the colony and the export of manufactured goods from the periphery. Only the relatively more autonomous 'settler' economies of Kenya, Southern Rhodesia and South Africa managed some industry during this (colonial) period.[23]

Africa's post independent analysts should have by now almost exhausted their chorus of disapproval of the legacy bequeathed upon us by the colonial economy. It is time to move on and ask why it is still difficult to unpack and correct the structure of the economy we inherited 40–50 years ago.

Like in most countries in Sub-Saharan Africa (SSA), Zimbabwe has failed to play her role of providing conditions for the majority of its citizens to engage in formal productive sector activities, hence the continuation of a narrow minority economy. They have failed to shift these countries' focal point of progress from the agricultural to the industrial sector, in the sense of Fei and Ranis who believed 'that the ideal shifting takes place when the investment funds from agricultural surplus and industrial profits are sufficiently large so as to purchase industrial capital goods like plants and machinery'.[24] They have also failed to provide the legal and political environment that supports the majority of the population's assets to transform into the formal property system, thus becoming effective and dynamic capital. Recent thinking is that, if this would happen it would unleash the majority of the country's business activities, starting from the micro, small and medium-scale enterprises (MSMEs) and direct them at other economic actors. Through the resulting interaction, initiating actors will first commit their own resources and get access to resources committed by other actors thereby ushering in the spiral dynamic of capitalism. When this happens and the process becomes successful, all actors build long-term co-operative relations based on trust, mutual understanding, and shared views. Failure of this process to happen has meant that the maintenance or even widening of economic dualism as the majority of economic actors remain outside the modern capitalist sector.

Economists normally advise that underdeveloped countries can have an industrial strategy that mobilises all the important factors that directly influence the growth and diversification of these economies, namely: the political level (nature of the state, governance, non-state actors), macroeconomic level (fiscal and monetary, trade, social and regulatory policies) and meso-level (infrastructure, science and technology, labour and education) factors. Buttressing these segments of the economic engine with well thought-out incentives/regulatory policies, the ensuing economic environment will impact positively on the competitiveness, diversification and performance of a country's enterprises (see Figure 7.1 for an integrated policy making space). Through this diagram one can visualise the interactions of the key drivers in economic and social space: politics, economics and social actors.

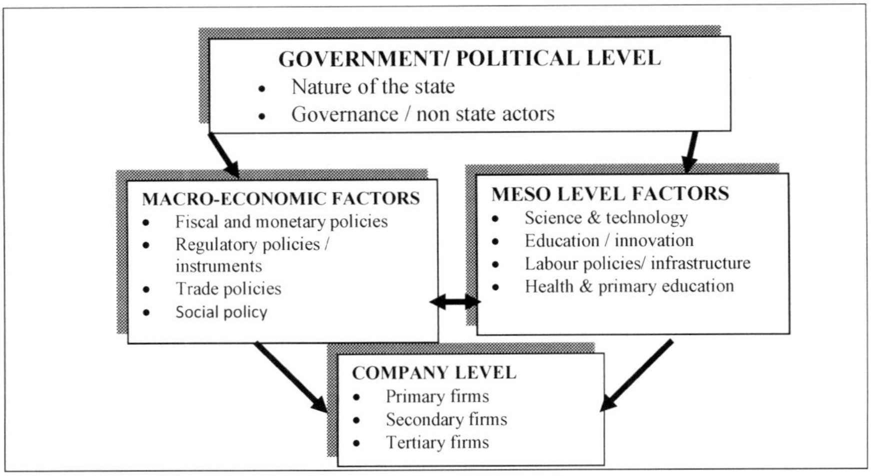

Figure 7.1 An integrated policy-making space.

Source: Developed by the author to illustrate the functioning of an integrated policy space.

The factors that directly influence the growth and diversification of these economies can be illustrated using a hypothetically constructed 'integrated policy making space diagram', namely: the political level, non-state actors, macroeconomic level, and meso-level factors. Through the interface of this policy making space, we can enhance change and growth of the backward agricultural sector and link it with the dynamic modern sector, employ value chain analysis, and thereby close the 'missing link in the development puzzle'. Further, in order to enhance the development of the whole economy there is need to address the issue of legal property rights of the majority of the people. This is so in order to enable them to efficiently function economically, once they are registered under the country's legal property systems.

Further, as economists we also advise governments and policy makers to tilt growth towards enhanced integration with the regional and global economies, in the form of export growth and openness to foreign capital inflows. We talk about the need for an overall improvement in productivity and competitiveness combined with a diversified and balanced industrial growth in a wider, well-linked economic space that allows for the efficient and effective use of factors of production on the basis of increased value addition.

Absence of linkages and connectivity of value chains at the national and regional levels

A central observation in the literature inspired by the global commodity value chain approach is that the highest value added is concentrated in the marketing and design functions of the value chain and no longer in manufacturing, let alone raw material processing, while increasingly the governance of value chains rests with companies controlling the former functions.[25]

The developments in the capitalist economies are increasingly being organised in a variety of different business systems and global commodity chains approaches, building on distinctive institutional contexts and through co-ordination of economic activities across national boundaries On the contrary, the majority of African firms including those in Zimbabwe are still predominantly producing in isolation of each other even at the domestic and regional level. The latter countries' firms are not only lagging behind other regions of the world in the upgrading of their products through diversification of manufacturing activities, many of them have lost a sizable chunk of the value chains which were developed during the import substitution phase of their economies. The quote below is telling:

> the value of exports of agricultural machinery and equipment steadily grew from Z$1.1 million in 1980 to Z$2.9 million in 1984. Exports to SADC region included ploughs, cultivators, harrows, planters and seeders and parts of agricultural machinery. Zimbabwe also exported various quantities of railway rolling stock and other equipment to the East and Southern African region.[26]

By the turn of the millennium, most of Zimbabwe's metalworking industries built under the import-substitution era had closed down. What is fundamentally lacking in all these attempts is an integrated development value chain approach. The normal situation is that with active channels of business transaction, communication and dialogue, the networks or value chains share specialised infrastructure and labour markets. Most of the African industrial cluster developments are hardly noticed or recognised by domestic institutions, particularly the regulatory and legal property laws meant to bring on board all the players in the sector. In the sections below, we discuss the causes behind the inability of domestic firms to trigger linkages and connectivity of value chains at the national and regional levels.

A missing link in the development discourse puzzle

What rarely gets mentioned or discussed in the development discourse is what the Peruvian economist Hernando De Soto has been concerned with, that is how do we expect the huge assets belonging to the majority of our citizens to count as effective capital if these are not in the records and titles that formal property systems provide?[27] If these assets do not appear in a nation's codes of conduct, are not embedded in the formal property systems, how do we expect them to combine and be linked to other assets in the form of collateral and credit leveraging?

De Soto in many ways reveals the essence of capital:

> When advanced nations pulled together all the information and rules about their known assets and established property systems that tracked their economic evolution, they gathered into one order the whole institutional process that underpins the creation of capital. If capitalism had a mind it would have located it in the legal property system. But, like all things pertaining to the mind, much of capitalism today operates at a sub-conscious level.[28]

It is at this juncture that we encounter serious difficulties in applying the commodity value chain analogy to a country like Zimbabwe or other developing countries. We are told and advised to imitate the conditions of life as it transpired in the developed capitalist countries of the West, that all we should do is to create conditions of stable currencies, open markets, private sector development, all the objectives of macroeconomic stability and structural adjustment reforms. Let's try and understand why macroeconomic reforms are not working in these countries in our region. Why have our rich and enduring mines, agricultural farms and to a lesser extent our firms produced billions of dollars but the value chains have stalled? Why is it that the money we have received from the outside world in the form of development aid has failed to kick-in production value chains, as has happened in the other regions of the world? Why is it constant that a significant capital formation is only possible in the small segment of our economies and not in the whole economy?

The local and foreign investors we are attracting do have capital; their assets are more or less integrated, fungible, networked and protected by the formal property systems. But these are only a tiny minority of our countries' total population of assets – the majority is left outside the closed ring of legal property rights. It is in this respect that Fernando de Soto critically observes that:

> (these) are only a tiny minority – those who can afford the expert lawyers, insider connections and patience required to navigate the red tape of their property systems. The great majority of people, who cannot get the fruits of their labour represented by the formal property system, live outside Braudel's bell jar. The bell jar makes capitalism a private club, open only to a privileged few, and enrages the billions standing outside looking in. This capitalist apartheid will inevitably continue until we all come to terms with the critical flaw in many countries' legal and political systems that prevent the majority from entering the formal property system.[29]

Quite unlike the experience of Europe and Asia, in SSA the emerging industrial clusters and their MSMEs lack the institutional and legal mechanisms that formally fix their assets in records governed by rules contained in the property system. The assets of the poor and those of the small enterprise that governments appear to glorify and create ministries to craft policies for them are all but assets whose economic and social aspects are not fixed in a formal property system. It is, therefore, extremely hard to move such assets fluidly in the market. Until we address this dualism in the economic system, our African peasant farming sector, rural services, and the sprawling urban informal sector enterprises will remain an add-on appendage, and not a central pivot for the integration of our countries' non-formal sectors into the formal economy. Such a situation also undermines the prospects of creating synergies to close the missing links and subsequently creating robust clusters and value chains between SMEs and formal sector firms.

A pertinent question to be asked is why is it that the African region has failed to stratify into an industrial organisation that allows its small industrial clusters, housing the MSMEs to participate competitively in wide trade networks? Empirical earlier evidence from countries like Italy and Germany and more recently from some Asian countries gives attributes of successful clusters, or industrial districts. These include 'geographical proximity among firms, sectoral specialisation, close inter-firm collaboration, inter-firm competition based on innovation, a socio-cultural identity which facilitates trust, active self-help organizations, and supportive regional and municipal government'.[30]

Firms, large and small have five functions all focusing on other actors and their relations, *namely*: procurement; organisation and management; technology; marketing; and economics/finance. Typically in a large firm, each of the section managers of these functions interacts with corresponding managers of other firms or non-firms. In small firms, entrepreneurs enter into any level of the value chain and combine these functions. As long as there continues to be a legal failure that prevents the majority of enterprising people to freely negotiate and contract with strangers, this defeats the division of labour and relegates the poor and extra-legal businesses to a small circle of specialisation and low productivity of labour. A point to emphasise is that a firm, whether large, medium, small, or micro, does not constitute a black box. It is a serious interactive partner with other firms and non-firm actors in economic and social development.

In addressing the issue of inclusiveness in industrial strategies and the challenges faced by the concept of a value-chain industrial processes, there is need for a system that automatically allows the market to spontaneously widen as new entries approach it. Such a channel is one that allows growth through inclusive business networks. This follows the dictate of Adam Smith that, the wider the market, the more minute the division of labour can be. If there is no obstruction to this condition, both national and regional industrial value chains would follow the logic of the five pillars of development listed below: (a) deepened national and sectoral value chains, (b) competitive business climates, (c) improved regional infrastructure,

(d) reliance on special economic zones, and (e) enhanced capacity building of the economy.

Under the direction of a conducive macroeconomic and institutional settings, activities of firms are directed at other actors and through the resulting interaction, initiating actors first committing their own resources and get access to resources committed by other actors. If the process is successful, both actors build long-term co-operative relations based on trust, mutual understanding, and shared views, thus forming the foundations of the concept of social capital in business relationships. At the business level, these relationships are akin to what is defined as social capital – the network of social connections that exist between people and their shared values and norms of behaviour, which enable and encourage mutually advantageous social cooperation.

The theoretical concepts enunciated above are founded on the idea that each and every market is unique. Whether a market economy will be successful or not will depend on its historical conditions, and the interplay between the background institutions: the immediate social institutions, notably Government and the organisation of the business systems proper. It is for this reason that we have set the discussion of Zimbabwe's dualism development from the country's unique and specific conditions.

A conundrum of a schizophrenic attitude of governments

As it will be shown below in the Zimbabwean case, the outmoded system of legal property that was introduced under colonialism and was at the heart of economic dualism in the colonial economy has not changed. Instead, this erstwhile colonially imposed economic dualism has continued to be reinforced now by the post-independence ruling elite. With Zimbabwe's independence, slowly but surely a surge of people from the impoverished rural peasant economy have pushed themselves into the larger economic space of the modern sector. The conditions for the expansion of the rural peasant agricultural sector where the mass exodus of people are coming from continues to deteriorate, while at the same time the rate of growth of the industrial sector and the modern economy is insufficient to absorb the people, a new form of economic dualism is being entrenched. Thus, prevented from integrating into the formal legal system, the poor have created their own extra-legal system – a myriad of workshops, small crafts-workers shops producing essential goods and services, informal manufacturing and retail distribution, building and transportation. However, where these shops are operating there is no legal property rights or an attempt to make this happen.

A review of the literature suggests that the reallocation of jobs across the country's sectors is central to the process of structural change and upgrading productivity. The growth in labour productivity can come either from changes arising from the reorganisation of production within sectors through, for example, the adoption of new machines and technologies that raises output without changing the amount of labour. This can also happen from the reallocation of jobs across sectors ('structural change') as workers move from low- to high-productivity sectors (e.g. from agriculture to industry or services) – the structural bonus.

It was expected that Zimbabwe would experience a process of structural change that would be the centre of sustainable enhancement of the standards of living of the population, enabling more people to benefit from higher productivity levels in more advanced segments of the economy. In this way, structural change is the most effective driver of growth that reduces poverty in both the short and long run. The across-sector labour productivity component of growth is therefore strongly associated with the speed at which vulnerable employment and poverty are reduced.[31]

Instead of the expected structural changes as anticipated following the country's independence in 1980, Zimbabwe, like most of its peers in the Southern African region, has experienced a structural regression characterised by increasing dependence on natural resources, de-industrialisation and informalisation. In its State of the Manufacturing Sector Survey, the Confederation of Zimbabwe Industries (CZI) observed that: 'Industries in Zimbabwe are under serious threat. De-industrialization has reached catastrophic levels, with dire consequences to the state of the economy'.[32]

Admittedly, around 60–80 per cent of the Southern African region's economic players are micro businesses thus falling outside the formal legal systems. This provides ample evidence that, so as long as there is legal failure that prevents the majority of enterprises from fully participating in the recognised national legal property system, this will continue to defeat the division of labour, relegate these businesses to smaller circles of specialisation, smaller networks and low productivity.

When faced with this formidable apartheid of formal law, the people pushed into the informal economy cannot operate within the law. They cannot hold property efficiently, or enforce contracts through the courts. They cannot reduce uncertainty through limited liability systems and insurance policies. They cannot raise money for investment through mortgage and collateral to achieve economies of scale or to enter into new ventures to enhance their initial capital assets. The economic effects of this legal apartheid are most strikingly visible in the lack of formal property rights over real estate. These extra-legal asset owners are denied access to credit that would allow them to expand their operations – an essential step towards starting or growing a business in advanced developed countries.

On the surface it appears that the Zimbabwean government has tried its best in the circumstances. It has provided regulatory institutions, promotional institutions, all focusing on facilitating the internal or external affairs of the firms, e.g. working conditions, financing the market mobility of workers, etc. However, at other times, the government has reacted by demolishing what they perceive as shanty towns and illegal businesses. The

Zimbabwe government launched 'Operation Murambatsvina', referred to as *Operation Restore Order in May/June 2005*, resulting in the destruction of homes, business premises and vending sites. A United Nations report estimated that some 700,000 people in cities across the country lost their homes, their source of livelihoods or both.[33] A similar action has been taken elsewhere, even outside of Africa. In August 1999 Bangladesh authorities demolished 50,000 shanties in Dhaka. In various forms of shades and intensity, this sort of schizophrenic attitude by governments goes on. Where demolition fails to work, governments have supported microfinance programs that are transforming residential areas into extra-legal industrial zones, without even an inkling or noticing, that this avalanche of people into shanty towns, open spaces to construct their lives (homes and businesses) is here to stay and will not be tamed by police and administrators.

It is ironic that when migrants from developing countries move to advanced developed countries, well developed institutions eventually absorb them into networked property systems that help them to produce surplus value. Countries in our region cannot integrate migrants from the village in the same country into the formal sector, fix their assets into fungible forms that allow them to interface productively and generate capital within a large legal market.

Unlike in the capitalist economies of the West, where virtually all production is geared to the output of commodities, this contrasts sharply to the present-day African economy, where commodification is only restricted to the country's formal sector. In this set-up, introduction of the productive sectors, (mining, commercial or plantation farming, manufacturing, services, etc.) has not produced change in the structure of these economies.[34] On the contrary, because of the high level of commodification in the capitalist economies, pressure from industrialisation and falling domestic rate of profits, the developed countries continue to want to maintain the narrow trade relations with the African formal sector. The old colonial trading relations with a minimum development of the required infrastructures and ancillary services continue to be maintained in the formal sector enclaves, bearing little relation or at best consenting relations to the larger non-formal sectors of the economy.

The paradox of the matter is that, it is not true that African countries like Zimbabwe do not have the necessary legal structures that can embrace all the economic players within their jurisdictions. The laws exist, but there is the other side of the coin. In one case, it is claimed that the majority of the people choose to stay out of the legal environment and even most of them opt out of the formal system for the extra-legal social contracts. The question is why do they do so? The popular sentiment is that people take cover in the extra-legal or underground sectors to avoid paying taxes, or that they are running away from registering their real estate assets, etc. The truth of the matter is that existing laws, however elegantly written, do not address the aspirations of the poor, small entrepreneurs, or that of the small property owner. Hence the latter opt to stay out of that uncertain environment where their assets are continually taxed though without benefiting from the country's property laws. This is especially the case where they subdivide their assets into uneconomic parcels which they continually hide from the authorities. It is, therefore, the bad legal and administrative system which keeps people outside the legal system. As they remain outside the legal system, the assets of the poor are not covered by the national laws that connect assets into financial and investment circuits, despite the ever-constant rhetoric to do so. As the poor remain out of the 'bell jar', they are crying out for change and simplification of regulations which would bring them inside the system.[35] There is still the other side of the coin. Because of the central government's inertia, municipalities and local authorities have not demarcated the stands or sites where the poor operate from, hence the extra-legals do not have property title deeds over their pieces of land and hence they can be moved in and out any time at the authorities' whims.

In summary, the lack of enforceable property rights reduces the small informal entrepreneurs' investment horizons and prevents these small businesses from becoming bigger. The poor remain at the same level, as they have houses but no titles, crops but no deeds; and businesses without licences. This status quo remains, despite the existence of laws, the technology for planning and bringing in the extra-legals into the bell jar exists. The satellite imaging technology designed to map up the whole of our cities, settlements (urban and rural) in order to identify, profile and map the densely occupied settlements exists. These settlements, whether business stands or housing stands can be easily upgraded, decongested, registered and included into every nation's legal property register.

For this connection to happen, the national legal codes must recognise and connect with extra-legal arrangements and the existing social contracts that have developed. At the superficial level, this requires many disciplines – economists must get the numbers and costs right; urban planners and agronomists to assign priorities; mappers, surveyors and computer experts to provide the necessary information. But ultimately the connections must be concretised in the prevailing laws of these countries.

However, the primary role of leading this process must be assigned to the political role, at the highest level. History shows that this process only succeeds if it is supported by well thought out political strategies led by the apex in political leadership. It was President Thomas Jefferson who transformed Virginia at the end of the eighteenth century when he increased fungibility by abolishing, among other things, the practice of entail (not being able to transfer property outside the family). On a larger scale, in 1862 the United States Congress passed the celebrated 'Homestead Act' and other property laws that resulted in expanded markets and capital needed to fuel explosive economic growth.[36]

In the European continent, Stein and Hardenberg set the stage for universal property in Germany at the beginning of the nineteenth century, and

Eugen Huber in Switzerland at the beginning of the twentieth century who began to integrate all property systems in his country.[37] Japan was only able to complete its integrated national legal property code in the 1950s. In all these cases, the job of changing the historically inherited asset ownership structures is the job of political leadership. The political leaders are the only ones who can synchronise change, empower the majority and usher in a dynamic change that will power growth of the economy. They are the only ones who can make the much needed property revolution by taking the perspective of the poor, co-opting the elite and ultimately deal with the legal and technical bureaucracies that are the current custodians of the status quo.

As historical and empirical evidence shows, by guaranteeing property rights to the poor, the political leaders would have made their citizens into a co-sovereign. Historically there is evidence that societies with a wide distribution of property, notably land, residential housing and businesses are stable, more resilient to upheavals and without any inhibition to engage in productive value chain activities of all sorts – whether agricultural, forestry, mining or industrial. This can only happen when the properties of the majority can begin to talk to all other properties within a nationally globalised property system, a condition that reduces the costs of transactions. Just as the Nobel Prize Laureate Ronald Coase established that costs of transactions can be substantially reduced within a controlled and coordinated context of a firm.[38] Coase established that costs of carrying out transactions can be substantially reduced within the controlled and coordinated context of a firm. In this sense property systems can be likened to Coase's firm in that controlled environments reduce transaction costs, as succinctly captured below:

> Naturally, a point must be reached where the costs of organising an extra transaction within the firm are equal to the costs involved in carrying out the transaction in the open market, or, to the costs of organizing by another entrepreneur.[39]

Continued economic dualism in the Zimbabwean case

My original approach to the analysis of economic dualism in the Zimbabwean case was based on a historical analysis, i.e. dualism from the standpoint of the historical perspective.[40] Second, as pointed out in my hypothesis then, the dualistic development was induced by policies of the colonial government. Third, in the Rhodesian colonial experience, economic dualism was explained by events in the land market which formed the basis for dualism in the remaining other factor markets.

One of the most important indicators of economic dualism at the national level was manifested by land concentration in a minority group while the majority of rural farmers were relegated to small farm holdings.

The methodology was to establish the source and existence of economic dualism in the land market and thereafter its percolation into other factor markets. The historical roots of economic dualism that caused imperfections in these factor markets are to be found in colonial policies with respect to land, labour and capital, and discrimination in the marketing arrangements of agricultural produce. Specific attention was paid to the role of the government policies and monopoly elements in the hands of the relatively few large-scale farmers. Economic dualism in these factor markets was analysed in connection with its consequences on the economy.

The discussion on dualism wound up with an analysis of the interdependent relations in the economic structure working to pull down the standards of living or per capita incomes of the country's majority. Dualism in the colonial Zimbabwean economy was shown to have a tendency to be illustrated by five interlocking components that interact to create falling incomes per capita in the economic system, namely:

- Land alienation policies and discrimination in the provision of infrastructure and services.
- Population pressures in the African rural areas and environmental degradation leading to soil erosion.
- Low productivity.
- Migrant labour, discrimination and low wages.
- Falling incomes per capita.

One of the most important factors influencing almost all sectors of the Rhodesian colonial economy was the way in which agricultural development and land policies were related. Land alienation was probably the decisive force in the economic system. Economic dualism was triggered by the historical land alienation actions of the white colonial settler governments. Land alienation led to a rising man–land ratio where population pressure of both humans and livestock on the designated African rural areas led to environmental degradation and soil erosion. Naturally, the increase in population in a given land area in combination with land degradation and soil erosion effects made for low productivity in the traditional agricultural sector. Per capita incomes were affected as well since in the African land area man-hours worked on the farm per family member also decreased and off-farm work increased. Thus, the utilisation ratio of farm family labour tended to decline with the decreasing land area, and the result was a gradual creation of a labour surplus in the modern economy. The stagnant conditions in the traditional agricultural sector and discrimination and dualism in the labour market drove down the wage level of the fast accumulating number of job seekers in the modern sector. As more labour turned up due to the lack of cultivable land in the agricultural sector, the wage rate was further lowered. It is in this sense that the most important of the five factors listed above appears to be dualism in the land market, a dualism that has direct consequences for the income distribution in the traditional agricultural sector as well as for the incomes earned by African workers in the modern sector.

An analysis of economic dualism that incorporates its historical causes and effects has the advantage of showing not only the heterogeneity of the sectors in the economy, but also the interdependent relationships between the sectors in the dual economy. As the interdependence of the traditional sector with the modern sector is inevitable, policies that neglect the development of the former have adverse distributional consequences for the country's majority. Second, if the modern sector depends on the traditional sector for a significant part of its food and raw materials. Thus the neglect of the latter sector creates a bottleneck of necessities due to the inelasticity of agricultural production. Third, as the increase in employment implies generation of additional incomes, an increase in food prices becomes unavoidable if no adequate increase in agricultural output is forthcoming. In this sense, the level of agricultural production may set a definite limit to employment possibilities even of a capital–saving type. As Michal Kalecki noted: '… the demand for necessities increases, because either the wages of newly employed will be higher than their previous consumption, or the income of the peasants who remain in agriculture will increase, or both'.[41]

There is still the latter statement by Lewis that he had changed his attitude in relation to his earlier thesis on the possibility of producing a higher output per acre with fewer people on the farm without an improvement in techniques. 'The moral for policy makers is of course not to rely on "trickle down" to benefit the traditional sector, but to attack the problem of that sector directly.'[42] Latter generation of development economics has totally changed from the earlier stance of theories on dualism of only dealing with focus on expanding agricultural production in the fight against the problem of underemployment in underdeveloped countries. Improvement in techniques or organisation or both, has become necessary so that those transferred to off-farms occupations are fed and for the maintenance of inter-sectoral balance in development. Thus, given the consumer preferences of the typical worker, the output generated in the two sectors must be such as to prevent a 'shortage' of food or of industrial products.[43] Inclusive growth as currently shown by research findings draws us to conclude that the most distinct feature of the African economies remains that of a lop-sided nature in their patterns and size of production, consumption and trade. This characteristic distortion of a dualistic economy which affects the way which the formal sector relates to the larger informal sector, resulting in internal disarticulation for the whole economy, is discussed below.

The discussion in this chapter shows that both the theory and phenomenon of dualism has been at the centre of the development economics for over 60 years, i.e. since the publication of Lewis's pioneering article in 1954. The recognition of the heterogeneity of the economic sectors in the process of development was an important contribution of the dualism models. In the main model, classical dualism as originated by Lewis, the concentration is on the conditions for growth and distribution of income inside the modern sector. The subsistence sector was generally treated as a backlog in the economic system, having the main functions of providing labour supplies to the modern sector at a more or less constant wage rate.

In the experiences of most underdeveloped countries output growth and capital formation have increased more or less according to the predictions of the original dual model. The share of national income devoted to savings has increased. There has been little improvement in the standard of living of the people in the subsistence sector of the economy, since the distribution of income has tended to be unequal with the share of wages in the national income falling, while the combined share of profits and rents have risen. But as seen in this chapter, this adverse distributional consequence of the dual model was also predicted by Lewis model since the latter does not necessarily involve an equalising of the existing distribution of income. The rising capitalist incomes have continued to be accompanied by a declining share of income going to the members of the subsistence sector.

Most of the criticism of the dualism model has been centred on the adverse distributional consequences of the model for the peasant subsistence sector. The principal issue is not to expect a 'trickle down' effect of growth from the modern sector to the traditional sector, but that both sectors must grow and develop more or less simultaneously. Second, though the dual model was presented within a historical framework, the historical roots of economic dualism in underdeveloped countries as well as the reasons for its relative strength and weaknesses were neglected by the theory.

The recent literature on economic dualism in the African economy is now increasingly situated in the structural disarticulation analysis, whose most distinct feature is the lopsided nature of these countries' pattern and size of production, consumption and trade. This feature of 'modern economic dualism' continues to constitute the basic problem for transformation of these economies. A stubborn characteristic of their economic structure is their failure to disentangle themselves from this structural disarticulation and successfully embark on a sustained structural transformation, like what has happened recently to the economies of East Asia.

The ECA reported that the African agricultural trade was highly concentrated on a few primary commodities and that diversification into more dynamic products was required, but the report lamented that 'Africa has so far failed to achieve the necessary transformation for broad based growth'.[44] As has been argued elsewhere, the answer to this 'sodden state of the African economy' lies in the disarticulated colonial inherited economic structure of its economy whose logic was set to determine the pattern of the future of the continent's post-colonial development.[45] A disarticulated economy is one whose parts are not complementary, contrary to a coherent economy where there are domestic and/or regional sectoral complementarities and reciprocities. In a generally articulated economic system the exchange mechanism and sectoral/regional reciprocities become pervasive following on the total commodification of the economy driven by forward and backward linkages of production.[46]

A dualistic economy is characterised by a narrow and disarticulated production base with ill-adapted technology, poor manufacturing capabilities, declining market share in both the domestic, regional and international markets and sluggish growth. However, because of the lack of understanding or obscure appreciation of the machinations of the 'grafted capitalist' mode of production of a typical African economy, contradictory relations emerge in the functioning of African enterprises, in direct opposition to the pace of their integration into the global economy. Quite unlike the original capitalist mode of production, often referred to as 'endogenous' capitalism, Africa's post-colonial capitalist mode of production or 'grafted capitalism' lacked the historical roots of the cradle of capitalism, i.e. feudalism that already had embedded commodification of capital, labour, consumption and market penetration into the total mode of production.

In the case of the European experience, already under the endogenous capitalism, virtually all production was geared to the output of commodities, when industrial revolution occurred it produced substantive change in society in terms of economic and social cohesion. But in the present-day post-colonial Africa, where commodification was only restricted to the country's modern formal sector, introduction of the productive sectors, (mining, commercial or plantation farming, manufacturing, etc.) has not produced change in the structure of these economies.[47] On the contrary, because of the high level of competitiveness and globalisation in the capitalist economies, pressure from industrialisation and falling domestic rates of profits, it is normal that the developed countries will continue to want to maintain the narrow trade relations with the African formal sector. The old colonial trading relations with a minimum development of the required infrastructures and ancillary services continue to be maintained in the formal sector enclaves, bearing little relation or at best acquiescent relations to the ever growing and expanding informal economy.

In Figure 7.2 it can be shown that the formal sector (FS) is linked to the global economy through exports, imports, foreign direct investment (FDIs) and technology. The FS generally has lower surplus labour and higher average incomes than the informal sector (IS) and the rural agricultural subsistence or the communal sector (CS),[48] which both lag behind the formal sector incomes. There is high surplus labour in both the informal and communal sectors, and these sectors act as a buffer to surplus labour for the FS. The former sectors also provide a ready pool of labour for the formal sector if and when required. The informal and communal sectors form the non-formal sector (NFS), which is not linked beneficially to the FS, though contributing significantly to the survival of the people's economic and social well-being.[49] In the post-independence era, this phenomenon has now been

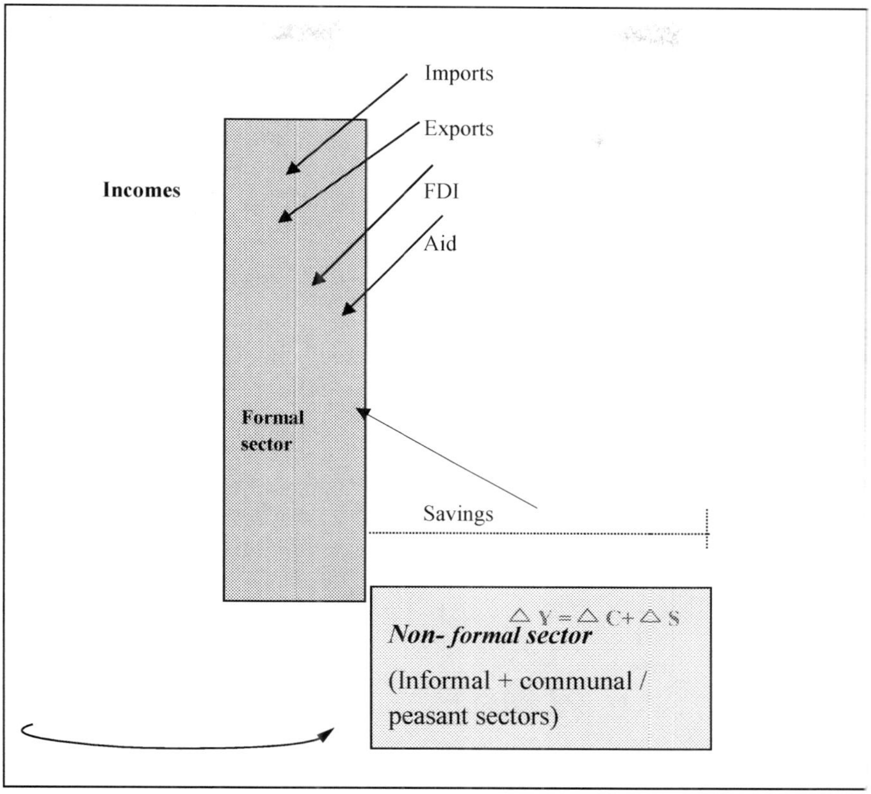

Figure 7.2 The duality of the African economy.
Source: Ndlela, 2007: Figure 4.1, p. 89.

entrenched and enhanced by policies implemented by the African state, oblivious of the expected role and mission of the post-colonial state, which was to address and effectively destroy inherited the dualistic economic structure of their economies. These are distortions in the way in which the FS and NFS of the economy relate to each other. There are also disarticulations internally, which have generally been overlooked in research compared to external disarticulations that have been studied extensively.

Three levels of disarticulations are easily discernible, namely: those within the different sectors of the economy (microeconomic distortions), between the sectors (structural and distributional distortions), and those caused by the external environment (mainly macroeconomic distortions). In spite of the pervasiveness of these distortions, African governments usually focus on the formal sector through policies and expenditures that provide systems and infrastructure mainly beneficial to that sector. The formal sectors of most of these economies are interlinked through various forms of infrastructure: roads, rail, air and telecommunications, mainly geared at fostering trade in exports and imports. Yet domestically, consumption between the different sectors is weakly linked, and regional formal sector linkages are weaker than those between themselves and centres in developed countries.

The most dynamic sector of the African economy is the formal sector, which generally contributes less than 20 per cent of total employment (except in a few countries like South Africa where it reaches 45 per cent). As already alluded to above, the formal sector of the African economy, however, cannot be readily expanded because of its inherent structural rigidities. This is invariably the case, in spite of the neo-liberalism argument that the African manufacturing sector can be expanded to enhance employment, given its linkages with the global economy. However, the argument against neoliberalism should be taken with a caveat. For growth to be shared and occur unimpeded, the African economy will undoubtedly need to be unshackled by liberal economic reforms which lowers the current trade barriers, tax rates, breaks monopolies, unshackles industry and competition in order to open up to regional and global markets. But in order for this to happen, there is need for a 'strong state' that must enable the markets to reshape society while the state pushes back on the illiberal aspects of social order.

The FS is biased towards high capital intensity, even though labour-intensive production processes might still be viable, while Africans cry out about the labour-intensive products coming out of East Asia and China. No matter how high the growth rate of the FS is, this remains a short-term phenomenon and will be unable to grow large and fast enough to eat away the NFS.

Generally this is because of the structural distortions characterising post-colonial economy, namely: (a) the unequal access to resources (asymmetrical distribution of factors of production); (b) productive and more efficient use of labour in the FS for capitalist gains; (c) failure of capital to enhance local and regional value chains to allow benefits of growth to trickle down to non-formal sector; and (d) high unemployment and under-employment resulting in net loss to the economy in terms of lost production and net loss in aggregate demand. This ultimately beckons and entails African leadership to embark on development and implementation of a strategy to graduate informal enterprise into the formal sector and promote business linkages between formal and informal enterprises including segments of the peasant or communal agricultural sector. It has been noted in the literature that in the nineteenth century Japan successfully destroyed that country's dualism by connecting its two sectors of the economy through the presence of a decentralised rural industry which was often linked to urban production.[50]

The link between dualism in the African colonial experience and in particular in the Zimbabwean colonial experience and dualism in the post-colonial era, forms the bedrock of the ensuing discussion in the chapters following below. The Zimbabwean experience of continuation with the Rhodesian economic dualism is a typical and even 'classic' example of the African post-colonial state's 'normalising the abnormal', i.e. continuing with dualistic structures of the economy as a new normal, while loudly blaming colonialism and imperialism of having planted and perpetrated underdevelopment.

This phenomenon was historically entrenched and enhanced by policies implemented by the successive governments from the colonial era to the post-independence period. This situation led to massive distortions in the way in which the formal sector (FS) and the non-formal sector (NFS) relate to each other. In spite of the pervasiveness of disarticulations both internally within sectors as well as external ones, the post-colonial state has focused on the FS through policies and expenditures that provide systems and infrastructure mainly beneficial to that sector. Yet domestically, consumption between the different sectors is often poorly linked, and these countries' formal sector linkages with the non-formal sector are weaker than those it has with similar centres in developed countries.

Thus the solution to the informal sector businesses does not lie in occasionally bashing them around, policing them, but in nursing them to grow their businesses to formality. An enabling environment for the informal sector should see these small businesses being given sufficient and relevant infrastructure, institutional support, and technology. They should be provided at various levels, infrastructure to do what the informal sector does best, to produce goods and provide services, that is special spaces or business stands, electricity and water. These specialised areas and spaces for various clusters of informal sector businesses will enable them to be provided with standards, networks, etc. to grow their businesses into large enterprises. As will be argued in the remaining chapters, the success of this will depend on giving the whole spectrum of non-formal enterprise, access infrastructure, technology and right to legal property titles.

Notes

1 Fei and Ranis, 1966:8
2 Lewis, 1979:212.
3 Ibid.
4 Myint, 1970; Lipton, 1977; Griffin, 1972, 1974, 1976.
5 Myint, 1973: Chapter 5.
6 Myint, 1973:97.
7 Lipton, 1977.
8 Ibid.:67.
9 Ibid.:97.
10 Ibid.:98.
11 Ibid.:72–73.
12 Byres, 1979:217.
13 Lipton, 1977:77–86.

14 Byres, 1979:218.
15 Lipton, 1977:339.
16 Ibid.:336. It is interesting to note that unlike in an earlier work. Lipton, 1968:142, the author has now done away with land reform as one of the solutions of the rural–urban inequality gap. It is said that the land reform is unpopular with the urban elite because it will cause the rural poor to consume more of the agricultural output and thus reduce marketable surplus. Lipton, 1977:107.
17 Kalecki, 1976:17–19.
18 Ibid.
19 Griffin, 1972, 1974, 1976, 1978.
20 Ibid.:1972:10.
21 Ibid.:24.
22 Ibid.:25.
23 Mkandawire, 2011.
24 Fei and Ranis, 1966:14–22.
25 Gereffi and Korseniewicz, 1994; Gereffi, 1996.
26 Ndlela, 1987.
27 De Soto, 2001.
28 De Soto, 2001:65.
29 De Soto, 2000:67–68.
30 Schmitz and Musyck, 1994.
31 AfDB, 2013; UNECA, 2015.
32 CZI, 2014:6.
33 UN, 2005.
34 Relevant to the Zimbabwean economy, value chains that matter are those that thrive to integrate the country's modern 'formal sector' to the regional and world economy. The larger non-formal sector of the economy is left outside of the dynamic circle with very little capacity for capital accumulation.
35 De Soto, 2001:66–68.
36 De Soto, ibid.:199.
37 Ibid.
38 Coase, 1937.
39 Ibid.
40 Ndlela, 1981.
41 Kalecki, 1976:18.
42 Lewis, 1979:216.
43 Fei and Ranis, 1966:24. For an analysis on the manifestation of disequilibrium in consumer markets resulting from redistribution of income, see Griffin and James, 1979:250–252.
44 Economic Commission for Africa (ECA), AERC and OAU's Report. 2001:1.
45 Ndlela, 2007:87.
46 Ibid.
47 Africa's 'grafted capitalism', thrives to integrate its modern 'formal sector' to the world economy, while over 70 per cent of the economy is left behind in the non-formal sector, fraught with distortions: (external, structural and micro-economic) with no virtuous links with other sectors of the economy, and no capacity for capital accumulation. Thus, so long as the non-formal sector remains large, the system is self-constraining, has no dynamics for change and is continuously left outside the trading and value chain relations both internally at the individual country level and externally in terms of regional linkages and connectivity.
48 Though this terminology is typically of the Southern African economies, in the rest of the African continent it should be understood as the traditional 'rural' or peasant economy.

49 As argued in Ndlela (2007) in many African economies, informal sector business may generate as much as half or more of GDP, handle as much as 40 per cent of all foreign exchange and over 40 per cent of exports and imports, support as much as 60–70 per cent of the people. It is also the main provider of transport for the people and meets the basic housing requirements of poor. But the NFS remains a secondary economy reproducing disarticulated subservient relations with both the domestic FS and external economy.

50 Fei and Ranis, 1966.

References

African Development Bank (AfDB). 2013. *Report of the African Development Bank by the Directors of the African Development Bank and the African Development Fund*. Abidjan, Côte d'Ivoire: African Development.

The African in Southern Rhodesia. 1992. Issued by Authority of Southern Rhodesia Government, Salisbury, 1 January–31 December.

Byres, T.J. 1979. 'Of Neo-populist Pipe Dreams: Daedalus in the Third World and the Myth of Urban Bias', *The Journal of Peasant Studies*, Vol. 6, No. 2:217.

Confederation of Zimbabwe Industries (CZI). 2014. *State of the Manufacturing Sector Survey*. Harare, Zimbabwe: CZI.

Coase, R.H. 1937. 'The Nature of the Firm', in *Economica New Series*, Vol. 4. No. 16. November:390–394.

De Soto, Hernando. 2000. *The Mystery of Capital: Why Capitalism Triumphs in the West and Falls Everywhere Else*. London: Black Swan.

De Soto, Hernando. 2001. *The Mystery of Capital: Why Capitalism Triumphs in the West and Fails Everywhere Else*. London: Bantam Press and Black Swan Edition.

Economic Commission for Africa (ECA), AERC and OAU's Report. 2001. *Africa and the World Trade Organisation (WTO): Doha and Beyond*. Addis Ababa: ECA.

Fei, J.C.H. and Ranis, G. 1966. *Agrarianism, Dualism and. Economic Development* Center Discussion Paper, No. 2, Yale University, Yale.

Gereffi, G. 1996. 'Global Commodity Chains: New Forms of Coordination and Control Among Nations and Firms in International Industries', *Competition and Change*, Vol. 4:427–439.

Gereffi, G. and Korseniewicz, M. 1994. *Commodity Chains and Global Capitalism*. Westport, CT: Praeger.

Griffin, Keith. 1969. *Underdevelopment in Spanish America*. London: George Allen and Unwin.

Griffin, Keith. 1972. *The Green Revolution: An Economic Analysis*. London: United Nations Research Institute for Social Development.

Griffin, Keith. 1974. *The Political Economy of Agrarian Change: An Essay of the Green Revolution*. Cambridge, MA: Harvard University Press.

Griffin, Keith. 1976. *Land Concentration and Rural Poverty*. London: Macmillan.

Griffin, Keith. 1978. *International Inequality and National Poverty*. London: Palgrave.

Griffin, Keith and James, Jeffrey. 1979. 'Problems of Transition to Egalitarian Development', *Manchester School*, Vol. 47:250–252.

Kalecki, Michal. 1976. *Essays on Development Economics*. London and New York: Cambridge University Press.

Lewis, W. Arthur. 1979. 'The Dual Economy Revisited', *Manchester School*, Vol. 47: 211–229.

Lipton, Michael. 1977. *Why Poor People Stay Poor: Urban Bias in World Development.* London and Canberra: Temple and Australian National University Press.

Mkandawire, Thandika. 2011. 'Rethinking Africa's Re-industrialization and Regional Cooperation: What Is the Best Way Forward?' in Mbeki, Moeletsi (ed.), *Advocates for Change: How to Overcome Africa's Challenges.* Johannesburg: Picador.

Myint, Hla. 1970. 'Dualism and Internal Integration of Underdeveloped Economies', *Banca Nazionale del Lavora. Quarterly Review*, Vol. 23, 1970:17.

Myint, Hla. 1973. *The Economics of Developing Countries.* 4th (revised) edition, London: Hutchinson.

Ndlela, D.B. 1981. 'Dualism in the Rhodesian Colonial Economy', *Lund Economic Studies*, University of Lund.

Ndlela, D.B. 1987. *Technology Imports and Indigenous Technological Capacity Building: The Zimbabwean Case, The Zimbabwean Case*, in Technology and Employment Programme, World Employment Programme Research, Working Papers, WEP 2–22/WP 173, International Labour Office, Geneva, March 1987.

Ndlela, D.B. 2007. 'Africa's Industrialisation: An Alternative Approach', in J.C. Senghor and N.K. Poku (eds), *Towards Africa's Renewal*. Hampshire: Ashgate Publishing Limited.

Ranis, Gustav and Fei, John C.H. 1961. 'A Theory of Economic Development', *The American Economic Review*, Vol. 51, No. 4:545–546.

Schmitz, H. and Musyck, B. 1994. 'Industrial Districts in Europe: Policy Lessons for Developing Countries', *World Development*, Vol. 22, No. 6:889–910.

United Nations Economic Commission for Africa (UNECA). 2015. *Economic Growth, Inequality And Poverty In Southern Africa: Issues and Policy Options.* Southern Africa Office, Addis Ababa. Web.uneca.org.

UN. 2005. *Report on the Fact-finding Mission to Zimbabwe to Assess the Scope and Impact of Operation Murambatswina*, by the UN Special Envoy on Human Settlements Issues in Zimbabwe, Mrs Anna Kajumulo Tibaijuka, New York: United Nations.

8 The consequences of economic dualism

Background

The chapter focuses on the main argument in the book, that colonialism invented and entrenched the present economic dualism model. When the Europeans clashed with the African peoples in the Southern African region, the traditional African economy that was based on land-intensive activities was reduced to an enclave economy, parcelled out into was to be called 'Native reserves'. Both the South African 1913 Natives Land Act and the Rhodesian 1930 Land Apportionment Act had one thing in common: that no African could purchase or rent land other than in areas 'scheduled' for Africans.

The analysis in the chapter subsequently establishes the existence of dualism in other factor markets, namely labour, capital and produce markets.

In contrast to the preceding chapters, where we have dealt with causes of economic dualism in the Rhodesian colonial economy, the present chapter is concerned with an analysis of its consequences. The analysis will focus on the interdependent relations in the economic structure working to lower the standards of living or per capita incomes of the country's majority, while raising the living standards or per capita incomes of the colonial white minority. Economic analysis has long paid attention to the cumulative process in the economic system and to the fact that all parts of the economic system are intimately and interdependently related to each other so that it is generally not possible to separate the causes and effects in a rigorous way.[1] Empirical evidence in the Zimbabwean colonial experience provides five interlocking components that interact to create falling incomes in the African sector, namely:

1 Land alienation policies and discrimination in the provision of infrastructure and services.
2 Population pressure in the African peasant areas and land degradation mainly due to soil erosion.
3 Unlimited supplies of labour.

4 Discrimination and low wages.
5 Falling per capita incomes.

These relations can be explained in the first place by the influence of relative factor prices that led to different factor price ratios that were used by the African and European farmers. In the long run, due to the prevailing set of relative factor prices, new, superior, and capital-using technologies were accepted by the white farmers since it was cheaper for them to use more capital than labour. On the other hand, a relatively higher price of capital in relation to labour made it expensive for Africans to accept new technologies.

The different responses to new technologies, however, were not only factors behind the income gap between Europeans and Africans. One of the basic conclusions we arrive at in this book, is that dualism the Rhodesian economy was historically achieved through land alienation policies and in particular the conditions reigning in the land market. The existence of dualism in the land tenure system thus formed the basis for economic dualism in the rest of the economy. Through land alienation, the African population was forced to grow in an artificially limited land area (the African reserves). Increased population pressure of both humans and livestock in the African rural areas was created as a result of a policy where the whites gradually took over African lands and drastically changed the production conditions in the original 'traditional' economy to the point where it is almost appropriate to speak of destruction.

The increased man–land ratio in African areas led to an environmental land degradation and soil erosion. As the man–land ratio increased, the per capita income on the African sector tended to fall. This sequence of events made it possible to lower wages and call forth an 'unlimited' supply of African labour which by means of discriminatory legislation was confined to unskilled jobs in the 'modern' sector. In the Marxian tradition, the 'unlimited' labour phenomenon leads to the swelling of labour influx into the urban areas thereby increasing the enlargement of labour reserves. This subsequently contributed to the worsening of the proletariat which was the country's process of primitive accumulation. In the case under review, growth inflows of capital gave rise to permanent impoverishment of the local agrarian peasantry. This was in many ways the prevailing capitalism growth as we know it today – globalisation and accumulation through encroachment of the poor peasantry space.

Thus, the most important of the five factors listed above appear to be the land alienation policies, which triggered off a dualism that had direct consequences for income distribution in the traditional agricultural sector as well as for incomes earned by African workers in the modern sector. The stagnation conditions in the African rural areas and 'discriminatory' dualism in the labour market combined to lower the wage level of the ever increasing numbers of job seekers in the modern sector. As a result, African incomes and working conditions in both the traditional and the modern sector of the Rhodesian economy progressively became grossly inadequate.

In concluding this section, consideration is given to a possible transformation of the dualistic economic structure. This discussion begins with some broad policy objectives and then goes on to review policy recommendations that have emerged from previous studies. Finally, we discuss the direction of desirable structural changes in both the agricultural and modern sectors.

Technological change

Differences in factor price ratios

The evidence presented in Chapters 3 to 5 shows that the Europeans and Africans did not face the same relative factor prices. The question is how these different groups of farmers responded to the prevailing relative prices operating in the sector. We shall now attempt to provide an answer to this question.

The relative factor prices prevailing in the economic systems are translated into economic forces as the different producers explicitly or implicitly use them in reaching their decisions. In other words, the consequences of the dualistic pattern of relative factor prices were translated into a set of differing relative factor proportions, i.e. into differences in the techniques of production employed by the African peasants on one hand and European farmers on the other.

As established in the foregoing chapters, Europeans and Africans faced entirely different sets of factor prices, in terms of access to land, credit and produce markets. Due to land concentration among the white farmers, the implicit rent or shadow price per hectare was lower for the white farmers than for the African peasant farmer. Quantitative rationing along racial lines excluded many Africans from access to credit. In terms of implicit relative factor prices, the price of capital became infinitely (or at least prohibitively) higher for the majority of Africans.

Second, the wage rates for African workers in the European agricultural sector, though at penurious levels, were still somewhat higher than the wage obtained by African workers in the African farming sector. In the majority of cases, African farmers used family labour, but those who did hire labour actually paid a lower wage than that paid by white farmers.[2] Furthermore, due to the poorer economic conditions among African farmers (both APAs and TTLs), the imputed price of family labour in the African areas was lower than the wage received in the European areas.

It then follows that for the European farmers, land and capital were cheap in terms of labour, while for the African farmers the opposite was true. Consequently, the former chose techniques of production which required more land and capital per unit of labour. As a result, European farms were more land and capital intensive than the African farms. In this sense, the relative factor prices have encouraged labour intensive forms of production in the TTLs and land and capital intensive techniques on the large-scale European farms.[3] These inequalities and ratios can be summarised in the form of the following symbols:

1 $r_E < r_A$
2 $i_E < i_A$
3 $w_E > w_A$
4 $\left(\frac{T}{L}\right)E > \left(\frac{T}{L}\right)A$
5 $\left(\frac{K}{L}\right)E > \left(\frac{K}{L}\right)A$

where r = rental rate of land or shadow price, i = interest rate, w = wage rate, E = European farms, A = African farms, T = land or terrain, L = labour, K = capital.

These markedly different factor proportions of the two groups of farmers in a dual agricultural economy stem directly from the prevailing set of relative factor prices. In addition, the system creates allocative inefficiency, since the conditions for free competition are violated when all producers do not face the same relative factor prices. The big farmers in the European sector tend to adopt techniques of production that are characterised by excessively high land–labour ratios.[4] On the contrary, the small peasant farmer will combine less than the socially optimal amount of land and capital with his labour. Thus as a result of the effects of dualism on factor price ratios, there were pronounced differences in the techniques employed and, even more important, in the response to technical change between the European and African farmers in Rhodesia.

The influence of relative factor prices on technological change

Economic models have in one way or another incorporated technical progress as one of the main ingredients of the growth process. But most of these models have taken technical progress as given, and have failed to look into the causes and factors that inhibit technical progress in many societies. As Mats Lundahl emphasised:

> If we are to understand why certain economies develop and others do not, the presence or absence of technical progress cannot be taken for granted. Some kind of systematic treatment of the reasons behind either state must be provided as well.[5]

In this section an analysis will be made of the reasons behind the different responses to technical change in the Rhodesian economy. Our analysis will be based on the evidence gathered in Chapters 3 to 6 and will show that imperfections in the land and other factor markets, as well as outright discrimination, had the effect of increasing the likelihood that if an innovation did occur, it would be the large white farmers who adopted it. The African peasants could not adopt the new innovations because of the problems connected with differing relative factor prices. The influence of the relative factor prices, indivisibilities and risk aversion hampered the adoption of new techniques, inputs or crops in the African peasant sector, thus leading to different responses (along racial lines) to technological change.

At the beginning of colonisation there were no technological differences between the European and African farmers, as Giovanni Arrighi observed:

> Prior to 1903–1904, those Europeans who were interested in agriculture were either part-time farmers devoting themselves to more profitable activities or, as it was the case with many Afrikaaners who had trekked to Rhodesia, they were subsistence cultivators indistinguishable (by style of life, technique of production, crops cultivated) from the African peasantry.[6]

In a latter article Arrighi has added: 'In the rare instances in which they (the whites) engaged in agricultural production, they used techniques with lower yields per acre than those used by the Africans'.[7] However, in the long run there was an adoption of new capital-using technologies by European farmers since it was relatively cheaper for them to use more capital than labour. On the other hand, the high relative price of capital for Africans made it more expensive for the latter to adopt new technology.

The prevailing relative prices of the factors of production, especially that of labour and capital, are an important determinant of whether a (given) technology will be adopted or not. The influence of technological changes has been emphasised by Keith Griffin in his study of the Green Revolution.[8] Griffin's argument can be summarised with aid of production isoquants and isocost lines (relative factor prices) represented in Figure 8.1. The main point in Griffin's argument is that new technology is potentially useful if it displaces all or part of the original isoquant towards the origin.[9] It is possible to determine the technique that will be adopted and, if so, by whom. On the vertical axis we measure the employment of capital (K), and on the horizontal axis we have the employment of labour (L).

Let us assume that the relative prices of labour and capital are represented by the price lines P_0P_0 and P_1P_1 (capital relatively cheap), and P_2P_2 and P_3P_3 (labour relatively cheap)[10] and that the technology at the disposal of Africans and Europeans is indicated by the isoquant TT. In this situation the European will choose the combination of labour and capital indicated by point A, the point at which the isoquant TT is tangential to the price line P_0P_0. The Africans will select the combination of labour and capital given by the point B, also a point of tangency, but between isoquant TT and price

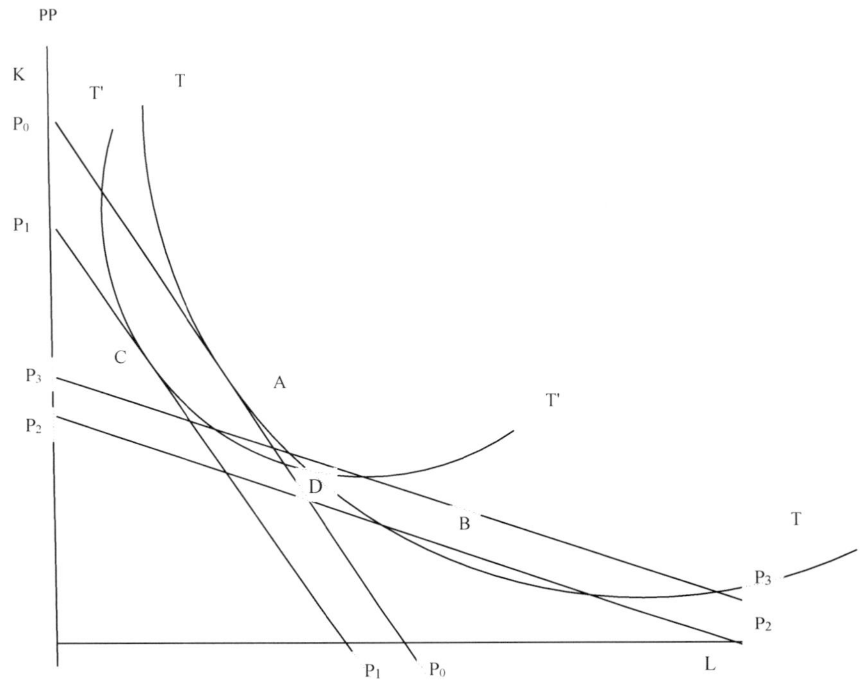

Figure 8.1 Production isoquants and isocost lines (relative factor prices).
Source: Ndlela, 1981:185.

line P_2P_2. Assume next, that a new, capital-using technology, indicated by isoquant T'T' (where T'T' indicates the same amount of output TT) is introduced in the economy. By whom will it be adopted?

It is clear from the diagram that given the different relative factor prices which confront the Europeans and Africans respectively, the new technology will be adopted only by the Europeans (at point C).[11] The cost of capital and other material inputs will be lower for the European farmer and hence he has an incentive to innovate. The Africans can choose between their 'original' technology at point B and the new technology at point D, but they will not be able to innovate because the movement from B to D is associated with a rise of total costs since the isocost line P_3P_3 lies further from the origin than P_2P_2. Given the respective relative factor prices, producing at point D is a more expensive option than remaining at point B.

In contrast with the Africans (who are left on the old isocost line), the Europeans were, therefore, able to produce more cheaply than before (i.e. on a new isocost line closer to the origin). The resultant expansion of European agriculture was thereby accompanied by a corresponding decline in the African share of total output.

Thus, the lower the relative cost of capital inputs, the more widespread will be the adoption of an innovation, i.e. the more readily will farmers invest in capital which embodies an improved technology.[12] A low level of interest rates, a low price of capital or high wages will tend to induce farmers to abandon their old techniques in preference to new ones which are more intensive in their use of capital inputs.[13] On the other hand, when the cost of capital is high in relation to the cost of labour, new innovations will not be widely used and the sector will remain 'traditional', in the sense of retaining the old technology. This is because the introduction of an innovation requires expenditure on fixed and working capital and this type of expenditure will not occur when capital inputs are expensive in terms of labour.

In the Rhodesian case, as was seen in the empirical chapters, the price of capital in terms of labour was high. Economic dualism in land tenure and in the capital and produce market had a tendency to create surplus labour and make this factor relatively cheap. In such circumstances, even if technical change is biased in a capital-using direction neither the large white farmers nor the small peasants will have a high propensity for innovation. This is because the market structure in the rural areas has produced a low wage economy. However, as shown by the differing factor price ratios above, the white farmers who were invariably facing a lower relative price of capital than the majority of the African farmers were expected to be more 'progressive' because their real costs of innovation were lower.

The ability of white farmers to acquire both land and capital on easier terms than their African counterparts meant that the former were in a better position to combine resources in order to meet the changing economic conditions than the latter. This can be illustrated by the case of tobacco and maize:

> Between 1951 and 1957 acreage under tobacco cultivation in the six major tobacco producing areas declined by 10 per cent but yield per acre rose by 60 per cent; in the major corn-producing areas acreage under cultivation expanded by 17 per cent and average yields rose by more than 40 per cent. These high yields through intensification of land use involved heavier expenditure in yield increasing products, principally fertilizer, and improved techniques of production.... Technologies of production in the African areas are as different from those in the European areas as day is from night. The family is the labour unit.[14]

The lack of property rights in the Tribal Trust Lands were also important in discouraging investment, a situation that has not been resolved in Zimbabwe's post-independence period. The adoption of a specific innovation such as fertiliser applications, or the use of hybrid selected seeds, or overall modernity may be associated with a variety of particular characteristics of farmers, such as educational attainment, land ownership patterns and the like. After a survey of African evidence, Gerald K. Helleiner observes that the following characteristics are positively related to the adoption of innovations:

> farm size, wealth, tenure status, extension contact, participation in the local organisation, use of communications media, degree of full time commitment to farming, commercial expenditure and modernity. Among the factors tested but found to be unrelated to adoption were age, educational attainment, religion, sex, work or farming experience.[15]

As the analysis above shows, the reason for a differential in the propensity for innovation along racial lines in the Rhodesian case lies first and foremost in the relative factor prices of labour and capital faced by the different groups of farmers. However, we have also seen that under the discriminatory price policies of Marketing Boards, African producers were not encouraged to improve their crops or cattle stock since the price mechanism invariably placed the latter's produce at the same (lower) level.

Indivisibilities, complementarities and risks

The complexity of the problem of the factors inhibiting innovation may also be elucidated further by the notion of indivisibility, complementarity and ability to take risk. Agricultural innovations entail important indivisibilities both in research and in actual implementation:

> the rapid shifts in technique that are now occurring in some countries result from work in research laboratories and experiment stations, usually maintained by government, whose results are then disseminated among farmers through field agents. Further, technical change is usually embodied in new or improved inputs of water, fertiliser, seed, pesticides and so on.
>
> ... Even pure subsistence farmers can benefit from improved supplies water control system, and research and international facilities.[16]

The problem of indivisibilities in the context of agricultural innovation largely stem from the fact that the individual producer unit is often too small to support an inventive activity. As in other ancillary activities – provision of processing facilities, transport networks and sources of finance – economies of scale in producing inventions and given agricultural research all fall under the properties of public goods. The optimal scale of an ancillary activity like carrying out agricultural research, experimentation and dissemination is usually so large that for the most part it is a government responsibility. The attitude of the government in its recognition of this need and its willingness to allocate resources to it, provides an important influence for productivity trends in the agricultural sector. Small-scale production units such as family farm units can attain optimal efficiency only when embedded in a framework of supporting activities organised on a much larger scale. But as we have seen, this was not the case in the Zimbabwean colonial system where a dualistic pattern that emanated from the government policies hampered the introduction of new technologies, i.e. the indivisibilities were not reduced.

In an article entitled 'Technology and the Economic Development of African Agriculture in Rhodesia', J.P. Danckwerts does not mention the historic causes hampering the acceptance of technology by African farmers, but instead states that the rate of technological development is dependent on two specific social factors, i.e. on the willingness and ability of the population to sustain technological advance.[17] The social factors emphasised include 'the need to set aside income to provide increasing quantities of capital; the necessity for more regular and accurate application of work; the need for longer periods of learning to equip workers for increasingly complex duties'.[18]

Since Danckwerts does not explain why the aforementioned factors came about, his approach, as we have seen, does not provide more than a limited explanation. However, he points to an important obstacle to innovation when he stresses indivisibilities.

> The differences between the technological sophistication of the appliances used in the traditional African and modern, or European agricultural sector in Rhodesia are readily apparent. The latter are able to use a wide range of some of the most modern machinery in the world and are to able achieve high levels of productivity through the application of mechanical power to a variety of extremely complex machinery.... Traditional agriculture is largely confined to the use of a limited range of simple tools and machines dependent on human or animal power and limitations of stamina which this implies.... The small size of production units militates against the private ownership of the larger units of capital which frequently offer the greatest economies.[19]

The indivisibilities with regard to farm size and use of machinery and other permanent forms of investment were a consequence of economic dualism. With regard to the APAs, Roger Riddell noted:

> The units are too small to be capitalised efficiently – the majority are too small to warrant the purchase of a tractor. This is not altogether surprising considering that the majority of farms were located without a view to creating viable economic units.[20]

The success of an irrigation scheme (an indivisibility) e.g. depends on the purchase of complementary agricultural inputs (e.g. seed), which in turn requires an efficient credit system as well as working a delivery system to facilitate the provision of inputs.[21] Thus, given the complementarity of factors necessary for the innovative behaviour largely due to the presence of indivisibilities, any solution of the dualistic problem in Zimbabwe will have to tackle these problems as well.

At this point, we may also relate the analysis to the discussion of the ability to take risk or uncertainty. John Weeks has analysed this in terms of Lipton's concept of 'surviving algorithm' to show that in the market organisation of economic society there is an inherent tendency for the benefits from economic development to be distributed systematically in favour of the richer groups in the society.[22] Weeks has summarised the conditions for the survival algorithm as followed: (a) under conditions of imperfect knowledge (uncertainty) there is no single marginal physical product for each factor, but there is a large probability range within which the actual marginal physical productivity for any factor will be located in a given period; (b) in these circumstances profit maximisation does not necessarily involve a unique marginal value product to the price of each factor (which also may vary), but rather equates the marginal expected value product to the expected price of each factor; (c) this involves profit maximisation over a period of several growing seasons, some of which may be prosperous, others of which may not be so; and (d) for most cultivators the failure of an innovation may be quite disastrous – starvation or loss of land – because they lack accumulated wealth to cushion the impact of a bad crop year. That is, risk aversion is caused by the state of poverty and the 'risk premium is an increasing function of risk and decreasing functions of assets'.[23]

Frequently, risk-taking will be avoided by the poor groups that apply a survival algorithm instead of profit maximisation. Because of the heavy negative weight given in their objective functions to the losses they might incur if a new technique is tried, the poor farmers will refrain from the new invention, and hence lose the gains from innovative behaviour. Thus, despite the fact that economic profitability (defined to include the risk factor) is a necessary element in smallholder adoption of innovation, farmers with large asset holding and annual incomes are in a better position to bear risk than small farmers. For instance, new high-yield seed varieties involve greater risk of failure through inadequate water supply, destruction by local pests and diseases, i.e. a sort of dangers against which traditional seed varieties have become immunised over many generations. Yet it is in the latter area where the benefits of innovative behaviour are mostly likely to be found.

In the Rhodesian colonial experience, poverty among the African peasants and its consequences with regards to low risk bearing ability, presumably hampered the adoption of new innovations by the African peasants. For example, in a document circulated by the directors of African Farming Development Company (after it ceased its operations), it was stated that when farmers were hit by a drought in one year, 'unfortunately the arrangements for drought relief were not extended to Tribal Trust Lands (TTL) cash farmers and heavy backlogs of indebtedness were clocked up by most of the farmers in the scheme'.[24] Given the poor land resources in the African areas and the lack of other factor inputs, African farmers were more likely to be risk averse than the European farmers. In fact, only a few APA farmers could afford a loan programme 'covering all elements of "input" necessary to successful "output" – ploughing, seed, fertiliser, pesticides, picking and transport to market'.[25] In this way the problem of risk aversion is a consequence of dualism since it is directly connected with low production in the African areas hence the elimination of economic dualism will have to take into account the problems of indivisibility, complementarity and risks affecting the African agricultural sector.

Population pressure in the African rural areas

The differential response to technological change was an important factor behind the widening gap between the European and African per capita incomes. Of equal importance, however, was the cumulative tendency for output per worker to fall in the African areas due to the increase in the man-land ratio. In the long-run historical perspective, one of the most profound effects of dualism in the Rhodesian African agriculture was the development of population pressure on the designated African areas. The typical Rhodesian agrarian entry became the antithesis of inclusive growth. Instead of incorporating the African peasantry, it displaced it by de-linking it from the original entry of the modern domestic market economy and eventually from into the evolving regional and international markets, i.e. globalisation.

The interrelationship between population growth and agricultural change has often been analysed with the aid of the concepts of 'optimum population density'. This concept has attracted many writers, though it has proved difficult to define and measure.[26] The optimum population has been defined as that population at which with given natural and capital resources and a given technology, output per capita is maximised. The concept may be useful in the following way: suppose that a given agricultural community has a finite amount of land and a given range of techniques and that output per capita is at a maximum. As the labour force increases over time, the marginal and average products will tend to fall in the absence of increased inputs of other factors.[27] However, a community may be expected to make an effort to maintain the equilibrium position. But suppose the labour supply increases beyond the optimum. Although total output may continue to rise, the average output per capita declines as does the marginal productivity.[28] At this point in time, the community is overpopulated in terms of optimum population theory.[29]

D.B. Grigg argued that after the population pressure rises above the optimum, conditions are created that begin to force the farming community to change either its technology, its resources, or its numbers, so that it returns towards the optimum density or establishes a new optimum.[30]

However, regarding the application of the concept of optimum density to peasant communities, it should be taken into consideration that these societies are sensitive to the decline in the marginal productivity than commercialised societies. That is, as long as the additional labourers can produce food for their needs plus a small surplus for sale, they will go on increasing their labour inputs regardless of whether marginal productivity is declining or not.[31] They may begin to alter their condition when pronounced physical symptoms of overpopulation begin to appear.

The relevance of the concept of population pressure in a limited land area may be particularly illuminating in the case of Rhodesia. The African population was forced to grow in an artificially limited land area as a result of economic dualism in the land tenure system. Thus, already by the 1930s, signs of overcrowding and overstocking had become increasingly apparent in many African rural areas (Cf. Chapter 3). From the 1940s up to the 1970s, the problem of population pressure of both humans and livestock intensified in the African rural areas. This artificial creation of population pressure on the African land areas was in sharp contrast to the scanty population densities in the white rural areas. As Roger Riddell pointed out, that vast amounts of commercial farm land were not cultivated, i.e. as much as 60 per cent or even more of the country's best land owned by the whites was left unused.[32] On the other hand, overutilisation of land occupied by Africans led to cumulative land degradation and soil erosion. This follows from the condition that land was a scarce factor relative to labour and that a decumulation of land resources results from artificial population pressure and labour force confined in the limited land area.

With time the soil quality deteriorated to such an extent that additional inputs of labour no longer added much to output. There was also a change in the socio-economic structure affected by the creation of an unlimited supply of labour. As the African population increased and the land available diminished, people in the long run were forced to leave the Tribal Trust Lands and migrate into the modern sector – towns, and mining settlements.

Soil erosion

Following the massive land alienations, particularly after the Land Apportionment Act of 1930 (Cf. Chapter 3), the signs of excessive population pressure of both humans and livestock became pronounced. This led to a deterioration of land resources, which in turn resulted in soil erosion particularly visible already in the early thirties as Arrighi noted:

> Already the first signs of possible deterioration of the land in the native areas from cumulative evils in the shape of soil erosion, the drying up of springs, the extirpation of the valuable pasture grasses through overstocking, and the exhaustion of fertility were discernible in some of our

> more congested native reserves, and it is plain that we must take more positive control, if we are to see an increase, and not reduction in the life supporting capacity of our native areas. The cumulative evils of population pressure on the land soon materialized: in an attempt to maintain output, land began to be brought back into cultivation before the soil had a chance to regenerate fully and grazing areas were destroyed as the number of livestock increased.[33]

This process continued and accelerated throughout the thirties, so that by 1943, 63 per cent of reserves were classified as 'overpopulated' by the Department of Native Agriculture, and 50 per cent were carrying excessive cattle stock.[34] The government made several attempts to stop the spread of soil erosion but without much success. One of the aims of the Natural Resources Board in 1941 was to combat the spread of erosion. The Native Husbandry Act (1951) sought to regulate the construction of conservation works, such as contour ridges as well as regulate African farming in relation to soil conservation methods of cultivation and grazing. The Land Husbandry Act also provided for a centralised village scheme where arable lands were neatly laid out, separated from grazing land and protected against storm damage and erosion. However, the implementation of this Act met with resistance from the African peasant farmers. The latter criticised the Act on the grounds that it required continuous cultivation of the already over-used poor soils. Reallocation of land meant that some good farmers had to leave their well-tended fields and start on new ground. In most African reserves the average arable acreage per family was six to eight acres (2.4 to 3.2 hectares), which given the soil exhaustion, lack of equipment and other material inputs and knowledge, was usually inadequate for African rural households.[35]

With further land alienations during the 1950s and 1960s, population pressure increased in the African reserves. Thus, with a higher man–land ratio, there was also greater pressure on the soil, which resulted in more soil erosion, which was presumably self-generating as well. The overstocking of grazing areas got worse in the 1960s and 1970s, and this becomes even more serious if account is taken of the fact that 90 per cent of the TTLs lie in the more arid Natural Regions III–IV.[36] Thus by 1965, the grazing areas were classified as follows: 13 per cent as absolutely bare, 36 per cent as heavily overgrazed, 15 per cent as being in a more moderate condition and 36 per cent as being good. But the latter categories include stretches of land infested by tsetse fly, which could not be grazed at all. A survey carried out by the Department of Conservation and Extension showed that in 1976–1977 the cropping potential of 12 per cent of the TTLs had already declined and further 41 per cent was in imminent danger of deterioration. About half the TTLs had their fertility seriously impaired.[37] Thus, in 1976 the Natural Resource Board declared that progressively serious desiccating effects, due to overgrazing had appeared,[38] and that grazing schemes aimed at soil conservation and upgrading of pasture lands, had generally failed. E.G. Cross has summarised the state of the TTLs in the following statement:

> Tribal Trust Land provides homes for nearly 60% of our population, and a social security system for over 90%. Over the past 15 years it has absorbed 64% of the population growth. But the limit has been reached. It can no longer support its expanding population, and food has to be imported.... The Tribal areas are overgrazed, subject to excessive population pressure and are close to ecological collapse in many districts.[39]

Thus due to overgrazed and overcrowded lands in the communal areas, the changeover from the shifting system to permanent cultivation could not provide a solution. This situation forced farmers to adopt some other means of maintaining soil fertility, but such changes have by no means always taken place.[40] In this connection, P.M. Grant has argued that if manure was applied together with nitrogen fertiliser in the Rhodesian peasant farming this would result 'in high yields in the first season and for many years of continuing cropping'.[41] However, as shown in Chapter 5, it was virtually impossible for the majority of the African farmers to either have enough savings or have credit facilities in order to purchase fertilisers. The consequences were, therefore, further generation of soil depletion leading to more soil erosion.

Unlimited supply of labour

A further consequence of land alienation was that it created surplus labour in the sense that the majority of the working population were limited to tiny holdings in the traditional agricultural sector. Beyond the point at which family labour time could not be fully utilised in the family farm, off farm sale of labour became necessary. Because of the decline in per capita income in the traditional sector, unskilled labour was forced out of that sector in order to seek alternative incomes in the modern sector.

As further land alienations took place, a successive decumulation of land resources ensued and once more traditional labour was pushed into the modern sector, shifting the supply curve of labour to the right (Cf. Chapter 6). In the long run, the growth of African population and shortage of land forced people to leave the reserves to seek employment in the modern sector. However, the actual number of persons living in the traditional sector did not decrease since the dependents of migrant labour working in the modern sector remained in the traditional sector. In fact, the number of persons in the rural African sector has increased during the last two decades.[42]

The unlimited supply of labour was also reinforced by the development in the produce market, where as shown in Chapter 4, a given labour effort of African participation in the produce market gave in the long run a lower financial return than it had done earlier. This lowered the per capita incomes in the traditional economy and made the alternative of wage employment more attractive than participation in the produce market. But the concrete case of unlimited supply of labour is first and foremost a consequence of land alienation process. The latter did not only have the effect of forcing people out of the traditional sector. As demonstrated in Chapter 6, it was also essential for establishing the uneven power relations in the market for unskilled labour. The creation of discriminatory laws and a colour bar in the market for unskilled labour might perhaps have taken place even without land alienations, but they would not have been effective, for Africans would have had the alternative of falling back on a traditional economy that allowed for much higher standard of living than has actually been the case.

Incomes

The influence of dual relative factor prices in the agricultural sector and the 'discriminatory' dualism in the labour market may be particularly useful in explaining the fall in agricultural incomes as well as the incomes earned in the modern sector. The following concepts of income may also be examined in relation to the consequences of dualism in the Rhodesian case: distribution of personal income by size between the different racial groups and between the modern and traditional sectors, distribution of income between different regions of the country, distribution of income between the factors of production, and the distribution between urban and rural dwellers.[43] In this section the discussion is limited to an examination of the consequences of dualism in so far as they affect the distribution of incomes per capita between the European and African rural areas, the wage and salary differentials in the modern sector and the ensuing differentials in the standards of living. The ultimate consequences of dualism in the Rhodesian case appear to be the falling per capita incomes for Africans in the rural areas, the increasing income differential between Europeans and Africans and the growing insufficiency of incomes for Africans in both urban and rural areas.

Output shares in agriculture

In the long-run perspective, agricultural incomes of the Europeans and Africans were influenced by the differences in the relative factor prices prevailing in the agricultural sector. As a result, the European farmers were able to lower their production costs as compared to the Africans, thereby enabling the former to expand production while the latter saw their share of total output lowered. Second, the low output levels in African agriculture as compared to European output can be explained as a consequence of the increased man–land ratio and the concomitant erosion process. Thus, as early as by the 1930s, the agricultural economy of the Africans in Rhodesia had begun to show signs of ailment. This trend continued unabated in the post-1945 period:

> the marked European prosperity of the post-1945 period was achieved, as in South Africa, as a direct result of African poverty. In the years 1937–1958 the volume of European agricultural output increased by 259 per cent and its value, thanks almost entirely to tobacco, by over 1,000 per cent. African productivity meanwhile limped behind, barely able to provide for the rapidly growing population, which was eking out a living on increasingly overcrowded and deteriorating reserves.[44]

Judging from the empirical data of the 1960s and 1970s, a further widening of the differences in production performance between the Europeans and Africans took place.[45] The Africans' share of agricultural output remained at 20–30 per cent of the total. This is, to a large extent, a result of dualism.

Official government data show that the average African agricultural output as a proportion of total output was 24.5 per cent between 1954 and 1976.[46] (This was in spite of the fact that there were 700,000 African peasant farmers compared to 6,000 European farmers.) The European farming sector produced most of the commercial marketed output and employed most of the wage labour in agriculture. While the APAs supplied most of the output from the African areas marketed through official channels, production from the TTLs has been an unknown quantity. Until 1976 it was assumed to equal subsistence.

Total agricultural production increased at an average rate of 8.0 per cent per year between 1967 and 1976 (Cf. Table 8.1). During the same period, production on the European farms increased much faster than African production, 10.4 per cent per annum, as compared to 4.4 per cent for African agriculture. These differences in the production figures along racial lines reflect the consequences of dualism in the factor markets. As a result of the increased man–land ratio in the African areas and the consequential erosion process, a low level of production in the African areas became more pronounced. Weather variations between different regions, as seen in Chapter 3, provide another explanation for the fluctuations in agricultural output.

Table 8.1 African and European agriculture (including forestry): share in total output 1967–1976

	1967	*1968*	*1969*	*1970*	*1971*	*1972*	*1973*	*1974*	*1975*	*1976*
European	54.7	63.3	61.0	64.0	62.3	62.7	70.3	64.0	70.5	67.7
African	45.3	36.7	39.0	36.0	37.7	37.3	29.7	36.0	29.0	32.3
Total	100.0	100.0	100.0	100.0	100.0	100.0	100.0	100.0	100.0	100.0

Source: Rhodesia, National Accounts of Rhodesia, 1976.

Further declines in African sales, was due to crop failures which are in turn attributed to adverse weather conditions. The decline in African output was more severe during such periods, partly because of poor soils and because the African areas were located in the drier regions of the country. As a result of these declines in output African rural areas were increasingly forced to import food in the recent years.[47]

The rising share of European agricultural output during the colonial period can also be illustrated by the figures in Table 8.1, which include forestry.[48] Between 1967 and 1976, the contribution of agriculture to the GDP fluctuated between 15 and 20 per cent.[49] However, despite this more or less constant share of agriculture to GDP, the average share of white agricultural production (when including forestry) to total output increased from 60 per cent in 1967–1969 period to 67.4 per cent in the 1974–1976 period, while the share of production from African areas fell from 40 per cent to 32.6 per cent (Cf. Table 8.1). African agricultural output was marked by more severe annual fluctuations than European agriculture. This was partly due to distortions in the allocation of all those factors that might have compensated for verse weather conditions. But it is probable that the fundamental reasons for the low output levels in the African agriculture were the increased man–land ratio and accompanying soil erosion process in combination with stagnant technology.

Falling per capita incomes in the African rural areas

The evidence presented in Chapter 3 shows that at the beginning of the twentieth century, African peasants in Zimbabwe sold large amounts of surplus agricultural produce to the towns and mines. But the growth of the peasantry's surplus produce was soon to be curtailed. This took place through the alienation of African lands and consequent eviction of Africans from their previous good quality lands along the high-veld to the drier regions of the country, where in addition they were far away from the markets. Thus, most of the characteristics of structural underdevelopment of contemporary Zimbabwe, which created a pattern of regional and sectoral inequality, were achieved as a result of land concentration in the white hands and shortage of land in the African reserves.

The consequences were soon to be seen in differentials in the land distribution between European farms on the one hand and African farms on the other (Cf. Chapter 3). Our interest in the empirical data of the inequality in land distribution lies in the effects it had on falling incomes per capita in the African rural areas. Further evidence demonstrates that if access to resources, particularly land, is severely restricted and population pressure is rapid. The consequences may be an absolute decline in the per capita incomes of the rural areas.[50] Thus, African rural incomes were estimated to have fallen 'from £15 per capita in 1956, to £11 in 1968'.[51] Further, because of population pressure in the African rural areas, the natural growth in numbers could no longer be absorbed in the TTLs without a reduction in the per capita product. Thus, A.J.B. Hughes has observed:

> Many tribal areas are becoming relatively densely populated, and local tribal authorities are unable to give allocations of arable land of the sizes which are regarded customary. The reduction of the sizes of existing allocations has not been favoured, which has meant that many of those who are seeking land cannot be granted rights to use any for a considerable time, thus creating a landless class.[52]

The fall in the per capita product for Africans in the rural areas was a consequence of rural population pressure in these areas which led to low production. As shown in Chapter 4, this fall in the per capita incomes was not only limited to the TTLs, but it was also experienced in the labour market for unskilled jobs in the modern sector. This was partly caused by a shift to the right in the supply curve of unskilled labour which depressed the wage level in the modern sector. Another important cause of low African incomes deriving from work in the modern sector would appear to be the discriminatory controls that made it possible to fragment labour markets in such a way that bargaining power was systematically altered in favour of the employers and the white employees.

Wage and salary differentials

The purpose of this subsection is to show that wide differentials in wages and salaries were a consequence of the dual structure of the economy and the ensuing levels of economic activity between the African rural sector and the modern sector. As we have argued above, the low level of African wages in the modern sector was a consequence of land alienation policies which created an unlimited supply of labour. With further land annexations, a growing number of job seekers turned up in the modern sector, which further depressed the wages of the unskilled Africans.

Through discriminatory laws, the colour bar and other institutional controls in the labour market, the wage gap differentials widened in those sectors of the labour market where union formation and minimum wage laws were not applicable. Thus, the highest wage differentials were found in farm and domestic services, which had their employment conditions regulated by the Masters and Servants Act of 1901 (Cf. Chapter 3).

The ILO Report has a breakdown of employment of the two major racial groups in the modern sector.[53] From 1964–1975, there was an increase in the number of African workers although aggregate employment fell in the 1975–1976 period.[54] The number of 'industrial workers' (all workers outside agriculture and domestic service) also increased in the post UDI[55] period, probably as a result of the government's industrialisation policies, based on import substitution. This increase also persisted in spite of a substantial rise in the capital-labour ratio which occurred in the post war mining industry, as the role of small owner-workers declined in significance. However, as can be seen from the ILO Report, much of the expansion in the 1970–1975 period was in the agricultural and domestic service sectors. The latter sectors employed over 50 per cent of all employees in the modern sector, that is, three to four times as many as any other single sector. But as shown above, the agricultural and domestic service workers came under the Masters and Servants Act, and were subject to severe restrictions with regard to unionisation, collective bargaining and rights to organise.

According to the Economic Survey of Rhodesia, April, 1976, the European (including Asian and Coloured) – African wage ratio in the 1966–1977 period further widened.[56] A major feature emerging from the data is that African wages were substantially lower than those of Europeans, and this situation was fund in all sectors. The disparity in the average earnings between whites and blacks between 1966 and 1977 mounted on the average to 10 : 1 (with variations between sectors). This was more pronounced in those sectors of the labour market in which union formation and wage bargaining were not applicable, as in farm and domestic service sectors.

The trend during the 1960s and 1970s is more or less in line with the trend during the earlier decade. (Between 1955 and 1962, the European–African average earnings ratio in mining, manufacturing electricity and water supply was 11 : 1.[57] African wages were generally higher among 'industrial workers' than among the domestic service and agricultural labourers because of the fact that the latter were excluded by the Industrial Conciliation Act of 1959 and thus remained under the Masters and Servants Act of 1901, which did not recognise union formation and wage bargaining.

In terms of constant 1964 prices, the 'industrial workers' average earnings increased by 318 per cent over the 1946–1970 period.[58] By contrast, the share of the African wage bill accruing to the plantation and domestic service workers fell from 1946–1947 from more than 50 per cent to 28.5 per cent in 1970 and to 26.2 per cent in 1975. This fall persisted despite the expansion in the volume of employment, as the numbers of farm workers doubled from 142,000 to 290,000 from 1946 to 1970, thereafter rose to 353,700 in 1975. The wage bill of this group hardly increased more than six-fold in current prices up to 1970 and by another 51 per cent by 1975.[59]

As a result of the stagnant conditions in the African agricultural sector earned incomes were much lower than incomes obtained on the European commercial farms. Whereas the European farmers used hired labour and paid low wages in comparison to other sectors of the economy, the African farmers mostly used family labour. Further, their implicit wage presumably was lower than earnings of Africans in the European farms. Thus, in practice the lowest wage in commercial farming was to be found among APA farmers who often combined family labour with hired labour. This provides further confirmation to the argument that the cause of wage differentials was to be found in the dual structure of the economy which led to stagnation in the African rural sector as a whole.

As seen above, dualism began in the land tenure system and provided a rural economic structure that ensures a regular and an abundant supply of cheap labour for the labour market. The plight of the unskilled workers was made worse by the discriminatory dualism in the labour market that served to depress their wages even further. Thus, as a consequence, dualism has directly led to a widening of wage gap between white and black workers on one hand, and also between the various sectors of African labour (e.g. between farm labour and industrial workers) on the other.

The inadequacy of wages

As shown in the preceding analysis, an important consequence of the dualism in the land and labour markets is reflected in the vast gap between European and African earnings in the modern sector. This subsection attempts to relate African wages to the concept of the inadequacy of these wages in the modern sector, particularly in urban areas. Whether a wage is adequate or inadequate is a relative concept in that it assesses the relative sufficiency of the wage in relation to the minimum necessary costs of subsistence for the worker and his family and these costs vary in space and time. In more general terms, the concept draws a comparison between wages and the basic needs of the workers and their families. The effect of the wage level on the incidence of poverty may be explained by the notion of the Poverty Datum Line (PDL).

Basically the PDL enquires into what poverty is and how one can determine at what level minimum wages should be set. The PDL can be defined as an 'objectively' determined measure of the amount of income a family of a given size and composition requires, within a defined environment, in order to live at a given minimum level of health and decency.[60]

Before going any further, it ought to be mentioned that the issue of the PDL and its relationship to wages is a rather tricky question. The PDL is need-oriented, and income requirements are dependent on family size and composition, while wages are determined by the conditions in the labour market. But, as Verity Cubitt emphasises:

> the PDL can be a useful indicator for the employer against which to compare minimum wage levels … the PDL is exactly that, a *datum line* below which a family would be in poverty and above which they would not.[61]

However, the PDL should not be used as a basic 'minimum wage standard' but rather as an orientation point above which wages can be said to ensure a minimum level of health and decency. If, for example, a working man cannot reasonably expect to earn within a reasonable period of time a wage that would enable him to support a family of moderate size, the wage structure can be said to be inadequate.

Another conceptual framework dealing with the basic needs of the lowest income groups in underdeveloped countries is the Basic Needs Approach (BNA). The BNA was summarised in the resolution of the World Employment Conference held in 1976:

> Strategies and national development plans and policies should include explicitly as a priority objective the promotion of employment and the satisfaction of the basic needs of each country's population.... Basic needs include two elements. First, consumption: adequate food, shelter and clothing, as well as certain essential services provided by and for the community at large, such as drinking water, sanitation, public transport and health educational and cultural facilities.[62]

The BNA was, thus, mainly concerned with the provision of the minimum requirements for consumption and essential services by the community, as well as providing the opportunity for mass participation in the decision-making process and productive employment for the poor.[63] This framework is, however, considered inappropriate at this stage of our analysis since we are dealing only with the poverty that affects the wage earners and their families in the urban areas. Above all, the lowest paid segment of the labour force – the farm workers – are not included in this section. We shall return to the concept of the BNA when we consider a question of eliminating poverty which in itself a consequence of dualism. In this sub-section the analysis relies on data provided by studies on the PDL in the Rhodesian colonial setting.

The first of the PDL studies in Rhodesia was conducted by Edward Batson in 1944,[64] and this was followed by a similar study in 1958 by David Bettison.[65] These pioneering studies were followed by the later comprehensive studies conducted by Verity S. Cubitt and Roger Riddell in 1974, by Roger Riddell and Peter Harris in 1975 and by Cubitt in 1979.[66]

The studies by Cubitt and Riddell, and by Riddell and Harris were more elaborate and comprehensive than the previous similar studies.[67] The authors have included nine categories of the basic items in their assessment, namely: food, clothing, fuel and lighting, personal care and health, replacement of household goods, transport, accommodation, education and provision of post-employment consumption.[68] The final PDL was arrived at by converting the figures of each of the costs of the items into monthly costs. Strict precaution of the urban African consumer price index should be taken into account.

A conservative estimate of the average size of an African family in Zimbabwe in the pre-independence period was put at six persons.[69] With the extended family relationships, there is no doubt that many families were larger than this estimate. At the time, this average family size would require about $70 to $75 per month to satisfy their necessary minimum requirements. In June 1973, it was estimated that 89 per cent of the industrial workers received less than $70 in the form of cash wages.[70] However, this does not mean that all these families were living below the PDL. Some families were well below the average size, some received non cash benefits (free transport to work, free or subsidised housing), while other families would be engaged in some forms of illegal and informal trading. Even a casual observer could easily notice in the urban townships of Zimbabwe (including some Tribal Trust Lands) illegal or private taxi operators, curio makers, vegetable hawkers, backstreet bicycle repairers, watch repairers, sheeben queens (persons running illegal alcohol drinking establishments), shoe-shine boys, herbalists and a host of other operators, mostly small-scale commodity producers and people providing services, all of whom are ignored in the official definitions of economic activities.[71] One of the worst forms of the manifestations of this form of economic dualism is the lack of property rights protecting these peoples' assets. Regarding the lack of legal property mechanisms necessary to generate capital, Hernando De Soto remarked that 'The disastrous economic effects of this legal apartheid are most strikingly visible in the lack of formal property rights over real estate'.[72] However, with generous allowance of these factors, the fact still remains that over 70 per cent of workers in the modern sector lived under a regime of poverty with their incomes unable to take them above poverty-stricken state.

The inadequacy of wage structure was a deep seated consequence of economic dualism in Zimbabwe. As a result the wages of unskilled labour in the pre-independence period, it was most likely that this trend would continue to be the same, at least until changes in the dualistic structure of the economy begin to take place and become effective. As shown in the next chapter, dualism inherited from the Rhodesian colonial economy has continued to prevail long after the country's independence in 1980.

Conclusions

In conclusion, the chapter presents the consequences of economic dualism, focusing on the interdependent and interlocking relations emanating from dualism in the country's economy. The end result of these interlocking relations, starting from the discriminatory land tenure system, through economic dualism in virtually all the factor markets has been the lowering of standards of living or per capita incomes of the country's poor majority, while raising the living standards or per capita incomes of the colonial white minority. These relations emanated from the influence of relative factor prices which in turn led to different factor price ratios that were used by the African and European farmers. The result was the setting of superior, and capital-using technologies at the disposal of the white farmers since it was cheaper for them to use more capital than labour. On the other hand, relatively higher prices of capital in relation to labour prevented African peasant framers from adopting new technologies, thus leading to the latter adopting inferior and less productive technologies.

It was the consequences of the dualistic pattern of relative factor prices that were translated into differences in the techniques of production employed by the African peasants on one hand and European farmers on the other. The imperfections in the land and other factor markets, as well as outright discrimination, had the effect of increasing the likelihood that if an innovation did occur, it would be the large white farmers who adopted it. These disparities set the tone for the likely continued and unabated economic dualism in Zimbabwe's post independent period. The situation will only change with the obliteration of the dualistic structure of the economy.

Notes

1 See Myrdal, 1944:75–77, 207–209, 1957:12, 1968: Appendix II.
2 Weinrich, 1978:12 noted that employees in the APAs 'are exceedingly poorly paid. Many of them are kinsmen who are given little more than their upkeep; unrelated hired labourers get an average of some R$3 a month, often paid in kind than in cash'.
3 An analogous case was demonstrated by Griffin in the Colombian case, see Griffin 1974:98–100.
4 Cf. Griffin, 1972: Chapter 1, 1974:36–37.
5 Lundahl, 1979:558.
6 Arrighi, 1970:209.
7 Arrighi, 1979:172.
8 Griffin, 1972, 1974.
9 For a detailed exposition of the classification of technical progress, see Södersten, 1980: Chapter 11.
10 The relative factor prices ratios P0P0 and P1P1 are the same (P0P0 is parallel to P1P1), but these ratios differ from the factor price ratios P2P2 and P3P3 which are also the same.
11 For an analogous situation, see Griffin, 1974:47.
12 Ibid.:46.
13 Ibid.
14 Yudelman, 1964:87–88.
15 Helleiner, 1975:49.
16 Reynolds, 1977:58.
17 Danckwerts, 1970:18.
18 Ibid.:20.
19 Ibid.:23.
20 Riddell, 1978:52.
21 Lundahl, 1979:585.
22 Weeks, 1970; Lipton, 1968:2.
23 Weeks, 1970:29.
24 Hughes, 1974:287.
25 Ibid.
26 Grigg, 1976; Carr-Saunders, 1933; Sauvy, 1968; Peacock, 1955; UN, 1953.
27 Grigg, 1976:140.
28 Ibid., Reynolds, 1977:87–89.
29 Grigg, 1976, Ibid.; van de Walle, 1965.
30 Grigg, ibid.

31 Ibid.
32 Riddell, 1978:64–65.
33 Arrighi, 1970:217.
34 Ibid.
35 Because of the land shortage in the African reserves only those who were actually cultivating were allocated arable and grazing lands under the Native Land Husbandry Act, 1951.
36 See Rhodesia Herald, 1978.
37 Rhodesia Herald, 1978.
38 Ibid.:4 August 1979.
39 Cross, 1977:185.
40 Grigg, 1976:160; Boserup, 1965:41.
41 Grant, 1976:252.
42 Cross, 1977.
43 Paukert, 1973.
44 Palmer, 1977:244.
45 Ibid.
46 Rhodesia, 1977 (Monthly Digest of Statistics, April 1977: Table 7.1).
47 Nziramasanga, 1980:37.
48 While by law, forest land in both the African and European areas could be occupied and leased on terms and conditions prescribed by the appropriate Minister (Land Tenure Act.1969: Sections 12 and 26), in practice all forestry production was in the European area.
49 UN, 1980:30.
50 See also Griffin, 1976:4.
51 Loney, 1975:60.
52 Hughes, 1974:28.
53 ILO, 1978: Table 34.
54 This probably indicates the strain in the economy as a result of the war of liberation. All evidence suggests that from 1977 to the end of 1979 there was an even greater decline in employment figures.
55 UDI refers to the Unilateral Declaration of Independence by the Ian Smith, the Rhodesian Prime Minister on 11 November 1965, which on paper gave the Rhodesian colony its unilateral independence under white settler rule from the British Government.
56 These wage ratios are calculated from the average earnings (which include cash evaluation of all payments and kind – food, clothing, housing, etc.).
57 Southern Rhodesia – The Census of Production, 1962: Table 2.
58 ILO, 1978:95.
59 Thus, the change in the average earnings of farm and domestic service labour has in real terms been marginal and in the case of farm workers lower real wages registered in 1978 compared to 1963. Ibid.
60 Cubitt and Riddell, 1974:5; Riddell and Harris, 1975:12.
61 Cubitt, 1979:59.
62 ILO, 1977:2.
63 Ibid.
64 Batson, 1945.
65 Bettison, 1960.
66 Cubitt and Riddell, 1974; Riddell and Harris, 1975; Cubitt, 1979.
67 E.g. Bettison, 1960 reached his PDL assessment in relation to food, clothing, light, cleaning material, transportation, taxation and rent requirements. This enumeration made no allowances for examples in education, personal care and health and other non-biological basic needs of life.
68 Riddell and Harris, 1975:25, Table 5.

69 Harris, 1974: 27.
70 Ibid.
71 Cf. Davies, 1978. The ILO mission also found the informal sector quite substantial in Kenya, ILO, 1972.
72 De Soto, 2001:85.

References

Arrighi, Giovanni. 1970. 'Labour Supplies in Historical Perspective: A Study of the Prelotarianization of the African Peasantry in Rhodesia', *The Journal of Development Studies*, Vol. 6, No. 3:217.

Arrighi, Giovanni. 1979. 'Peripherilization of Southern Africa, I: Changes in Production Process', *Review*, Vol. 3, No. 2:161–191.

Batson, E. 1945. *The Poverty Datum Line in Salisbury*. Cape Town: University of Cape Town.

Bettison, D.G. 1960. 'The Poverty Datum Line in Central Africa', *Rhodes Livingstone Journal*, Vol. 27:21.

Boserup, E. 1965. *The Condition of Agricultural Growth: The Economies of Agrarian Change under Population Pressure*. London: George All & Unwin, Ltd.

Carr-Saunders, A. 1933. 'Some Aspects of the Population Problem', *Geography*, Vol. 18:536.

Cross, Eric G. 1977. 'The Tribal Trust Lands in Transition: The National Implications', *The Rhodesian Science News*, Vol. 2, No. 8:185.

Cubitt, V.S. 1979. *Supplement of the Urban Poverty Datum Line in Rhodesia: A Study of the Minimum Consumption Needs of Families (1974)*. Salisbury: University of Rhodesia.

Cubitt, V.S. and Riddell, R. 1974. *The Urban Poverty Datum Line in Rhodesia*. Salisbury: University of Rhodesia.

Danckwerts, J.P. 1970. 'Technology and the Economic Development of African Agriculture in Rhodesia', *Rhodesian Journal of Economics*, Vol. 4, No. 4:18.

Davies, Rob. 1978. *From Rhodesia to Zimbabwe No. 5: The Informal Sector. A Solution to Unemployment*. London: Catholic Commission Relief.

De Soto, Fernando. 2001. *The Mystery of Capital: Why Capitalism Triumphs in the West and Fails Everywhere Else*. London, Sydney and Auckland: Black Swan.

Grant, P.M. 1976. 'Peasant Farming on Fertile Lands', *The Rhodesian Science News*, Vol. 10, No. 10:252.

Griffin, Keith. 1972. *The Green Revolution: An Economic Analysis*. Geneva: United Nations Research Institute for Social Development.

Griffin, Keith. 1974. *The Political Economy of Agrarian Change*: An Essay on the Green Revolution. Cambridge, MA: Harvard University Press.

Griffin, Keith. 1976. *Land Concentration and Rural Poverty*. London: Macmillan.

Grigg, D.B. 1976. 'Population Pressure and Agricultural Change', *Progress in Geography*, Vol. 8:180.

Harris, Peter S. 1974. *Black Industrial Workers in Rhodesia: The General Problems of Low Pay*. Mambo Occasional Papers, Socio-Economic Series No. 2, Gwelo.

Helleiner, Gerald K. 1975. 'Smallholder Decision Making: Tropical African Evidence', in Lloyd G. Reynolds (ed.), 1977. *Agriculture in Development Theory*. New Haven and London: Yale University Press.

Hughes, A.J.B. 1974. *Development in Rhodesian Tribal Areas: An Overview*. Salisbury: Tribal Areas of Rhodesia Research Foundation.

ILO (International Labour Office). 1972. *Employment, Incomes and Equality: A Strategy for Increasing Productive Employment in Kenya*. Geneva: International Labour Organization.

ILO (International Labour Office). 1977. *Poverty and Landless in Rural Asia. Vol.1*. Geneva: International Labour Organization.

Lipton, Michael. 1968. 'The Theory of the Optimising Peasant', *The Journal of Development Studies*, Vol. 4:327–351.

Loney, Martin. 1975. *White Racism and Imperial Response*. Harmondsworth, Baltimore, Victoria, Ontario: Penguin African Library.

Lundahl, Mats 1979. *Peasants and Poverty. A Study of Haiti*. London: Groom Helm.

Lundahl, Mats and Ndlela, Daniel B. 1980. 'Land Alienation. Dualism, and Economic Discrimination: South Africa and Rhodesia', *Economy and History*, University of Lund, Sweden, Vol. 23, No. 2:110.

Moyana, H.V. 1975. *Land Apportionment in Rhodesia*. Unpublished PhD thesis, Columbia, New York.

Myrdal, Gunnar. 1944. *An American Dilemma, The Negro Problem and Modern Democracy*. New York: Patheon.

Myrdal, Gunnar. 1957. *Economic Theory and Underdeveloped Regions*. London: Patheon.

Myrdal, Gunnar. 1968. Asia Drama: *An Enquiry into the Poverty of Nations*. New York: Patheon.

Nziramasanga, M. 1980. 'The Agricultural Sector in Zimbabwe: Prospects for Change and Development', in UN – United Nations. Zimbabwe, Towards a New Order: An Economic and Social Survey. Working Papers, Vol. 1, United Nations, 1980.

Palmer, Robin. 1977. *Land and Racial Discrimination in Rhodesia*. London: Heinemann.

Paukert, Felix. 1973. 'Income Distribution and Different Levels of Development: A Survey of Evidence', *International Labour Review*, Vol. 108, Nos 2–3:97–125.

Peacock, A.T. 1955. 'Economic Theory and the Concept of Optimum Population', in J.B. Cragg and N.W. Pirie (eds), *The Numbers of Man and Animals*. Edinburgh: Oliver and Boyd Series.

Southern Rhodesia – The Census of Production.1962. Salisbury: Government Printers.

Reynolds, Lloyd G. 1977. *Image and Reality in Economic Development*. New York: Prentice-Hall, Inc.

Rhodesia. 1976. *National Accounts of Rhodesia*. Salisbury: Central Statistical Office (CSO).

Rhodesia. 1977. *Monthly Digest of Statistics*. Salisbury: Central Statistical Office.

Rhodesia Herald. 1978. Newspaper, Salisbury, 27 August 1978.

Riddell, Roger C. 1978. *The Land Problem in Rhodesia. Alternatives for the Future*. Mambo Occasional Papers, Socio – Economic Series No. 11, Gwelo.

Riddell, Roger C. and Harris, Peter S. 1975. *The Poverty Datum Line as a Wage Fixing Standard: An Application to Rhodesia*. Mambo Occasional Papers, Socio-Economic Series, No. 4, Gwelo: Mambo Press.

Sauvy, A. 1968. 'Population Theory', *Encyclopaedia of Social Sciences*, Vol. 12:8.

Södersten, B. 1980. *International Economics, Second Edition*. London and Basingstoke: Macmillan Press.

UN (United Nations). 1953. *The Determinants and Consequences of Population Trends*. New York: United Nations.

UN (United Nations). 1980. *Zimbabwe, Towards a New Order: Economic and Social Survey*. Working Papers, Vol. 1–2, United Nations.

Weeks, John. 1970. 'Distribution in Peasant Agriculture', *The Journal of Development Studies*, Vol. 7, No. 1 29.

Weinrich, A.K.H. 1978. Agricultural Reconstruction in Zimbabwe, (unpublished paper).

Yudelman, Montague. 1964. *Africans on the Land: Economic Problems of African Agricultural Development in Southern, Central and East Africa, with Special Reference to Southern Rhodesia*. Cambridge, MA: Harvard University Press.

9 Destroying dualism

Introduction

The chapter starts from the stark realisation that the inherited economic and social structure from colonial dualism has continued to exhibit its adverse consequences for the standards of living of the majority of the people long after the end of Rhodesian colonialism. With this insight, our basic proposition in the chapter is that transformation of the inherited colonial economic and social structure is the elimination of economic dualism. This implies merging of the different socio-economic sectors, the levelling of the factor markets and the integration of the two the visible economic sectors (the dynamic modern sector and the communal and informal sector) into the framework of a single organic and dynamic economic system. In the remaining sections of the chapter, we sketch out the different policy scenarios and end up with some policy recommendations on the elimination of dualism.

While the gaining of independence and the ending of colonial political ties became a fairly rapid affair, though after a protracted independence liberation struggle, the transformation of the distorted economic dualism structure inherited from the colonial system appears to be a more complicated and essentially a long-term task. The inherited economic and social structure has continued to exhibit its adverse consequences for the standards of living of the majority of the people, so that the economic potential of the country cannot be mobilised for the benefit of the entire population. The question that arises is what measures or development strategies should be employed to deal with economic and social problems that have resulted from several years of neglect and exploitation of the African peasantry and working people? The attempt in the remaining pages of the book is to sketch out possible patterns of future reforms designed to reduce and eventually destroy the dualism in the economic system. The measures used should be judged by their ability to restructure the dual agrarian sector and all other sectors of the economy in order to effect, in the shortest possible time, rapid economic and social changes leading to marked improvements in the condition of life of the hitherto deprived African majority.

In order to tackle the historical economic dualism of the Rhodesian colonial type one has to address the plight of the people who still remain and work on the colonially designated land areas. As demonstrated in the chapters above, Zimbabwe along with most of African countries still has the majority of its people coming under the nomenclature of peasants, that is people with certain rights on the land and working on the land but not part of the unbounded opportunity-seeking modern market economy. During the colonial era, African rural peasants were parcelled out of their traditionally preferred lands to the designated 'native reserves', latter to become Tribal Trust Lands (TTLs).

In the case of Zimbabwe, after independence from the colonial era, African designated peasant lands have remained as they were during the colonial period, only changing the name to 'communal lands'. What is today identified as the 'traditional' sector in the contemporary economy was created as result of a policy where the whites gradually took over African lands. In essence, the colonial shaped and crafted peasant farming sector has continued to derive the right of income from working on the ever crowded agricultural lands, with many of them increasingly becoming landless labourers. Whether led by the post independent political elite or other social and economic classes including monopoly capitalism, the post-independence struggles of land still hover around the agrarian question to liberate the peasantry from the stranglehold of the interests of the narrow capitalist class and the 'new post-independence' bourgeoisie.

If we postulate from the viewpoint of the global trajectories of accumulation, the pre-capitalist African peasant economy remains under the whims of the world capitalist system as the integral nature of capitalist accumulation. In this vein, there is absolutely no excuse for the post-colonial state to dismally fail to curtail this form of dualism-induced primitive accumulation. The latter has continued to be sustained by the post-colonial governments in cohorts with monopoly capitalist classes. The African peasants have continued to give up ground rent[1] (paying rents for lands alienated from them), their labour and hence leaving the capitalist squeezing into the consumption basket of the poor peasant farmers.

There may be solutions that simply gloss over the actual transformation of the dualistic structure of the economy, i.e. solutions which merely conceive of marginal rather than structural changes that are meant to alter the fundamental character of the country's economy. Under these types of solutions, the majority of the poor African peasants will remain more or less at their present living conditions, being largely untouched by modern sector development. Before going on to discuss the alternative policy proposals of the transformation of the dualistic social and economic structure, I propose to look at some concrete tasks, raised by this transformation process.

From the point of view of development, meaningful transformation involves the integration of the traditional with the modern sector, which cannot be achieved without structural changes in both the former and the latter. Because of the market imperfections and distortions existing in the economy, structural changes cannot be expected to take place within the existing market structure and its mechanisms. Consequently, purposeful development policy actions can be taken only by a strong liberal state intervention. This is because the redistribution of lands and allocation of investments cannot be left to the spontaneous activity of the market mechanism. This will require a centrally coordinated development programme and/or government intervention to remove the existing market imperfections which were originally imposed and crafted by the colonial state.

In a long-term development strategy, events cannot be merely left to the unplanned allocation among sectors on the basis of an assessment of individual profitability but it must also include the explicit elimination of economic dualism. In fact, the selection of development projects and the assessment of their profitability and efficiency must also take into account this requirement. As the UN Report on the eve of Zimbabwe's independence correctly emphasised:

> Future development proposals by the government of an independent Zimbabwe must go beyond mere statements of objectives. They must make provisions for structural changes and fundamental policy reforms.[2]

Some policy recommendations from the colonial era

Many of the policy proposals for future development that were made during the colonial period, failed to deal with the crucial problem of structural reforms. The objectives of these proposals were limited to such improvements in African conditions that could be accommodated within the prevailing colonial economic dualism structure. The proposals were based on 'the prevailing philosophy which attempted to attribute African poverty to African values and attitudes rather than to the economic and social restrictions imposed on the African farmers'.[3] The theoretical justification of African poverty is thus exemplified in a document prepared for the Rhodesian government in 1967:

> Economic development is fundamentally a function of the religious, social and cultural values of a society and the psychological traits of its members, which together constitute a way of life. A study of the Bantu people of Africa reveals the absence at this stage of most of those elements which are conducive to economic development as an endogenous process.
>
> ... The resultant low income level may not be an undesired situation, in the sense that it constitutes equilibrium between marginal disutility of effort and marginal utility of income.[4]

The above justification is typically of or akin to the original notion of satisficing peasant who does not respond to economic incentives, explained in detail in Chapter 4. Thus, having neglected the existing dualistic structure in the land tenure and the discriminatory dualism in other factor markets as being responsible for African poverty, the Report went on to suggest that the African living conditions could be improved by measures 'to modernize farming in the subsistence sector and raise its productivity' and also 'generate employment opportunities outside the subsistence sector'.[5] These measures, however, would be sufficient only as long as foreign interests and European immigrants continued to make further encroachments, investments, expanding, among other things, European agriculture, manufacturing and mining activities.[6]

Although more a bit 'progressive' than the above Report, the Whitsun Foundation (a Rhodesian-based institution) also preferred to gloss over the deep seated structural problems of economic dualism. The Whitsun Foundation's policy suggestions were based on the premise that while an increasing proportion of the Africans would in the future both reside and be employed in the modern sector, a growing absolute number would continue to live in the rural areas. Thus, in order to halt the degradation of land resources and personal incomes, certain measures would have to be undertaken. These included among others: (a) more training of Africans in technical skills in order to enhance their employability; (b) promotion of African advancement in industry by removing racial barriers and what was described as a 'positive' policy regarding immigration which would ensure that immigration did not endanger the principle of giving to local labour first priority of employment in jobs for which they are qualified; (c) priority was to be given to investment funds in the urban sector in order to create employment opportunities there; (d) lifting of racial discrimination in the allocation of land, with access to property rights being given to those African with potential to employ land productively and without resource depletion.[7]

Thus, the Whitsun Foundation raises the issue of land reform only in order to dilute it. It is said that only a small amount of land is potentially available for reallocation, which is contrary to all available evidence in Zimbabwe. Second, the argument allegedly based on economic grounds, that reallocation of land should only be available 'to users who would farm the land productively without resource depletion' may not be justified for three reasons:

a African farmers in Zimbabwe, whether in the APAs or TTLs or wage employees in the European farms have demonstrated skill and ability in farming.[8]
b Lower yields in the TTLs are largely the result of poor soils, soil erosion resulting from overcrowding of both humans and livestock and lack of credit and services rather than from lack of skills.

c Those to be resettled would not replace those working in the presently farmed commercial areas, but rather they will be going into areas which have been lying fallow.[9]

Therefore, there may not be much risk of lowering productivity on the part of those to be resettled, especially if the land reform should include the whole package of complementary inputs such as credits, extension service and marketing facilities.

In a study by the German Democratic Institute (GDI) policy proposals were made on the basis of the Basic Needs Approach (BNA). The BNA was defined as consisting of three elements: (a) minimum requirements for consumption, i.e. adequate food, clothing and housing; (b) the provision of essential services by community (health, education, public transport, etc); (c) mass participation in the decision making process. The GDI study assumed that these objectives, though not explicitly defined by the liberation movement were 'contained in all programmes of the liberation movements and (were) indeed the major goals of the entire developing world'.[10] Roger Riddell also took as his objective the BNA on more or less similar grounds. Riddell chose the BNA because 'it was then the specific strategy which the ILO World Employment Conference in Geneva proposed that all developing countries should adopt for the next twenty-five years'.[11] Thus, these studies proceeded from well-known policy prescriptions, but the question that remained was how these prescriptions could be adapted to the specific needs of Zimbabwe.

As far as land reform was concerned, the GDI study recommended (a) the redistribution of land and settlement of African peasants from overcrowded TTLs onto the present white land. The new settlements would take the form of small holdings and they would preferably be created on land suitable for intensive farming (Regions I, II, and III), and also on land presently under irrigation. (b) The large-scale farms would be maintained and would be allowed 'an orderly transition of ownership and management' either to state ownership, local corporate ownership, cooperative ownership or remain as private enterprises or leaseholds. Thus, a mixed farming system in both ownership and production structure was envisaged.

A more detailed transformation of the agricultural sector was found in the work of Roger Riddell. In dealing with alternatives for the future, Riddell dealt with land reform in more detail than in other similar studies, and outlined a system of land tenure to provide for (a) security of tenure for all; (b) the control of land and of any surplus produced by those who work on the land; (c) participation in decision making relating to land; (d) equality of income and land distribution; (e) a 'thorough going land reform' to be carried out under a socialist economic framework which was expected to lead to a more equal distribution of land and income. Riddell's recommendations were thus couched as long-term policy options:[12]

a The means of production should be nationalised and come under 'social ownership' in order to evolve a system of equal access for all those engaged in land cultivation, full employment, equal distribution of income as well as achievement of self-reliance.

b A resettlement of Africans from the present overpopulated areas to the unused and underutilised 'white' areas was proposed. This measure was said to have the advantages of increasing the potential for agricultural development and the easing of land pressure in the African areas which itself leads to a greater potential for the development of these areas.

c Rural communes were proposed throughout the rural areas. Communes were preferred to small holdings because it was said that such cooperatives were more efficient in the utilisation of the division of labour. Furthermore, as technical progress on agriculture is not scale-neutral but has a bias in favour of larger acreages, communes would be ideal for Zimbabwe. Riddell argued that the communes had the advantage of providing a more rational and efficient framework for the provision of extension service, credit and other necessary inputs such as fertiliser and seeds – as well as the marketing of the crop. The other advantage of the communes was said to be in product specialisation according to natural regions, as well as concentration of health facilities as compared to scattered small-holdings.

d Land and capital would be held in common and farmers would pay less taxes to the central government thereby sharing a greater proportion of the proceeds among themselves.

e After nationalisation of land the government would retain the small and large-scale European operators on their farms. One way would be to insist on Zimbabweans gaining managerial expertise and technical knowledge.[13]

Riddell also proposed that the government should finance necessary incentives to be paid to those white farmers who have been profitable so that they continue on their land.[14] This was important according to Riddell because 'It needs to be extremely profitable for farmers to stay in their land long enough to ensure that new management could be trained to run the farms competently'.[15]

Thus, the policy options reviewed above range from the conservative ones of the colonial government that aimed at maintaining the status quo to the more radical ones offered by Riddell. The policy instruments suggested here, especially those of Riddell, go a long way towards reforms needed in the transformation of Zimbabwean agriculture. But since these suggestions do not essentially deal with the problem of dualism, there is still lack a strategy that will lead towards an elimination of the differences within the dual economy.

Early strategies to eliminate dualism

A development strategy designed to reduce and eventually eliminate dualism must attempt to answer the following fundamental questions: (a) in what form should the transformation of the traditional agricultural sector take place? (b) how should the modern industrial sector be transformed so that it enhances technical progress or brings about rapid changes in technology and in product pattern of the traditional sector?

Regarding the first question the narrative in this book is concerned with the nature of the land reform and the type of innovations required in the transformation. The second question refers to the structural changes of the modern industrial sector and its capability to adapt and further produce the kind of transformations needed in other sectors of the economy, especially the agricultural sector. Technological progress in industry provides the main vehicles of technological progress in all the branches of the national economy.[16] The main concern will, however, be the transformation of the agricultural sector towards an integrated entity in terms of techniques employed, productivity and income distribution.

To be effective, the elimination of economic dualism must critically depend on the form or forms of structural changes in the African agrarian sector. As suggested in studies cited above, the most important means for obtaining a meaningful structural change is a radical land reform in which the provision of extension services and financial assistance will be part of the arsenal of the land reform. This needs no justification in view of the population pressure in the former TTLs now renamed communal lands and the existence of unused land in the former white areas, estimated to be as high as 60 per cent in 1980.

Bruce F. Johnston has argued that the most fundamental issue of agricultural strategy facing the underdeveloped countries in the choice between a bimodal strategy in which resources are concentrated within a subsector of large, capital-intensive units, or a unimodal strategy which is designed to encourage a slower but wider diffusion of technical innovations which more or less comply to the factor proportions of the sector as a whole.[17] The unimodal strategy emphasises sequences of innovations that are highly divisible and largely scale-neutral. These innovations can be adapted in an efficient way to small farms and can also be adapted gradually, i.e. they are appropriate to the progressive propagation of techniques within particular areas and extension of benefits to new areas. Johnston suggests that the propagation effect will take place via the spread of the new innovations, e.g. when irrigation facilities or improved market opportunities in one area are adopted by farmers in the neighbourhood.

The bimodal strategy, on the other hand, has the advantage of rapid adoption of a wider range of modern techniques. However, with this type of strategy, innovations are only usually adopted by a minority of large farmers, especially in those economies where there is a small demand for commercial goods because the majority of the working population are still peasants. Consequently, the bimodal strategy does not spread the use of techniques to the entire agricultural sector. Thus, the gap between the factor proportions used by the different farmers will widen further and the bulk of output will continue to come from the more capital-intensive farms.

On the other hand, under a unimodal strategy, the most advanced farms are supposed to display about the same factor intensities as average farms. Differences in output per unit of input may continue to be large, especially in the early stages of transition, although this will tend to reflect differences in the efficiency of production and management rather than major differences in factor proportions.

In the Zimbabwean case, the ultimate aim of eradicating economic dualism, must start with reducing the differences in factor proportions between farming systems. In a limited way, the unimodal strategy can lead to a reduction of the indivisibilities since the strategy emphasises highly divisible and scale-neutral innovations. However, as the aim is not only to reduce differences in factor proportions without at the same time increasing productivity rapidly, Zimbabwe must take advantage of using some of the less scale-neutral innovations already available in the country's agriculture. This means that, even though the unimodal and bimodal strategies are mutually exclusive, the solution may be the adoption of unimodal strategy for the whole country, but with a view to move on to use the machinery, irrigation systems and other complementary innovations at present only available to the commercial farms. The question of the implementation of such a strategy will critically depend upon the policy instruments employed by the government, particularly to move towards the use of machinery, irrigation system and other complementary innovations hitherto predominantly only available to the commercial farms.

On the other hand, the modern industrial sector should be transformed to provide the technical innovations needed in other sectors of the economy, and especially in the agricultural sector. As in the transformation of the agricultural sector, there may be a need for state intervention in the industrial sector if technical progress is to be in harmony with the economic conditions of the country. The recognition that technical progress in industry is the main vehicle of technical change in other sectors of the economy should compel the government to intervene in order to influence structural changes in industry. This may be particularly the case if there is need to create capital-goods producing industries[18] and research and development activity designed to spread technical innovations to other sectors of the economy. In this connection the UN Report on Zimbabwe stated that 'Direct government action will also be needed in the implementation of an appropriate science and technology policy'. The Report emphasised that if a science and technology plan should be part of the national development plan 'centres and institutions for the acquisition and adaptation, design and development of technology should be established to ensure that full advantage is taken of domestic possibilities in this sphere'.[19]

Zimbabwe may be fortunate to have an appropriate production capacity including technical and professional manpower to adapt technical innovations to the local conditions. Though the Rhodesian colonial system relied on foreign investment and control, the importation of technical skills and a very strict racial division of labour, there was also a relatively large industrial sector producing intermediate and producer goods (capital goods) with a certain capacity for internal technical innovation. The manufacturing industry's best performance during the post UDI period was in the basic metals and metal products. All the chrome produced in the country was processed into ferrochrome and the iron and steel industry increased its capacity to one million tons a year.[20] The products from the iron industry provided inputs into the mining and agricultural sectors. Thus, there already exists an appropriate production mechanism with a minimal research and development capability which can enable the country to provide the necessary inputs needed in the transformation of its dual economy. This was a necessary condition for the modern sector to orient itself towards the supply of innovations needed in other sectors of the national economy.

Post-independence strategies to eliminate dualism

With a population of Zimbabwe estimated to be 16.06 million in 2017, 52 per cent being female and largely dependent on agriculture, the land issue has remained at the epicentre of the country's socio-political and economic struggles since colonial times. As shown in the preceding chapters of this book, the racial distribution of land by the successive colonial administrations entrenched the structure of economic dualism.

This uneven distribution of the land was the driving force of the war of liberation that engulfed the country from the 1960s to 1980, culminating with negotiations for independence from the colonial master, at Lancaster House, London, England in 1979. In 1980, some 6,600 white farmers occupied 15.5 million hectares of prime land, while some seven million African people were crowded in the marginal and drier parts of the country.

At independence in 1980 the Government of Zimbabwe was thus faced with the task of restructuring these historical imbalances of racially skewed land distribution. The Land Reform Programme – Phase one of 1980–1989 – saw the acquisition of 3.6 million hectares of land under European occupation under the 'willing-buyer, willing-seller' basis, as part of an ambitious programme to resettle an estimated 162,000 families.[21] However, due to a number of constraints that included legal, financial and political limitations the speed and magnitude of land reform was petered down to low levels, at the beginning of the 1990s despite the unabated demand for land.

The land reform was later to be resuscitated under the 'Fast Track' Land Reform Program (FTLRP) launched in July 2000. Unlike its predecessors, this phase was characterised by little documentation in terms of plans and a quite haphazard implementation. It was also characterised by controversial land acquisition processes with instances of violence that were reported widely. Although the FTLRP was scheduled to 'officially' finish at the end of August 2002, largely because of its politically motivated stance and nature, it has been smouldering on, albeit, intermittently to the end of 2017, which coincided with the intervention of the military that removed Zimbabwe's sole post independent leader Robert Mugabe in a *coup d'état*, which came to be known as a soft coup (coup-not-coup). FLTRP was able to add some 145,775 new Model A1 farmers (each household with at least three, and maximum five hectares of arable holding and varied communal grazing) and 16,386 Model A2, farmers based on small, medium and large-scale commercial farms (ranging from 100 hectares to 1,000 hectares, although on average 500 hectares).

As can be easily seen, the A1 model scheme is a near replica of the old communal peasant farming model only by another name. Thus, the pre-independence institutionally induced dualism in the structure of the economy has continued to be pervasive long after Zimbabwe's independence in 1980. However, when it relates to its key segment of the agrarian sector, in quantitative terms the system has changed considerably with a preponderance of smallholder farm operations across the board. In terms of land tenure regimes, in 2014 the major pattern on the ground shows that: (a) Over 1.2 million family-held pieces of land under customary land tenure in the designated communal areas (previously termed Tribal Trust Lands) on 16.4million hectares; (b) Some 145,775 new Model A1 farmers joining 76,000 old Resettlement Model A1 farmers on a total of about 9.4 million hectares on permit tenure; (c) Some 8,000 freehold and leasehold tenure Small Scale Commercial Farmers on 1.4 million hectares; (d) Some 24,000 farmers on Model A2 'offer letters'/ leasehold tenure, on 2.98 million hectares; and (e) About 1,000 remaining freehold agricultural land holders and corporate agro-estates.

While the old system that was geared towards large-scale production in terms of both support to infrastructure (dams and transport), credit markets and price support lingers on, the transition to the predominantly smallholder production agrarian structure has met with a number of challenges and as such has yet to yield anticipated results.

As the World Bank, 2015 observed, the evolution of Zimbabwe's land tenure regimes from colonial to current post-colonial period have been evolving since the turn of the nineteenth century as follows:

a Freehold tenure, mainly in the LSCFs, the small scale commercial and peri-urban areas – where in land is accessed through market transfers.
b State-based leasehold tenure (with and without option to purchase) which operates mainly in the A2 farms and some SSCFs – where in

land is accessed through allocation by the State in the form of land leases.

c Customary tenure, which only operates in the communal areas – where land is accessed through customary tenure norms.

d Permit tenure provided to landholders on State-owned land mainly in A1 and Old Resettlement Areas – where land is accessed through allocations by the State in the form of permits.

e Unalienated land controlled by the State, devoted largely to gazetted parks and forests, but including some areas managed under concessions negotiated with private entities.

Despite the variations in the tenure systems shown above, the State has retained Powers of Eminent Domain over all land in Zimbabwe and has continued to hold allodial title (absolute right) to the land.[22]

The dominant tenure regime, instituted in the colonial era and continued to the independence date and beyond, is the LSCF land areas. While white commercial agricultural farming areas were empowered by the 'freehold' system to use, mortgage, raise capital from banking institutions, dispose and acquire as well as bequeath as inheritance, there were differences in the other tenure regimes. In the LSCF areas there was a vibrant land market, which was predicated on the 'freehold' rights pertaining to that tenure regime. Individuals and corporates were able to buy and dispose of their 'commercial' properties, with legal basis ensuring that these transfers were recorded with the Registrar of Deeds under the Ministry of Justice and Parliamentary Affairs.

Within the SSCF areas black individual farmers were allowed to continue leasing the allocated lands, often with an option to purchase the same properties. They did record some economic successes that saw a number of them send their children to schools and other places of higher learning. However, during this period the SSCF Areas did not expand in terms of additional land allocations or deliberate state support for agricultural enhancement.

The communal areas where the customary tenure held sway has continued to be the absorber of all the African people that are not accommodated in the newly opening modern (urban) sector and mining establishments and commercial farming areas. Within the communal areas, allocation of land has continued to be entertained by traditional authorities (kraal heads, headmen and chiefs) and as such continued to be a buffer for all those who had been retrenched from formal employment and natural growth. As shown in Chapter 6, Zimbabwe's Constitution, the supreme national law of the land, appears to clearly exclude the communal lands from the dynamic jar of capitalism, in contrast to empowering other citizens holding agricultural land outside communal areas 'freedom to acquire, hold, occupy, use, transfer, hypothecate, lease, or dispose, of agricultural land'. It can be argued that the Constitution excludes and locks-in the country's poor majority in a situation where they cannot uplift themselves beyond the subsistence survival, as they do not hold title over their homes and houses. Thus the people in the communal lands are legally constrained in making a surplus and grow their assets within the communal land area.

In the Zimbabwean case, the land sub-divisions have become smaller and smaller as the population continues to grow over the years thereby exacerbating the man-land ratios which has led to environmental land degradation. Because of the growing population in the country and lack of opportunities, both rural and urban communities have been encroaching into the country's wet land areas a practice that is against the country's Constitution, as wetlands are protected under the Environmental Management Act.

Eradicating dualism through land reform and land tenure systems

To eradicate economic dualism, the first point of attack should be the colonial inherited structural distortion that gave birth to a relatively well-developed modern formal sector that existed alongside an underdeveloped and backward rural economy. The latter is the home of 70 per cent of the country's black population. It is this economic dualism that explains the perennial problem of the underutilisation of resources, implying structural disintegration and underdevelopment as shown in Figure 7.2 (Chapter 4). In this situation the modern formal sector is based on the behavioural and organisation rules of the market; while the non-formal sector relies partly on the market and traditional modes of economic behaviour and resource utilisation.[23] As argued in the preceding chapters, the assets of the latter are not protected by the formal property laws.

As shown in Chapter 3, Zimbabwe's dualistic land distribution situation had not changed much well into the second decade of the country's independence. The white dominated large-scale commercial farms (LSCFs) had remained concentrated in the productive Regions I–III, while communal land areas remained located in the marginal IV–V Regions.[24] According to Guy Mhone,

> The average farm sizes … are roughly such that the average LSCF is about 2,200 hectares, the average SSCF (small-scale commercial farm) is about 125 hectares, and the average Communal farm is 4.5 hectares. This is despite the fact that on the basis of studies undertaken during the colonial period, 6 hectares was officially recognized as the minimum requirement for an average communal sector household of about six people.[25]

The above is corroborated by the 1991 World Bank report that 3.5 million hectares in the fertile white agricultural areas remained unused.[26] Specifically on the communal areas, a 1994 'Report of the Commission of Inquiry into Appropriate Agricultural Land Tenure Systems' proposed that individuals could register their home plots and vegetable gardens but, in the long run, there would be no individual tittle deeds that would protect the land rights of women and would be administered by local chiefs.[27] By this act, the Zimbabwe's post independent government has accepted stock, lock and barrel the colonial 'inherited' land ownership in the communal areas. In the view of the government commission, communal land ownership was to exist side by side with freehold tenure in the commercial farming sector. In essence, what was being offered was a sense of ownership and a place but little freehold rights.

The task of facing Zimbabwe's land reform and restructuring the historical imbalances of racially skewed land distribution, has been both an intriguing and complex process for the new post-independence government. The Land Reform Programme – Phase 1 of 1980–1989 – saw the acquisition of 3.6 million hectares of land under European occupation under the 'willing-buyer, willing-seller' basis, as part of an ambitious programme to resettle an estimated 162,000 families.[28] The implementation process went through technical feasibility reports of the land to be acquired, followed by due legal process of acquisition, detailed planning, and appraisal by an Inter-Ministerial Committee composed of senior personnel in government agencies and development partner representatives prior to scheduled implementation. Due to a number of constraints that included legal, financial and political limitations, the speed and magnitude of land reform petered down at the beginning of the 1990s despite the unabated demand for land. There is no doubt that the problem caused by the historical injustices of the colonial regime and its white settler land grabbing was always going to be faced and extinguished so that the rightful owners of the land assets take back their historically stolen lands. Resolution of the land issue had been one of the principal targets of the liberation struggle and the new government that came to power in 1980 initially made promising moves towards addressing the gross historical imbalance in ownership that existed. The war of liberation was fought for this right to repossess the land. The people of Zimbabwe and the international community were acutely aware of this.

By 1999, only 76,000 families had been resettled in mostly Model A1 Schemes that were the bulk of the 3.6 million hectares acquired through legal acquisition of land from the Large Scale Commercial Farming Areas that still numbered about 4,500 white farmers. Thus by the turn of the twenty-first century, there were no other significant alterations to land tenure categories from what it was at independence in 1980. Only minor amendments to the legislation governing some aspects of land administration had been made. These included the Communal Land Act No. 20 of 1982; the Traditional Leaders Act (Chap 29:17); the Customary Law and Local Courts Act (Chap 7:05) revised edition 1996 and Rural District Act 1998 (Chapter 29:13) and the Revised edition of 1996. These Parliamentary

Acts sort to consolidate the administration of the communal lands by local authorities and traditional leaders.

During this period, commercial farmers were able to sell and buy land in the open market and have the transfers registered at the Deeds Registry. Indeed, during the studies leading to the 'Report of the Commission of Inquiry into Appropriate Land Tenure Systems',[29] it was discovered that 66 per cent of recorded land transfers at the Deeds Registry were intra-family, indicating the existence of a skewed land market.

But long before the Fast Track Land Reform Programme the government had tried several methods of dealing with the country's land reform, starting with the so called resettlement permits. In the first Phase of the Resettlement Programme of the 1980s the land remained in the hands of government, with beneficiaries given three permits, namely: (a) permit to reside and build a homestead, (b) permit to have access to arable land and (c) permit to de-pasture livestock on common pastures. This state of affairs was investigated during the studies for the Land Tenure Commission in 1994 and found to be a source of insecurity that grossly affected their commitment and long-term investment. It was noted that this made many beneficiaries not to surrender their communal area holdings.

However, the demand for land within communal customary tenure as administered by the traditional leaders and councillors had long started to increase. This was against the fact that the size of the communal lands had not been increased since independence. The size of these original 'Native reserves' set by the colonial regime when the Africans were forcibly moved out of their original lands had remained the same.

Tensions continued to build up as portions of communal land area were from time to time excised in the post-independence era, such as the cases of displacement of communities in the wake of the construction of Tokwe–Mukosi Dam, (Masvingo) and the ethanol project in Chisumbanje in Chipinge. Allocation and sub-divisions of land for both building of homesteads and arable lands has continued to be an on-going activity in the communal lands under the authority of traditional leaders. Demand for residential land in peri-urban communal areas has increased phenomenally, resulting in communities allowed by their traditional leaders, and the local Rural District Council authorities to sell both residential and arable plots to home seekers from the nearby cities.

Zimbabwe's Land Reform Program in the 2000 period

An important landmark in the Zimbabwe land question was the 1998 Land Conference. The Conference had been called under pressure of donors, bearing in mind that only 71,000 families had been resettled on 3.3 million hectares. The Conference had involved key domestic stakeholders, international donors and multilateral institutions. The Conference had also agreed on the key principles that would govern land redistribution:

transparency, respect of the rule of law, poverty reduction, affordability and consistency with the country's wider economic interests. On this basis, the government published an 'inception phase' document in March 1999, which was to run for a two-year period, but progress in its implementation was slow.

However, Zimbabwe's land reform took a political dimension when in January 2000, the government proposed an amendment to clause 57 of the draft Constitution, allowing compulsory acquisition of land without compensation. Although the Draft Constitution was rejected in a referendum vote a month later, the government introduced compulsory land acquisition through parliament.

The logic of Zimbabwe's land reform almost decisively followed the government's defeat in the constitutional referendum in February 2000. From this moment, the government had to deal with the land occupation, while also taking the legal route of Constitutional changes.[30] The Constitution of Zimbabwe Amendment (No. 16) Act (No. 5 of 2000), backed by amendments to Land Acquisition Act (No. 15 of 2000) allowed the state to acquire land compulsorily, without compensation for the land but only for improvements.[31] For the Government of Zimbabwe, the responsibility for compensation was transferred to the former coloniser, the British Government. However, the British Government, while acknowledging its debt on financing land reform, reneged on this responsibility as it vehemently opposed the Fast Track Land Reform programme.

The Fast Track Land Reform Program

Though, there are many and conflicting interpretations on Zimbabwe's land reform, there is virtually no dispute over the legitimacy of the Fast Track Land Reform Programme (FTLRP). The war of liberation was fought primarily to restore the people's lands that had been usurped by the Rhodesian colonial government. Zimbabwe's colonial land architecture had remained virtually the same in the country's post-independence period. This only changed when the government's one-party state came under threat from the opposition group in a constitutional referendum vote. Following this episode, a new era of change to Zimbabwe's rural and agricultural landscape had arrived in the post 2000 period, with the introduction of the FTLRP.

Zimbabwe's FTLRP drastically turned the landscape of the country as a whole. A bold step to tackle Zimbabwe's land reform had been tackled, albeit haphazardly, only after the scare of an election defeat heralded by the ruling party's loss of a constitutional referendum. The government embarked on a path of expropriating almost all individual commercial farms as well as a number of corporate-owned estates. In the process, the input, marketing and research institutions that had been built up over decades were weakened or destroyed and agricultural production collapsed across the board.

With its attendant merits and demerits, for the first time Zimbabwe's agricultural landscape quickly became dominated by the smallholder farming sector constituted as communal lands, old and new FTLRP resettlement lands as well as the small-scale commercial farming lands.[32] The reigning tenure regime in this subsector remained mostly the old colonial established customary system in the communal lands, followed by the Old Resettlement Areas, the Model A1s under the FTLRP and leasehold allocations in both A2 and small-scale commercial farming areas.[33]

In terms of land marketability (de jure), Zimbabwe's Constitution, the supreme national law of the land, passed in 2013, has clear provisions on how land should be dealt with in the national discourse, in terms of the right to own, transfer and hypothecate agricultural land in the country. In Section 72 the Constitution defines agricultural land as 'land used for agriculture – a separate piece of land on Deeds Registry' – but excludes communal lands, which is treated under Section 282 where the provisions of traditional leaders are given as 'to administer Communal Land and protect the environment', as well as resolve disputes.

In addition, Section 289(b) provides for real rights to every Zimbabwean regardless of ethnicity or gender. The Constitution thus empowers citizens holding agricultural land outside communal areas 'freedom to acquire, hold, occupy, use, transfer, hypothecate, lease, or dispose, of agricultural land'. In this way, the Constitution thus overrides all previous national laws promulgated before 2013, which became *ultra vires* to the national constitution, though these still have to be realigned.

While there is no formal land market in the communal lands under customary tenure, anecdotal indications reveal existence of informal land market where traditional leaders and at times Rural District Councils have been involved in land transfers. This, however, leaves the communal lands vulnerable and open to uncertainties and forces of the market. There has been expropriation of communal lands for mining purposes (i.e. Chiadzwa) and commercial sugar estate expansion (i.e. Chisumbanje). Attempts at compensating the people have been made through Community Ownership Trusts where operating companies are supposed to contribute financial returns to the affected communities. (i.e. Ngezi and Chiadzwa). The record has not been impressive with a lot of dissatisfaction voiced by community representatives. Thus, Zimbabwe's post FTLRP land tenure security in the various reigning tenure regimes remains tenuous to say the least, as the following tenure systems are in place:

Remaining large-scale commercial farming areas (LSCFA)

The LSCFA sector had been run as 'freehold' and has previously enjoyed the most 'secure' property rights in terms of transfer rights, but no longer enjoys these freedoms as a whole. At least up to the abrupt end of the tenure of President Robert Mugabe through a military coup in November

2017, without adequate political backing, there was always the possibility of takeover of the whole or part of a farm by government with the amended Land Acquisition Act. There was also uncertainty on the valuation of the property for compensation in the event of compulsory acquisition and the possible nature of acquisition (invasion) were still issues that define tenure insecurity in the sector. It can be said, however, that freehold owners who have title deeds to the land, have something to use as a tool for negotiating compensation for loss of their property.

Since the Land Acquisition Act (Chap 21) revisions of 1985 any commercial farming enterprise wishing to dispose of their land had to apply to the Ministry of Lands and Rural Resettlements (MLRR) for a Certificate of No Present Interest (CONPI) where the state is given the option of first refusal. Although no figures are available for the level of interaction it can be surmised that this requirement is presently not conducive for the development of a land market. At least up to mid-2018, the CONPI costs a fee of US$200 payable to MLRR per transaction.[34]

Land tenure and small-scale farming areas

The current tenure regime accorded to this group of settlers is an 'offer letter', which hopefully will be converted into a lease. In the meantime, however, those who have been settled in the A2 Schemes since 2000 are still not fully 'secure' due to perceived fears of possible eviction for not meeting the conditions of the lease application (i.e. proven and marketed production, perceived sub-letting, perceived under-utilisation), and possible subdivision of the lands they occupy. Some of the properties have remained under Court contestation by previous commercial owners as well as cases of fallout from political affiliation.

A2 farmers enjoy limited rights of use under the government permits issued through an offer letter, and the few that have 99-year leases, the fuller bundle of rights is still not within their grasp due to what can be perceived as obscure and at best murky governance issues. That the land can be repossessed by the State and re-allocated to new beneficiaries, has not been clearly articulated to the beginning of Zimbabwe's second Republic.[35] This was a result of the government insisting that farmers cannot be allowed to sublet lands that were allocated to them.

Customary communal tenure

The argument presented here is that the Rhodesian colonial governments successfully withheld the freehold rights to indigenous peoples because they wanted to control them. The colonial state feared that the ownership of capital in the form of land and buildings might empower them and encourage a challenge to colonial authority. This legitimate right of the indigenous rural people to hold land assets under freehold has again been withheld in the modern era by the post independent government of Zimbabwe, leaving the rural agricultural lands under communal ownership.

In the meanwhile, the widespread land degradation, and massive soil erosion already rampant under colonial rule continues to destroy much of Zimbabwe's potentially productive farm land. Under the practice of common ownership of land and free unfettered access, a massive man–land ratio compels people to cut down the few remaining trees for a variety of reasons, including wood fuel, fencing of agricultural fields, and in some areas – tobacco curing.

There is sometimes little understanding that modern agriculture and with it high yields and low costs is impossible without serious transformation of the current communal areas. First, the state must deal with the issue of over-crowdedness in the communal areas.[36] This can be done through provision of innovative farming methods, infrastructure, institutional reforms and security of the people's assets giving them property rights titles. I wish to argue that it does not make sense to withhold the majority of country's assets from the nation's legal property rights. The same goes for those tenure systems like communal tenure and those under the A1 that have little incentive to invest. The communal farmers may own tangible things but cannot exercise property rights on anything they have, their lands, livestock, fields and gardens.

Because of the lack of property rights in the communal lands, Zimbabweans are slowly but surely abandoning their rural areas in terms of making permanent improvements there. Those who have accumulated some resources largely move on to buy properties in the urban areas. This is because people could benefit and hold value of their assets by owning their own houses in urban areas.

It has been observed elsewhere that the contribution of land to economic growth depends upon the security, duration and enforceability of property rights. Knowing that property rights are secure provides an incentive for agricultural investment and helps develop markets for renting and selling land. This also supports the common wisdom that securing land tenure is important for poverty reduction.

A new policy to restore property title rights to land and extend those rights to the whole country, backed by a rule of law, will be one way out of the age-old problem of entrenched structural economic dualism trap. Until this happens and the rest of the country's population is integrated into the legal property system and have the same ability to use their resources in the open market, the poor will remain outside Hernando De Soto's 'bell jar'. As De Soto aptly concludes, 'If extralegal property rights are not accommodated, these societies may muddle along with their dual economies – with the so-called law abiding sector on one side and the impoverished extralegal sector on the other side'.[37]

On the land reform, our conclusion is in line with that of the broad agreement among authors of empirically grounded studies that Zimbabwe's

Fast Track Land Reform Programme (FTLRP) implemented during the 2000s did finally reverse the system of land based racial segregation, which had escaped reform at independence and remained virtually unaltered in structure until 2000.[38] By reallocating agricultural land that was not being effectively or fully utilised to over 1.3 million beneficiary families, land reform has more than doubled the productive use of land – and in this sense, land reform can also be seen as having intensified the productive use of national resources as a whole. This is especially so, with the introduction of the A1 and A2 farmers.[39]

In 1999 about 4,500 large-scale commercial farms, including plantations (estates) and corporate holdings owned over 9,000 farmland properties covering an area of about 11 million hectares. The FTLRP targeted five million hectares for redistribution. By 2009, less than 400 of individually owned white farms remained. The large agro-industrial plantations or estates and conservancies were not substantively expropriated, although they lost some land and/or were partially 'illegally' occupied.

However, what remains unsolved is the continued existence of the communal areas, which have remained under the colonial-shaped traditional system of tenure. What still remains undone is the bold attempts or measures to restructure the economy starting with the rural agricultural sector where economic dualism has its roots.

A major question that will continue to be asked is why is it that while we know that the solution to the land question is anchored on the land reform, in the case of Zimbabwe and other countries of the south, this has failed to resolve transformation and the emancipation of the peasantry. Second, while the agrarian question was seen, at least in the Marxist tradition as a question of the transition, the peasantry in the Global South has remained stuck in the same deprivation mode by the earlier colonial state and now by the indigenous and monopoly classes in these countries. In the case of Zimbabwe, there is still work to do in terms of following up the long-proposed land audit which hopefully is expected to deal with transparency and corruption issues that have resulted in multiple ownership of acquired farms by the political elite. But in all these developments, the African peasantry in the communal areas remains at the same place, in the same conditions as they were left there by the colonial state. As will be argued in the section below, the eradication of economic dualism in Zimbabwe and countries in similar conditions, demands a raft of measures ranging from institutional, inclusive infrastructural, technology and leveraging on legal property rights.

Policy recommendations

Zimbabwe's economic dualism cannot be successfully corrected by merely addressing its parts while retaining the disarticulated structure of the national economy. The opportunity to eradicate economic dualism lies in confronting head-on the current structural regression and disintegration that has laced the whole economy. As shown in the above section, Zimbabwe's economy has continued to carry its disarticulated structure where the modern sector is not complementary to the backward pre-capitalist peasant farming economy. In a generally articulated economic system the exchange mechanism and sectoral/regional reciprocities become pervasive owing to the total commodification of the economy as a whole driven by forward and backward linkages of production and services.

From the start, Zimbabwe's economic structure became fundamentally flawed, in that the foundation of its modern sector became characterised by a narrow and disarticulated production base. Though a thriving modern enclave, the national economy was founded on narrow-based manufacturing capabilities. It depended on migrant labour with little ability to deepen its domestic market share, and from this base expand to both regional and international markets.

Quite in the early years of colonialism, instead of embracing a vibrant though less developed indigenous market economy, the African peasant production for the urban markets was discouraged in favour of subsistence farming. In terms of building a national economy, here lay the shortsightedness of the colonial economic model, as Adam Smith saw it otherwise when he wrote:

> It is the surplus produce of the country only, or what is over and above the maintenance of the cultivators, that constitutes the subsistence of the town, which can therefore increase only with the increase of this surplus produce.... Upon equal, or nearly equal profits, most men will choose to employ their capitals rather in the improvement and cultivation of land than either in manufactures or in foreign trade.[40]

Contrary to the predictions of the classical economists, the reason for the colonial administration was to create conditions for the extraction of surplus labour from the impoverished African peasantry. This led to a situation where commodification was only restricted to the country's modern formal sector, (including mining, commercial, plantation farming, manufacturing, etc.), a situation that created and deepened the structure of economic dualism.

As shown in Chapter 7, Zimbabwe's modern formal sector (FS) was typically linked to the global economy through exports, imports, foreign direct investment (FDIs) and technology. The FS historically has had lower surplus labour and higher average incomes than the communal sector (CS) and subsequently the informal sector (IS). In the case of colonial Zimbabwe, surplus labour was created and nurtured in the communal land areas. In the post-independence period, high surplus labour progressively became evident in both the CS and the IS. These sectors now act as a buffer to surplus labour from FS and provide a ready pool of labour for the formal sector if and when required. Due to the shrinking of the formal economy through de-industrialisation in recent years, this has resulted in a huge informalisation of the economy. The share of informal employment to total employment has risen from 80 per cent in 2004 to 84.2 per cent in 2011 and 94.5 per cent in 2014.

At the sectoral level, getting rid of dualism in the Zimbabwean economy must start from a model that ensures transformation into a dynamic modern agricultural sector with an equal dynamic industrial sector both based on similar conditions in terms of access to technology, markets, legal and institutional support. As shown above, Zimbabwe has had a long established system of freehold in the large-scale commercial farming (LSCF) system, where the freehold tenure, was seen as the most secure tenure as it conferred full property rights. In the specific conditions of the country's post-independence period, the State found it reasonable that lands that remain under freehold should give government the option of first refusal for any proposed transfer or sale through a public proclamation at the behest of the seller. This was meant to ensure a measure of transparency in the land market.

Second, it became prudent that Zimbabwe should resolve all the outstanding land issues and come up with agreed options on the way forward. One such option was the resolution of the current 99 year leases. After the exit of Zimbabwe's first president, Robert Mugabe, the incoming government directed that all remaining white commercial farmers be issued 99-year leases instead of the five-year leases as per the previous arrangement and that all agreed-to applications for land should not discriminate (as per the Constitution) on the basis of political affiliation, race, gender, health or disability status.

At least at the level of political rhetoric, this was a promising start, as it leads to sorting out outstanding issues that resulted from the unplanned and in some ways chaotic land seizures from the turn of the millennium. It can be further argued that the transformation of Zimbabwe's agrarian sector into an integrated industrial economy cannot happen as long the communal lands remain a residual sector, purportedly run on traditional values, where the nation's modern property laws do not apply. The lagging behind of the communal farming sector in terms of technology, resource mobilisation, and incomes will remain an impediment to the desired inclusive growth and transformation of the economy. With relatively high surplus labour, the communal sector also acts as a buffer to surplus labour from formal sector, unlike the modern formal sector which is linked to the global economy through exports, imports, foreign direct investment (FDIs) and technology.

The Constitution of Zimbabwe (2013) states that under Traditional Leadership:

1 The institution, status and role of traditional leaders under customary law are recognised.

2 A traditional leader is responsible for performing the cultural, customary and traditional functions of a chief, headperson or village head, as the case may be, for his or her community.

Further, under Section 282 (2) of the Constitution 'traditional leaders have authority, jurisdiction and control over the Communal Land or other areas for which they have been appointed, and over persons within those communal lands or areas'.[41]

In drafting the Constitution, the Zimbabwean drafters appear to have been caught in upholding and bringing the village norms of 'chiefs and headman' into the modern society, thereby drawing the country's future growth model back to the often 'sordid' village customs. The present Constitution bestows political freedom, democracy, accountability and rule of law that is differentially enforced in one sector of the community and not in the other. The question is, how will the transformation of the historically entrenched dualistic structure of the economy take place when the colonial crafted 'traditional' system remains strong and is jealously safeguarding the authority of the chiefs and headmen in land allocations. Elsewhere, in drafting the Indian constitution the drafters insisted on the individual rather than the village to be the moral unit of the constitution. It was important to the drafters of the Indian Constitution, that 'The task of modern citizenship was to convert the partial loyalties of society to a loyalty to the modern state'.[42]

There is an alternative voice from some analysts who have recommended that communal areas should cease to come under the State administration – i.e. usufruct with State and local/traditional authority. The proposition is that the State should confer them as Traditional Freehold rights as follows:

a Deed of Grant should be issued to the Family for arable and residential land, in favour of joint ownership by both spouses.
b For grazing land and other common property lands the Deed of Grant should be made in the name of a Community Trust, which may or may not coincide with Village Development Committees, who will look after the natural resources and pass appropriate by-laws to exclude other communities encroaching on their common property.

In the event that the State wants to expropriate land in the communal lands it should do so in consultation with the traditional authorities (chiefs, headmen, etc.) and the elected community representatives. Communities should be promptly compensated for loss of use of the expropriated lands.

While this 'communal' ownership model sounds traditional as the allocation of land is entertained by traditional authorities (kraal heads, headmen and chiefs), it is still basically as was crafted by the colonial masters. It does not offer 'individual' property rights for the people living there to have title, develop and be able to dispose of their property through sale, thus leaving the majority of the people outside the modern 'capitalist' mode of production.

Yes, it is generally agreed that land to the Zimbabwean people is viewed, in particular, as a symbol of belonging, safety net for the rural masses, and abode of the ancestors. However, for the communal lands to produce surplus value, the notion of individual property becomes necessary as an inducement to their owners. This can only come when the nation takes a conscious decision to integrate its colonially crafted land use to be in line with the modern legal property laws. As shown in Chapter 7, this took at least over 200 years in Europe, more than 100 years well into the nineteenth century for the US government to pass special statutes that integrated and formalised US assets. More recently in Japan the national campaign to formalise the property of farmers began in the late nineteenth century and ended in the late 1940s.[43]

In the Southern Africa context, conscious efforts to formalise property laws has yet to begin. When this finally happens, the formal property systems will empower 'traditional' farmers to know what assets are available and what opportunities exist to create surplus value. In the case of Zimbabwe, this opens up enormous opportunities for people to freely access markets, and free them from dependence on the whims of the sometime parochial 'traditional' leadership, politicians and bureaucratic stranglehold.

There is the recent example of development of land reform in Rwanda, where the Government is reported as having handed out secure, legal title to millions of small scale farmers. The enactment of the 2004 Land Policy and 2005 Land Law constitute a reform in Rwanda. The 2004 Land Policy basically provides that: (a) all Rwandans will enjoy the same rights of access to land; (b) all land should be registered for security and titles that are tradable unless it fragments a plot to less than one hectare; (c) land use should be optimal; (d) consolidation of household plots is encouraged to ensure that each holding is not less than one hectare; (e) land administration is to be based on a reformed cadastral (registered title deeds) system; (f) a system of land administration is to be developed; and (g) marshlands are in the state's private domain and are to be allocated to individuals on concession by the Ministry of Lands (MINITERE) on condition of good management.[44] It is reported that the impact has been immediate and dramatic. It has also fostered democracy, established stability and overnight has turned millions of families into people with real assets and value.[45]

It is, therefore, clear that the Zimbabwean 'communal areas' model cannot be expected to respond to liberal economic reforms designed to unshackle country's rural farming sector into a modern industrialising economy. This is because the prevailing land-use rights are still entrenched in a non-market model. There is therefore a challenge to address the issue of this segment of the community outside the modern capitalist sector. Otherwise, growth will not truly follow and accelerate, spreading prosperity such that the 'communal areas' begin to speak with the modern sector of the economy on the same terms. This is a reminder that the rule of law and property rights must apply ubiquitously across the board and become the most prominent institutional pillar of economic growth and prosperity. Again in the words of Adam Smith

> My experience leads me to consider state-enforced property rights as the key growth-enforced property rights (and) as the key growth-enhancing institution. For if those rights were not enforced, open trade and the huge benefits of competition and comparative advantage would be seriously and dramatically impeded.[46]

To deal effectively with economic dualism, Zimbabwe and indeed other African states in similar situations will need a strong, effective, progressive and competent state which will enforce national embracing laws strictly and fairly, while relentlessly upholding the rule of law. Anything short of this will leave the majority of these countries' citizens under an archaic 'traditional' rule of law that allows government officials to have discretion to manipulate the poor peasant farmers, while leaving them perpetually poor with no tangible rights to their assets. While this was once acceptable in earlier traditional societies, it cannot be tolerable to exist side by side with more advanced forms of rights in the modern liberalised economy.

It is discernible that our constitutions continue to recognise the principle of 'one man one vote' common to all in society, but not 'one man one value' for all in the same society. In ethical and material terms, citizens in modern liberal states look to the state to make their lives more predictable. Those of our citizens living in the communal areas need to enjoy the same aspirations and levels of predictability as their counterparts in the modern sector of society. Society cannot lift itself to a higher level and sustained growth without the help of the state to infuse similar laws that regulate markets to enforce property rights, contracts and provide security of life across the country's landscape.

Notes

1 Rent as a category was regarded by Marx as one form of surplus value just like net interest income, net production taxes and industrial profits. As seen in Chapter 4, this is where peasant assets like their grain, animal stock are not graded and therefore purchased for a song by the capitalist classes.
2 UN, 1980:96.
3 Ibid.: Table 36.
4 Sadie, 1967, quoted in UN, 1980:190.
5 UN, ibid.
6 Ibid.
7 The Whitsun Foundation, 1975.
8 Cf. UN, 1980:192.
9 Thus, one of the prerequisites of change in traditional tenure patterns likely to cause a short-run decline in output will be offset by an increase in output as

more African labour is applied to the previous vacant land (Nziramasanga, 1980:59).

10 German Democratic Institute, 1977:9.

11 ILO, 1977:2.

12 Riddell, 1978:104–112.

13 Ibid.:115.

14 Ibid.:119.

15 Ibid.

16 Cukor, 1972:79.

17 Johnston, 1976:593–601.

18 Cf. Szentes, 1976:293.

19 UN, 1980:195.

20 For a discussion on the potential of technical innovations and technical skills, and the future development of Zimbabwean industry and its role as an intersectional link, see Wield, 1980, and Nyathi-Mdluli, 1980.

21 Moyo, 2007; Kanyeze *et al.*, 2011; Nyoni, 2016.

22 Nyoni, 2016:5.

23 See Mhone, 2000.

24 For the country's natural regions, refer to Chapter 3, section 3.3.

25 Mhone, 1997:15.

26 World Bank, Zimbabwe Agriculture Sector Memorandum, Vol. II, Washington, DC: World Bank, 1991:44.

27 O'Keefe and Moyo, 2007.

28 Kanyenze *et al.*, 2011.

29 Rukuni and Eicher, 1994.

30 Madhuku, 2004.

31 Kanyenze *et al.*, 2011:93.

32 For details see, Nyoni, 2016; Moyo and Maguranyanga, 2014; Sukume and Dengu, 2014; Vudzijena and Mishi, 2014.

33 Zimbabwe's A2 farms, averaging from 20–100 hectares and to over 500 hectares in dry areas are under freehold sector. These are also the areas where the political–military elite now firmly in power own land. This has resulted in a new agrarian structure, and in a massive increase of smallholder agriculture.

34 However, following the Elections of July 2018, the Ministry of Lands has been combined with Agriculture to become Ministry of Lands, Agriculture. Climate Change and Environmental Tasks.

35 Officially Zimbabwe's second Republic starts with the end of the Mugabe rule, which ended in November 2017.

36 The communal areas are crowded places. The population density in Chivi district was, for example, 46 people per km squared in 2012. In a dryland environment (average rainfall in Chivi is about 550 mm), land areas are not sufficient for extensive cropping and grazing areas are limited (Scoones, 2018).

37 De Soto, 2001:225.

38 See, Moyo, 2000.

39 A1 – are small family farmers that make up the largest group with 1.3 million households each holding an average farm of 20 hectares, and A2 – is made up of 31,000 middle farms about 140 hectares each and 1,371 large farms – 850 hectares each.

40 Smith. Reprinted, 1970:337.

41 Zimbabwe Constitution, 2013, Section 282:133.

42 Das, 2012:57.

43 De Soto, 2001:52, 112, 175.

44 Musahara, 2006.

45 Ibid.

46 Smith, 1776:251.

References

African Development Bank. 2013. *Report of the African Development Bank by the Directors of the African Development Bank and the African Development Fund*. Abidjan: African Development Bank.

The African in Southern Rhodesia. 1992. Issued by Authority of Southern Rhodesia Government, Salisbury, January 1–December 31.

Cukor, G. 1972. 'Long-Term Planning in Hungarian Industry', in Zoltăn Romăn (ed.), *Progress and Panning in Industry: Proceedings of the International Conference on Industrial Economics*, Budapest 14–17 April, 1970. Budapest.

Das, Gurcharan. 2012. *India Grows At Night: A Liberal Case for a Strong State*. Haryana, New Delhi: Penguin Books.

De Soto, Hernando. 2001. *The Mystery of Capital: Why Capitalism Triumphs in the West and Fails Everywhere Else*. London, New York: Bantam Press and Black Swan Edition.

German Democratic Institute. 1977. *The Economy of Colonial Zimbabwe and Policy Issues for Future Majority Government Part 1*. Berlin: German Democratic Institute.

International Labour Office (ILO). 1977. *Employment Growth and Basic Needs: A One World Problem*: Tripartite World Conference on Employment Income Distribution and Social Progress and ILO: Meeting Basic Needs – Strategies for Eradicating Mass Poverty and Unemployment. Geneva.

Johnston, Bruce F. 1976. 'Rural Development and Employment: The Case for a Unimodal Strategy', in Gerald M. Meier (ed.), *Leading Issues in Economic Development*. New York: Oxford University Press.

Kanyenze, G., Kondo, T., Chitambara, P. and Martens, Jos. (eds). 2011. *Beyond The Enclave: Towards a Pro-poor and Inclusive Development Strategy for Zimbabwe*. Harare: Ledriz.

Madhuku, L. 2004. 'Law, politics and the land reform process in Zimbabwe', in M. Masiiwa (ed.), *Post Independence Land Reform in Zimbabwe: Controversies and Impact on the Economy*. Harare: Friedrich Ebert Stiftung.

Mhone, G.C.Z. 1997. *Zimbabwe A Country Overview*. Presented to the LEAD International Conference on Leadership for Environment and Development, Zimbabwe Session – Cohort 4, 21 April – 3 May.

Mhone, G.C.Z. 2000. *Enclavity and Constrained Labour Absorptive Capacity in Southern African Economies*. Harare International Labour Office Southern Africa Multidisciplanary Team Advisory Team (SAMAT), Discussion Paper No. 12.

Mhone, Guy C.Z. 2003. *Developmentalism and the Role of the State*. Paper originally prepared for the workshop on Growth and Development for the Premier's Policy Development Unit of the Kwa Zulu Natal Provincial Government in February 2003.

Moyo, Sam. 2000. 'The Political Economy of Land Acquisition and Redistribution in Zimbabwe, 1990–1999', *Journal of Southern African Studies*, Vol. 26, No. 1:5–28.

Moyo, Sam. 2007. *Emerging Land Tenure Issues in Zimbabwe: Review of the Zimbabwean Agrarian Sector Following the Implementation of the Fast Track Land Reform Programme; AIAS*. Monograph series, Issue No. 2/07. Harare: The Agrarian Studies Institute of the South Harare.

Moyo, Sam and Maguranyanga, B. 2014. *Assessment of Zimbabwe's Land Administration System and Options for the Future*. Paper prepared under the World Bank's Agriculture Sector Technical Group (ASTG) and Multi-Donor Trust Fund (A-MDTF) Land Studies. Price Waterhouse Coopers. Harare.

Musahara, Harman. 2006. *Improving Tenure Security for the Rural Poor: Rwanda Country Case Study, Improving Land Tenure Security in Rwanda*. Paper prepared for the Food and Agriculture Organization of the United Nations (FAO).

Nyathi-Mdluli, 1980. 'The Manufacturing Industry in Zimbabwe Industry', in *UN – United Nations. Zimbabwe Towards a New Order: An Economic and Social Survey*. Working Papers, Vol. 1, United Nations.

Nyoni, J. 2016. *Land Tenure and Land Marketability in Zimbabwe: Policy Options and Recommendations*. USAID Strategic Economic Research and Analysis – Zimbabwe (SERA) Program, USAID/Zimbabwe.

Nziramasanga, M. 1980. 'The Agricultural Sector in Zimbabwe: Prospects for Change and Development', in *UN – United Nations. Zimbabwe, Towards a New Order: An Economic and Social Survey*. Working Papers, Vol. 1, United Nations, 1980.

O'Keefe, Phil and Moyo, Sam. 2007. 'Land Tenure in Zimbabwe', pp. 579–580, published online.

Riddell, R.C. 1978. *The Land Problem in Rhodesia: Alternatives for the Future*. Gwelo: Mambo Press.

Rukuni, M. and Eicher, C.K. (eds). 1994. *Zimbabwe Agricultural Revolution*. Harare: University of Zimbabwe Publications.

Scoones, I. 2018. Zimbabweland – The on-going Masvingo study research. Blasio Mavedzenge, Felix Murimbarimba and Jacob Mahenehene. Harare.

Smith, Adam. 1776. *An Inquiry into the Nature and Causes of the Wealth of Nations*. London: W. Strahan and T. Cadell.

Smith, Adam. 1970. *The Wealth of Nations* (in two Volumes, Volume One). London: Everyman's Library.

Sukume, C. and Dengu, Ebbie. 2014. *Land Use Policy Review*. Paper under the Land Studies Programme. PriceWatersCoopers and World Bank.

Szentes, Tamas. 1976. *The Political Economy of Underdevelopment*. Third, Revised and Enlarged Edition, Budapest: Akademiai Kiado.

The Whitsun Foundation. 1975. A Programme for National Development. Whitsun Foundation, Adult Literacy Programme. Salisbury.

UN. 2005. *Report of the Fact Finding Mission to Zimbabwe to assess the Scope and Impact Operation Murambatsvina by the UN Special Envoy on Human Settlements Issues in Zimbabwe*, Mrs Anna Kajumulo Tibaijuka. New York: United Nations.

UN. 1980. *Zimbabwe, Towards a New Order: Economic and Social Survey*. Working Papers, Vol. 1–2, United Nations.

Vudzijena, V. and Lloyd, Mishi. 2014. *Zimbabwe's Land Tenure Policy and Strategic Options*. Paper prepared under the World Bank's Agriculture Sector.

Wield, D. 1980. 'Technology and Zimbabwean Industry', in *UN – United Nations. Zimbabwe Towards a New Order: An Economic and Social Survey*. Working Papers, Vol. 1, United Nations.

World Bank. 1991. *Agriculture Sector Memorandum, Vol. II*. Washington, DC: World Bank.

10 Conclusions

Theoretical and empirical foundations of economic dualism

The concluding chapter attempts to link the theoretical foundations of dualism, as represented by the 'classical' model of dualism associated with W. Arthur Lewis, with the empirical development of dualism up to the present-day structural underdevelopment of the Zimbabwean economy. The Lewis model divides the economy into one capitalist sector and one subsistence sector. It demonstrates how the classical assumption that labour is in perfectly elastic supply to the capitalist sector leads to conclusions different from those based on the neo-classical assumption that the supply of labour is less than perfectly elastic. The examination of the theoretical propositions of dualism is weighed in terms of their relevance to the conditions of actual underdeveloped economies.

As pointed out in the criticism of the Lewis 'classical' dualism model, in its analysis of the long-term accumulation of capital, the latter did not succeed in incorporating the development of the 'traditional' sector. This is because the Lewis model was centred on the 'modern' capitalist sector and only related to the pre-capitalist sector in terms of its integral nature of capitalist accumulation. The chapter sets out to draw conclusions on the development of economic dualism from Rhodesia to the post independent Zimbabwe. The reality remains that economic dualism has continued to manifest itself in many ways and is an inherent part of the subject matter of underdevelopment. This is shown by drawing out lessons on the historical and empirical evidence of the development of economic dualism from Rhodesia to post independent Zimbabwe.

Over time, economic dualism has had profound effects and consequences on the whole economic and social structure of society and development of Zimbabwe's economy. In the long run, the dualistic pattern of the prevailing set of relative factor prices increased the possibility that if any innovation did occur, it was the European capitalist farmers who adopted it. On the other hand, African peasant farmers failed to adopt new technologies because it was expensive for them to adopt capital relative to labour intensive technologies. This led to different factor proportions being used between the European and African agricultural sector, which in turn had serious consequences for widening the gap in incomes of the two sectors.

As demonstrated in the previous chapters, the original dualism set up during the Rhodesian colonial era has remained intact. The sprawling sorry state of the rural peasant economy in the present-day communal areas, the depleted grazing pastures and degradation of the land due to soil erosion have continued to intensify over the years since the country's independence in 1980. This has been due to the increased man–land ratio in the limited land area occupied by the African peasantry. Hence the quality of the soil in overcrowded rural areas has deteriorated to such an extent that additional inputs of labour no longer add much to output. With communal ownership of the land, there is little or no incentive to preserve and improve the land and its adjacent resources endowment.

In addition to the land degradation processes described in the preceding chapters, the preservation of economic dualism has also been exacerbated to the extent that the formal sector has been decimated through persistent de-industrialisation and informalisation with the resultant extension of decent work deficits,[1] resulting in entrenched poverty. To this, has been added the fast-growing informal sector activities in the urban areas. The Zimbabwean economy has progressively become informalised, with 94.5 per cent of all employment informal by 2014. The unemployed and underemployed people have continuously escaped poverty in the rural areas and migrated to the towns and cities, to eke out a living in squalid and uncertain conditions.

At independence in 1980, the informal sector was relatively small accounting for less than 10 per cent of the labour force, which was mainly attributed to legal restrictions of movement of people from rural to the urban areas. Following the country's independence and the collapse of the formal sector, the informal sector blossomed. The post-colonial government initially chose to conveniently continue with the inherited dualistic structures of the economy as a new normal, while loudly blaming colonialism and imperialism for having planted and perpetrated this form of underdevelopment. While capitalism has continued to subsist and exploit the peasant economies of the south, there is no excuse for this process to be assisted by the current policies of the ruling elites of the post-colonial period. The dualism that characterised the colonial economy and continues to do so, explains the perennial problem of the continued underutilisation of the resources, which implies underdevelopment. This deliberate continuation with the colonial economic dualism model described in Chapter 9 above is a typical and even 'classic' example of the African post-colonial state's 'normalising the abnormal'. Together the communal and informal sectors form a huge non-formal sector economy, which is not linked beneficially to the formal sector, though contributing significantly to the survival of the people's economic and social well-being.[2] In most African countries, this phenomenon has been entrenched and heightened by policies implemented by the post-colonial state, continuing to display distortions in the way in which the formal sector and non-formal sector of the economy relate to each other.

This phenomenon of underdevelopment due to economic dualism has been typically of Southern Africa, especially South Africa, Zimbabwe and Namibia (erstwhile South West Africa). Most of the literature contends that the first economy, is the modern sector, which produces the bulk of these countries' wealth and is integrated within the global economy. The second economy (also known as the marginalised economy), is characterised by under-development, contributes little to the gross domestic product (GDP), contains a big percentage of these countries' population, incorporates the poorest of the rural and urban population. The latter is structurally disconnected from both the first and global economy, and is incapable of self-generated growth and development.[3]

The fact that the majority of the population experiencing food insecurity is located in Africa's rural areas, which is engaged in subsistence farming, speaks volumes of the need to change the current African rural farming model. In many respects, this is at the heart of the argument for changing the legal property laws in order to empower the people to freely integrate into the mainstream economy of their respective countries. Here also lies the trigger for the agro-industry-value-chains to turn the African rural farming sector from its current subsistence model into modern value-chain clusters producing for the domestic, regional and international markets.

This becomes even more critical since agriculture is the mainstay of the majority of the population in Africa and the relationship between its performance and that of the key economic indicators like GDP, trade flows and employment cannot be overemphasised. In addition, agriculture is an important pillar for the success of Africa's regional trade, because it forms a significant portion of the economies in the region. At the global level, the agricultural sector can contribute towards major continental priorities, such as eradicating poverty and hunger. It is noted here that based on trade volumes, only five countries play central roles in mobilising the intra-African trade – Algeria, Côte d'Ivoire, Egypt, Nigeria and South Africa – being responsible for 67 per cent of all intra-African traded volumes in 2015.[4]

As shown in the section below, the challenge to reverse the persistence of economic dualism in the typical Southern African economies hinges in fundamentally changing the social and economic structure of these economies. This means urging governments to come out from their present fanciful dreams and face the real plight of the mass of their people continually living on the edge of the precipice. Governments, academia and civil societies have to pluck the moral, social and political will and courage to address these countries' national legal systems of property rights, which were inherited from the colonial era. This can be achieved through taking on board all the economic players (rural farmers, small, medium and large) into one simplified national law.

Eradication of economic dualism

A strong contestation that runs through this book is the interpretation that assumes dualism as a natural starting position of an underdeveloped economy so that over time it is reduced by market forces as the capitalist sector advances and the subsistence or traditional sector shrinks. We argue that it was unrealistic to expect a 'trickle down' from the modern to the rural agrarian sectors. What is peculiar about countries trapped under economic dualism is that high growth in other sectors like extractive industry, services and other modern sectors will not be accompanied by labour-intensive industrial revolution that could transform lives of the majority of the people trapped in rural poverty.

As has been suggested in the preceding chapters, inclusive development has to occur in order to have positive distributional consequences for the majority of the population of an underdeveloped country. For this to happen, markets will need a network of regulations and institutions and the ability of a strong state to provide reliable and predictable environment, not the usual populist state that dishes out 'freebies' like food and other subsidies, particularly in times of elections. Usually this practice is meted out by not popular regimes but by negative populist ones.

Empirical evidence from many other underdeveloped countries starting with those in the Southern African region, points to the negative distributional consequences of development that neglects the 'traditional' farming sector in the growth process. It is therefore imperative that the restructuring of these economies must inevitably start with the rural agricultural sector where economic dualism has its roots.

However, for this to happen the colonially inherited administrative, institutional and legal environment have to be structurally overhauled. The economic dualistic structures can only be eradicated through a well-structured land reform and complementary activities needed to make it transformative. In the case of Zimbabwe, this can be brought about by the restructuring of the communal areas into a modern agrarian reform that is able to transfer labour from rural agriculture to the more transforming industrial sector. This implies that simultaneous development of the two sectors, the modern capitalist and the 'traditional' agrarian sector should take place. In this case the effects of one sector on the other will be of mutual benefit.

One characteristic of economic dualism's persistence is the lack the institutional and legal mechanisms that formally fix the people's assets in records governed by rules contained in the property system. It is important therefore that governments must stop muddling along with the current dualistic economies, and instead revisit the institutional and legal systems under which the majority of their people's economic activities operate. This is in particular with regards to the legal property system which is the primary operating environment of people in a functioning and thriving democracy.

The eradication of economic dualism must involve eliminating the continuing institutional and legal failure that prevents the majority of enterprising people to freely negotiate and contract with those outside their areas. For as long as this impediment exists, it defeats the division of labour and relegates the poor and extralegal businesses to a small circle of specialisation and low productivity of labour. In addressing the issue of inclusiveness of economic activities from rural agriculture to purposeful industrial transformation, we have to address the current challenge of the people's assets to come under the national property legal system. There is, therefore, need for a system that automatically allows the market to spontaneously widen as new entries approach it. But this cannot happen when the largest section of the community is left out of the inclusive business networks, which is a bastion and remnant of economic dualism.

As argued in Chapter 9, to deal effectively with economic dualism, Zimbabwe and indeed other African states in similar situations will need strong, effective and competent states capable of enforcing national embracing laws strictly and fairly, while relentlessly upholding the rule of law. Anything short of legally binding property laws for all the country's citizens, will leave the majority of its citizens under the archaic 'traditional' laws that allow government officials to have discretion to manipulate the poor rural farmers, while leaving them perpetually poor, with no tangible property rights. With regards to the informal sector, this leaves them open to the authorities' discretion to allow them to establish and come back at will and destroy them, which has become a norm in most of these economies. At many levels this nurtures the prevailing corruption which is a result of public officials enjoying too many discretionary powers, particularly in the unreformed sectors of the economy like the rural areas and urban informal sector.

Currently in Zimbabwe, the assets of the poor peasant farmers and those of the micro, small and medium enterprises are assets whose economic and social aspects are not fixed in the formal property system. The rural agricultural lands have continued to be held under communal ownership. The legitimate rights of the people to hold assets including land under freehold continue to be withheld, and this is being done by the post independent government. Under these conditions, it is extremely hard to preserve and grow the communal farmers' assets, let alone move them fluidly in the market.

An important argument in this concluding chapter is that, until this situation is addressed, the country's rural assets will remain an add-on appendage, and not central to the integration of the nation's non-formal sector into the modern formal economy. Such a situation also undermines the prospects of creating synergies to close the missing links and subsequently creating robust value chains between small agricultural producers, micro-enterprise and formal sector firms.

The need for restructuring the economy must inevitably start with the large sway of the indigenous 'subsistence' agricultural sector where economic dualism has its roots. As emphasised above, the nerve centre of gravity in the transformation of economic dualism of the African economy, with the Zimbabwean situation in particular, initially revolves around the nature of the land reform. This includes change in the structure of property rights on land assets, as well as the complementary activities needed to make these measures effective. As Ranis and Fei (Chapter 6) recognised that as both sectors co-exist in the economy, development can be brought about only by a complete shift in the focal point of progress from the agricultural to the industrial economy, such that there is augmentation of industrial output. This is done by the transfer of labour from the agricultural to the industrial sector, wherein the growth of the agricultural sector must not be negligible. Its output should be sufficient to support the whole economy with food and raw materials. In many ways this is likened to the Harrod–Domar model, where saving and investment become the driving forces when it comes to economic development of underdeveloped countries.

As repeatedly argued above, the transformation of the agrarian sector into an integrated industrial economy cannot happen as long the communal lands remain a residual sector, and lagging behind the formal sector in terms of technology, application of property rights, resource mobilisation and incomes. The current communal land areas cannot be expected under their current conditions, to transform their production and farming systems into the modern formal economy. Only under a transformed model, can we expect to promote business linkages between formal and informal enterprises including large segments of the peasant or communal agriculture. The inclusive model should embrace all segments of society, including non-state actors, voices of women, youth, and micro, small and medium enterprises, which are essential to this process.

In the case of Zimbabwe, it is pertinent to take note of the conclusions of the country's 1997 'Report of the Commission of Inquiry into Appropriate Agricultural Land Tenure Systems' proposals, specifically on the communal areas. The Report proposed that individuals could register their home plots and vegetable gardens but, in the long run, there would be no individual title deeds that would protect the land rights of women and would be administered by local chiefs. As it has been aptly observed by Okeef and Sam Moyo

> The conclusions are good for the Government but not necessarily Zimbabwe. More particularly, for politicians as ministers the conclusions relating to each of the four sub-sectors are logical outcomes although

> the politicians, simultaneously, manage to keep land as a political issue.[5]

One can also add that it is also strange that the rights of women will be protected by chiefs and village headpersons with no title deeds on their properties.

The plot is virtually lost in the provision of the 2013 Zimbabwe Constitution (Section 72), which defines agricultural land as 'land used for agriculture – a separate piece of land on Deeds Registry' – *but excludes communal lands*, which is treated under Section 282 where the provisions of traditional leaders are given as 'to administer Communal Land and protect the environment', as well as resolve disputes. In terms of social progress and economic terms, this is grossly inadequate and a divergent path to taking the country forward to a modern era, where social and economic rights should be equal for all people.

The two provisions cited above appear to preserve the enduring colonial economic dualism model, all in the name of the preservation of the political patronage system of traditional chiefs, by the ruling political elites. As cited above, it may well be the case that in drafting the constitutions and related laws the government elites were caught up in keeping and upholding the village norms of 'chiefs' and 'headman' into the modern society, all in the name of preservation of culture. This is more likely to keep the Zimbabwean growth model stark in the 'sordid' village norms, instead of focusing on the individual rather than the village as a moral unit of the Constitution. The legal provisions certainly appear to have missed the boat in focusing on the task of modern citizenship whose mission is to convert the partial loyalties of society to those of the modern state.

To eradicate economic dualism, which has its footprint in colonialism, purposive government actions should go far beyond the 'property rights' issue and address the structural impediments created by the dualistic system over generations. The system has resulted in structured poverty processes marred by challenges such as the following:

- a Presence of ineffective regulatory environments.
- b Inadequate physical infrastructure; poor transport and telecommunication network systems, chronic power cuts, etc., which create a difficult environment within which to conduct business.
- c Lack of knowledge and skills, i.e. lack of education often results in the poor being excluded from formal employment.
- d Limited access to financial services: the poor tend to always pay more for everything especially when it comes to borrowing. Many have no bank accounts, lack skills and knowledge to make project proposals needed to acquire credit and most fundamentally have no legally registered properties to leverage as collateral.

The proposed measures to eradicate economic dualism in both the agrarian sector and the fast emerging informal sector of the economy are meant to reverse the modern sector's growth momentum on its own, not relating to the non-formal economy in a manner that marginalises and impoverishes the latter. Such dualistic structural distortion implies that even in the presence of growth, the economy is unable to absorb the vast numbers of the un- and under-employed into the mainstream economy. A precursor to the proactive role of the state is to provide sufficient conducive environment for the mass economy actors to rise and get involved in productive commercial activities beyond the present day subsistence agriculture. This is needed to integrate the non-formal economy as well as endogenously nurture the growth process in a manner that allows the majority of economic actors and the labour-force to be in productive activities. Finally, this entails reallocation of labour across sectors, akin to structural change, which is central to the process of structural transformation and productivity upgrading. This is also central and necessary for sustainable improvements in living standards, as it allows more people to benefit from higher productivity levels in the more advanced parts of the economy.

In the case of Zimbabwe the introduction of secure property titles to the communal farmers can open up a lot of opportunities. The rebuilding agricultural value chains can come on stream and take advantage of the vast opportunities presented in a number of commodity industry groups or clusters, namely, (a) horticulture; (b) livestock and meat; (c) legumes and oilseeds; (d) tree crops; (e) grains; (f) cotton; (g) tobacco; and (h) forestry and timber. It thus becomes critical for the rural farmers to take advantage of the high correlation between their farming activities and agro-industrial processing where the potential to regain lost ground is high. At the same time, the country could target some of the jobs at the lower end of global manufacturing that are expected to be transferred from China where rising wages for unskilled workers and technological upgrading creates opportunities for such jobs to be off-loaded to low income countries of Asia and Africa. There is growing evidence of some African countries already taking advantage and benefitting from this development, namely Ghana and Ethiopia. But unless and until there is a meaningful transition and transformation in these economies, these countries will continue to integrate its peasantry into the narrow capitalist state thereby maintaining economic dualism.

Notes

1 Decent work involves opportunities for work that is productive and delivers a fair income, security in the workplace and social protection for families, including free will to organise and participate in the decisions that affect their lives and equality of opportunity and treatment for all women and men.

2 In many African economies, informal sector business may generate as much as half of GDP, handle as much as 40 per cent of all foreign exchange and over 40 per cent of exports and imports, support as much as 60–70 per cent of the people.

It is the main provider of transport for the people and meets the basic housing requirements of poor.

3 Mbeki, 2004:29, quoted in Bojabotsheha, 2011.
4 UNCTAD, 2017.
5 O'Keefe and Moyo, 2017.

References

Bojabotseha, Teboho Pankratius. 2011. 'Dualism and the Social Formation of South Africa', *African Journal of Hospitality, Tourism and Leisure*, Vol. 1, No. 3. ISSN 1819–2025.

Mbeki, T. 2004. 'Meeting the Challenge for the Second Economy', *New Agenda: South African Journal of Social and Economic Policy*, Issue 14, Second Quarter:29.

O'Keefe, Phil and Moyo, Sam. 2007. *Land Tenure in Zimbabwe*, pp. 579–580, published online.

UNCTAD. 2017. *Strategic tools to assist negotiations and agricultural policy design in Africa*. UNCTAD/WEB/DITC/2017/1.

Zimbabwe Constitution of 2013. in Constituteproject.org.

Index

Printed in the United States
By Bookmasters